Controversial Issues
in Social Work Ethics,
Values, and Obligations

Edited by

Eileen Gambrill

Robert Pruger

University of California, Berkeley

ALLYN AND BACON

Boston • London • Toronto • Sydney • Tokyo • Singapore

Series Editor, Social Work: Judy Fifer
Vice President and Publisher, Social Sciences: Karen Hanson
Editorial Assistant: Mary Visco
Marketing Manager: Joyce Nilsen
Sr. Editorial Production Administrator: Susan McIntyre
Editorial Production Service: Ruttle, Shaw & Wetherill, Inc.
Composition Buyer: Linda Cox
Manfacturing Buyer: Megan Cochran
Cover Administrator: Suzanne Harbison

Copyright © 1997 by Allyn & Bacon
A Viacom Company
160 Gould Street
Needham Heights, MA 02194

Internet: www.abacon.com
America Online: keyword: College Online

Library of Congress Cataloging-in-Publication Data
Controversial issues in social work ethics, values, and obligations /
    edited by Eileen Gambrill, Robert Pruger.
        p.   cm.
    Includes bibliographical references.
    ISBN 0-205-19095-2
    1. Social workers—Professional ethics.   2. Social service—Moral
and ethical aspects.   3. Social service—United States.
I. Gambrill, Eileen D., 1934–   .   II. Pruger, Robert.
HV10.5.C65   1997
174'.93613—dc20   96–14452
                                                                CIP

Printed in the United States of America

10 9 8 7 6 5 4 3 2 1   01 00 99 98 97 96

Contents

I Debates about Practice

IV Debates about Professional Education and Training

V Debates about Special Client Populations

Preface

This book has three major focuses: (1) to present different perspectives on a number of current ethical and value issues related to social work; (2) to demonstrate the value of presenting different positions concerning an issue in a debate format; and (3) to demonstrate that controversy can be carried out in a constructive manner. *Controversial Issues in Social Work Ethics, Values, and Obligations* is for social work educators as well as social work practitioners and students of social work. It is for readers who wish to deepen their understanding of ethical, value, and obligation issues that arise in day-by-day practice by considering opposing viewpoints on these issues. It is for use both within and outside of formal education programs. It could be used as a text in a course on ethics in social work or as an ancillary source of readings.

A representative set of ethical and value issues was selected that concern a broad array of situations. A myriad of different issues was possible for inclusion in this volume. We have selected nineteen that we believe represent important issues for consideration by social workers. Issues discussed are clustered into five areas. Debates about practice are included in Part I. These include "Does reliance on diagnostic labeling help clients more than it hurts them?" and "Should clients have a right to information in their mental health files?" Debates in Part II concern use of coercion. These include: "Does the goal of preventing suicide justify placing suicidal clients in care?" and "Does coercion have a legitimate place in the treatment of legally competent adults?" Debates in Part III include those related to the profession, such as: "Is the NASW Code of Ethics an effective guide for practitioners?" and "Is the Code of Ethics as applicable to agency executives as it is to direct service providers?" Parts IV and V include debates related to professional education and training and special populations.

Criteria for selection of topics included a decision that any issue was a proper professional matter, had a continuing controversial content, and that there were willing opponents to argue each side. Selection of issues shows that we are not persuaded that because something is, it ought to be. This can be seen by inclusion of questions such as "Should social workers work in managed-care services?" Some of the questions challenge well-accepted positions such as locking suicidal people up to minimize harm to them. We do not believe a policy or position is necessarily the best one simply because most people happen to believe it or because it has been in place as an accepted practice. That is, we are not persuaded that consensus is a sound basis for acceptance of a point of view. Too many popular positions have been found to be inaccurate. In fact, we hope that one effect of this book will be to encourage readers to question what is widely accepted as well as what is new and innovative. There is a special need in the helping professions to question views because they may work against rather than for client interests.

The format of debates plus replies offers readers an opportunity to consider the relevance of rejoinder points that are made. Questions can be raised, such as, Does the reply address points in the opposing statements? Are the replies well reasoned? Is any evidence presented in support of claims made? Have relevant facts been cited? Preparing this book highlights the substantial realm of controversy in social work concerning ethical and value issues that should be clarified and communicated to students as well as practitioners rather than glossed over. No single work could capture all significant ethical and value issues. We hope that other works will continue the task of identifying, organizing, and discussing controversial ethical and value topics in the field.

We hope that social workers of many different persuasions will find the dialogues interesting and useful in sharpening their understanding of issues they confront in their everyday practice. Simply reviewing the list of issues can show what point of view you favor currently. Reading the debates in the book can help you to sharpen your critical thinking skills. Familiarity with tendencies likely to result in errors (such as a tendency to searching only for evidence that confirms favored positions) as well as fallacies that evade, obscure, or distort positions will help you to appraise the soundness of arrangements.

There are two ways to read this book. One is to read only statements that support preferred positions. This approach will result in the least benefit. If you do this, you will essentially have your biases confirmed. Another way to read this book (which we recommend) is to read both statements and rebuttals on an issue, paying special attention to arguments against favored positions. Only in this way are you likely to avoid the confirmation bias, the tendency to see and recall only points that favor your preferred point-of-view.

We wish to thank our contributors for preparing statements and replies and for their enthusiastic reactions to the format of this book. We invite you to share your reactions to both the format and content of the discussions and to suggest topics for future issues. You will no doubt have your own views on topics discussed. We hope you enjoy the discussions in the book and that reading arguments on both sides of issues will deepen your understanding and appreciation of factors related to the questions addressed and provide an opportunity to enhance your critical thinking skills. Our greatest hope is that reading these debates and arriving at your own point-of-view will result in decisions that are faithful to the mandate of our profession: to help clients, and (we would add) not to harm in the process.

Introduction

Professionals have special privileges based on their presumed expertise to help clients address certain kinds of problems (see for example, Abbott, 1988). Special privileges may result in special harms. A key aspect of being a professional is personal discretion in making decisions on the assumption that those decisions honor professional codes of ethics. The very term *unprofessional* often connotes unethical. Ethics concern standards and principles related to making decisions about how to act in a situation. Ethical issues are moral–value issues in which it is suggested that some ways of acting are bad, good, wrong, or right. Values can be defined as the social principles, goals, or standards held by an individual, group, or society. They state preferences about certain goals and how to attain them. Values are reflected in ethical principles and related actions. For example, some views emphasize the importance of ensuring fairness for the least advantaged individuals. Utilitarian views emphasize pursuing the greatest good for the greatest number. Values are appealed to support decisions at many different levels (e.g., public policy, agency practices, individual helper decisions). The Preamble to the 1995 draft of the Code of Ethics of the National Association of Social Workers (NASW) states that "This code is based on the fundamental values of the social work profession that include the worth, dignity and uniqueness of all persons as well as their rights and opportunities" (1995, p. 1). Core values include: (1) service; (2) social justice; (3) dignity and worth of the person; (4) importance of human relationships; (5) integrity and (6) competence.

Professional codes of ethics are usually vague, allowing discretion in decision making that some argue is needed and others argue offers opportunities to harm rather than help clients. The very vagueness of professional codes of ethics highlights the importance of taking specific examples and exploring them in detail. This book is a call to professionals to think carefully about ethical issues involved in their everyday work with clients. It calls on them to do so in a candid fashion, recognizing constraints on service. For example, in Debate 12, Burt Gummer argues that social workers in public agencies are agents of the state, not agents of clients. He argues that the NASW Code of Ethics has nothing to say about the moral choices that arise in public agencies regarding allocation of scarce resources.

Only through candid appraisal of ethical issues including identification of involved parties and both short- and long-term consequences of different options are we likely to arrive at well-informed ethical decisions. Ethical dilemmas often arise in which two or more principles or values conflict or in which it is difficult or impossible to be faithful to an ethical principle. Should people who have repeatedly assaulted others, causing serious injury or loss of life, be paroled even though there is a high probability that they will continue such actions? Here the value of self-determination and the value of protecting others from harm may conflict. A key conflict in many questions discussed in this book is that between clients' rights and obligations, those of the state, and those of professionals. Clients' rights are at issue in questions such as "Does coercion have a role to play in social work?" or "Does the threat of imminent harm to self provide an appropriate reason to hospitalize clients?" The obligations and rights of professionals are of concern in debates such as "Should professionals provide some pro bono service to clients?" The new draft of the NASW Code of Ethics calls on social workers to do so. Should this be a requirement? Factors that should be considered include:

1. clients' interests
2. the interests and rights of other involved parties, such as family members or victims
3. professional code of ethics
4. personal values of the social worker
5. agency policy
6. legal regulations

No wonder that reaching decisions agreeable to all interested parties is difficult (or impossible). "Practitioners are asked to solve problems every day that philosophers have argued about for the last two thousand years and will probably debate for the next two thousand. Inevitably, arbitrary lines have to be drawn and hard cases decided" (Dingwall, Eekelaar, & Murray, 1983, p. 244). Prescribed action may be legally mandated. Legal issues concern legislated rights or obligations. These may or may not be possible to act on. For example, parents may have a legal right to educate their children at home but not be able to do so because of lack of money. Some rights are both moral and legal, such as the right to free speech; they conform to a standard of behavior and are legally mandated as well.

The greater the potential influence over clients, the greater the need to carefully consider questions of ethics, values, and obligations to ensure that clients receive needed services in a manner that does not intrude unduly on their rights. In *Cruel Compassion* (1994), as well as in his other books, Thomas Szasz argues that clients' rights are routinely infringed on by a coercive psychiatry that imposes unwanted treatment on children and adults even though there is no evidence that such treatment is effective.

Critical Thinking as a Guide

Those who value critical thinking highlight its role in arriving at ethical decisions (e.g., Baron, 1994, Brookfield, 1987; 1995; Popper, 1992; 1994). Honoring the code of inquiry shown in Exhibit 1 on pages xv–xvii will increase the likelihood of arriving at well-reasoned ethical decisions. Critical discussion (e.g., seeking clarity, questioning assumptions, and considering different perspectives) will help us to identify involved participants at different levels and their interests (e.g., clients, significant others, the agency, community) and the potential consequences of different options. This will help us to discover competing interests and to consider long-term as well as short-term consequences of given actions. We will be more likely to carefully consider other points of view and to spot questionable appeals and arguments that, if acted on, may harm rather than benefit clients. Questions include the following:

- What exactly is the issue (e.g., what resources are involved? freedom? money?)?
- Who is involved and in what ways?
- What are alternate options?
- What are the consequences of each option for each involved person (both current and remote)?
- What grounds should be used as a guide about what to do (e.g., equity in resource distribution)?
- What changes could be made at what levels (individual, family, community, agency, service system, policy) to honor ethical principles?

Valuing critical inquiry encourages us to value truth over ignorance and prejudice, to ferret out our biases, and to think carefully about our responsibilities and the degree of match between what we say, we value and what we do.

References

Abbott, A. (1988) *The system of professions: an essay on the division of expert labor.* Chicago: Univ. of Chicago Press.

Baron, J. (1994). *Thinking and deciding* (2nd ed.). New York: Cambridge University Press.

Brookfield, S. D. (1987). *Developing critical thinkers: Challenging adults to explore alternative ways of thinking and acting.* San Francisco: Jossey-Bass.

Brookfield, S. (1995). *Becoming a critically reflective teacher.* San Francisco: Jossey-Bass.

Dingwall, R., Eekelaar, J., & Murray, T. (1983). *The protection of children.* Oxford, England: Basil Blackwell.

Popper, K. R. (1992). *In search of a better world: Lectures and essays from thirty years.* New York: Routledge.

Popper, K. R. (1994). In M. A. Notturno (Ed.), *The myth of the framework: In defense of science and rationality.* New York: Routledge.

Szasz, T. S. (1994). *Cruel compassion: Psychiatric control of society's unwanted.* New York: John Wiley.

EXHIBIT 1

A Code of Conduct for Effective Rational Discussion

The Fallibility Principle

Each participant should acknowledge the possibility that none of the positions presented deserve acceptance and that, at best, only one is true or the most defensive position.

The Truth-Seeking Principle

Each participant should be committed to searching for the truth or at least the most defensible position on the issue. Therefore, you should be eager to seriously examine alternative positions, to look for insights in the positions of others, and to allow other participants to present arguments for or raise objections to any position held with regard to any disputed issue.

The Burden of Proof Principle

The burden of proof for any position usually rests on the person who presents it. If and when someone asks, the proponent should provide an argument for that position.

The Principle of Charity

The argument presented for any position should be one that is capable of being reconstructed into a commonly accepted or standard argument form. If an argument is reformulated by a challenger, it should be expressed in the strongest possible version that is consistent with the original intention of the arguer. If there is any question about that intention or about implicit parts of the argument, the arguer should be given the benefit of doubt in the reformulation.

The Clarity Principle

The formulations of all positions, defenses, and challenges should be free of any kind of linguistic confusion and clearly separated from other positions and issues.

The Relevance Principle

One who presents an argument for or a challenge to a position should set forth only reasons or questions that are directly related to the merit of the position at issue.

The Acceptability Principle

One who presents an argument for or challenges a position should attempt to use premises or reasons that are mutually acceptable to the participants or that at least meet standard criteria of acceptability.

The Sufficient Grounds Principle

One who presents an argument for or challenges a position should attempt to provide reasons that are sufficient in number, kind, and weight to support the conclusion.

The Rebuttal Principle

One who presents an argument for or challenges a position should attempt to provide effective responses to all serious challenges or rebuttals to the argument or position at issue.

The Resolution Principle

An issue should be considered resolved if the proponent for one position successfully defends that position by presenting an argument that uses relevant and acceptable premises that are sufficient in number, kind, and weight to support the conclusion and provides an effective rebuttal to all serious challenges to the argument or position at issue. Unless you can demonstrate that these conditions have *not* been met, you should accept the conclusion of the successful argument. In the absence of a successful argument for any one position, you are obligated to accept the position supported by the best of the good or near-successful arguments presented.

The Suspension of Judgment Principle

If no position comes close to being successfully defended, or if two or more positions seem to be defended with equal strength, one should, in most cases, suspend judgment about the issue. If practical considerations require an immediate decision, one should weigh the relative risks of gain or loss connected with the consequences of suspending judgment and decide the issue on those grounds.

The Reconsideration Principle

If a good argument for a position is subsequently found to be flawed in a way that raises *new* doubts about the merit of that position. you are obligated to reopen the issue for further consideration and resolution.

Source: Adapted from T. E. Damer. (1995). *Attacking faulty reasoning: A practical guide to fallacy-free arguments* (3rd ed.) (pp. 12–16 and 172–186). Belmont, CA: Wadsworth Publishing Company.

Should Clients Have Access to Their Mental Health Records?

EDITOR'S NOTE: Keeping written records about clients is a standard practice in social work and has been since the early days of the profession. Although records have been kept for a variety of administrative and professional purposes, until recently, clients were invariably denied access to them. Providing such access seems more in the spirit of modern times. Yet, as the following debate makes clear, there are strong arguments on both sides of the question.

Sheldon R. Gelman, Ph.D., MSL, says YES. He is Professor and David and Dorothy Schachne Dean at the Wurzweiler School of Social Work of Yeshiva University in New York City.

Michele Winchester-Vega, DSW, presents the NO case. She is Assistant Professor at the Wurzweiler School of Social Work of Yeshiva University in New York City.

YES

SHELDON GELMAN

Access to written records maintained by mental health professionals should be available as a general rule to the individual who is the subject of the record. Although the professional or the agency that employs the professional may own the file folder and the papers contained therein, the client has a "property right interest"

1

in the information contained in the record and is therefore entitled to access. Except in unusual and limited situations, professionals should feel comfortable in sharing with the client what is contained in the record.

Although recording is regarded as an essential part of social work practice and an important element in risk management activities (Gelman, 1992), it is a task that is rarely approached with enthusiasm. Recording and record keeping are not viewed as high-priority items by most social workers. Therefore, workers are often reluctant to share records with clients because they often do not reflect the actual process or interaction that occurred.

Unfortunately, relatively little attention is given to recording in social work training programs. Although records should provide a chronology of client problems and agency involvement, they are loaded with problems. Recording often is done after other "important" tasks are completed. Also, there is often no clearly identified or stated rationale that underlies record keeping or recording practices. Information is often collected for no clear purpose, and workers view recording as a bureaucratic imposition that has little relevance to their work, client needs, or the provision of services. Records are developed and maintained but often are not in a form that is usable by either the worker or the agency, let alone the client.

Records and Recording

Interestingly, social service departments hold more information about individuals and families than any other organization. The information, however, is often inaccurate, highly stigmatizing, or insulting. Social work records are known to contain contradictory opinions, value judgments, rumors, and allegations that are unsubstantiated by fact, are not up to date, and often do not do justice to the work that was done. It is often difficult to determine why a particular referral was made, the nature of the problem, or what was done for a specific client. The language of the record is often filled with professional jargon designed to maintain the status or power difference between helper and helpee (Gelman, 1980). The use of such language has created special problems in communication and has led to situations in which the services sought by the client cannot be satisfactorily addressed by the professional. Rather than allowing for a process of engagement, distance and distrust are created. Opening records permits the correction of errors, the expansion of relevant information, the opportunity to explore explanations for behavior as well as alternatives, and a way to engage the client in meaningful dialogue.

The record needs to be viewed for what it is—a means of communication. Effective communication is a critical element in the helping process. The record is a tool, but it is only as good a tool as the information contained within it. Client review of the record can contribute to both accuracy and relevance. When used appropriately, the record can serve as a means of client growth and enlightenment, of worker development, and of professional growth. Appropriately documented information can be used for planning purposes and as a means of ensuring service continuity and accountability (Kagel, 1984).

Paternalism and Self-Protection

An important element of record sharing is the attitude of workers, not only toward their clients but also toward themselves. When workers record information about clients, they are in part recording information about their own values, attitudes, perspectives, and skills. Additionally, their recording will reflect a somewhat biased picture of their own competence and effectiveness. Therefore, to open records to clients requires not only a belief in the appropriateness and value of such access, but a high degree of confidence in and comfortableness with their own professional skills. Workers who are unclear or uncertain about their skills, as well as those that are unclear as to their role, will find it awkward to open their records to clients. Rather than seeing the record as a working tool, to be used in interactions with clients, it may show their own inadequacy as workers. This concern is manifested in two ways: One is an unwillingness to record information about clients in detail; the other is a reluctance to actively inform clients about their rights of access and procedures to be followed for gaining access. In such circumstances, the intent of the open access policy is subverted. The client does not have the opportunity to fully exercise his or her rights and thereby hold the worker and the service provider accountable for the nature and quality of service offered, and it also prevents appropriate and effective worker supervision. It also leaves professionals in the awkward position of not being able either to objectively document their successful interventions or to petition for additional resources to meet unmet needs.

Clients who distrust workers or who are made to feel inferior by being treated as children or adults incapable of playing a role in their own treatment are more likely to feel dissatisfied with the process. Clients who believe that professionals are hiding things from them or are saying things about them are likely to leave treatment or to seek redress for real or perceived wrongs.

The Success of Access

Today, access policies are extensive and cover almost all records maintained by government and voluntary organizations. The 1974 Freedom of Information Act, the Federal Privacy Act (1974), and the Family Educational Rights and Privacy Act (1974) provide citizens access to various records maintained by agencies of the federal government and local educational authorities.

Access by patients to their medical or health care records has been granted in many states. In 1979, the American Psychiatric Association issued a "Model Law on Confidentiality in Health and Social Service Records" that endorsed a policy of access by patients to their records. The Code of Ethics of NASW states that "The Social Worker should afford clients reasonable access to any official social work records concerning them." (NASW, 1990). The Family Service Association, as part of their standard setting process, has since 1977 required that member agencies permit client access to records as part of the counseling process. A similar policy promulgated by the Child Welfare League of America has been in effect since 1984. At least in principle, these policies support the right of clients/patients to review written files as part of the therapeutic process. These policies affirm the rights of citizens to participate in a meaningful and informed manner in decisions that affect their future.

Client access to records is based on the following principles, which are supported by both law and professional standards:

- Access is implicit and essential in democratic societies.
- Access is essential to client self-determination.
- Access is a means of improving record keeping.
- Access is a means of assuring accountability.

Access policies vary and can be categorized according to the level or degree of access (full, partial, none) and whether access is an actively encouraged or passive phenomena (Gelman, 1991). Full access means that a wide range of social service records are accessible to clients on whom they are maintained. They may review, amend, and have copies made of their file. Partial access means that limitations are placed on access to certain types of records or that specific sections of the record are restricted (e.g., health, psychiatric, third-party contributions). In most instances, access to third-party contributions are withheld unless permission is received from that individual to share the information or the privacy or confidentiality is protected. Active access involves both the availability of information to clients and their active engagement in the creation and maintenance of the record. Passive access policies, such as those that limit access to certain categories of information, tend to be paternalistic and protective of bureaucratic and professional discretion. Under an active access policy, the record becomes an integral part of the therapeutic process. This means that records are shared with clients by the worker, who can provide clarification and interpretation when necessary.

Although numerous arguments have been advanced against granting access, such as psychological damage to client, practitioners know best, unsuitability of material, manipulation by client, need to protect third parties (Wilson, 1978), results have been positive in instances in which access has been permitted and encouraged. Reports of studies with medical patients who were routinely given complete copies of their medical records indicate that they were more cooperative and less anxious. Similar positive experiences with psychiatric patients who were provided access to their records also has been reported. Problem-oriented medical records have been made available to clients with individual and marriage problems as part of the therapeutic process, with favorable results. Positive results have been noted also by psychologists sharing psychological test results with child and adolescent psychiatric patients and their parents and with parents of mentally handicapped children as well as delinquent adolescents and their families. A number of authors suggest that shared recording can promote a partnership between the worker and the client and that sharing records is integral to more client-centered and effective practice.

Accountability

Records must go beyond the documentation of accumulated knowledge or speculation, for they are an evolving account of how agencies and workers do their "business." Agency records and the entries prepared by workers have become the object of legal, legislative, and public scrutiny. Records provide documentation of duties, obligations, and acts of omission or commission. Records or the lack thereof can be used to support or impeach the credibility of agencies and staff in meeting professional or legal obligations.

REFERENCES

Gelman, S. R. (1980). Esoterica: A zero sum game in the helping professions. *Social Casework, 61*(1), 48–53.
Gelman, S. R. (1991). Client access to agency records: A comparative analysis. *International Social Work, 34,* 191–204.
Gelman, S. R. (1992). Risk management through client access to case records. *Social Work, 37*(1), 73–79.
Kagel, J. D. (1984). *Social work records.* Homewood, IL: Dorsey Press.
National Association of Social Workers. (1990) Code of Ethics. Silver Spring, MD.
Wilson, S. J. (1978). *Confidentiality in social work: Issues and principles.* New York: The Free Press.

Rejoinder to Professor Gelman MICHELE WINCHESTER-VEGA

I agree with Dr. Gelman that records are an essential and important part of our professional functions. Beyond that, however, we have several points of disagreement.

Dr. Gelman defends his position of advocating that clients have access to their mental health records based on a fear of risk-management liabilities and based on legal rights. The truth is that unethical or inappropriate practice is what creates the liability concerns, not the written record (Berliner, 1989). This fear has fostered an arena in which some social workers have opted not to keep mental health process notes on client interactions. The nature of these notes should be to allow social workers the right of discovery in the treatment process. Often, delicate, controversial, or extremely private issues are recorded by the treatment pen. Very frequently these thoughts remain undigested on paper and synthesized into cogent ideas in the worker's mind or eventually on paper at a much later time.

Dr. Gelman states: "except in unusual and limited situations, professionals should feel comfortable in sharing with the client what is contained in the record," but fails to outline what would be "unusual" or "limited situations." I believe that it should be within the domain of the professional relationship that questions regarding the record be handled. This is more advantageous than a simple access release.

Perhaps the most compelling argument for not allowing clients access to their mental health records is discussed by Dr. Gelman. In spite of the fact that social work departments may hold more information than other professionals, "the information, however, is often inaccurate, highly stigmatizing, or insulting. Social work records are known to contain contradictory opinions, value judgments, rumors, and allegations that are unsubstantiated by fact and that often do not do justice to the work that was done." Exposing clients to information that is preliminary, hypothetical, conflicting, and unsubstantiated could be hurtful or premature and could disrupt the therapeutic relationship in a way that otherwise could be avoided.

The rationale for client access to records as a means of improving record keeping and assuring accountability is an unfair burden on those who come to us in their most vulnerable states. Clients should not be burdened with the responsibility of policing our practice. Professionals, through auditing, supervision, peer review, and quality assurance, should be our tool toward ensuring high services standards.

REFERENCES

Berliner, A. K. (1989). Misconduct in social work practice. *Social Work, 34,* 69–72.

NO

MICHELE WINCHESTER-VEGA

Record keeping has been a significant part of social work practice from the beginning of our profession (Richmond, 1917). Perhaps as far back as then, the debate regarding client access to records began. The original purpose of keeping a professional record was to document professional procedures and to provide continuity of care. The chart (versus memory) was to be a place where one could recall accurately, fairly, and reasonably what occurred in the sessions. Additionally, the chart was to provide other professionals with accountability of services and data regarding the client's history and experiences in seeking assistance. Therefore, the domain or ownership of the record was that of the professional/agency. Today, these same records have become the domain of legal, legislative, and public arenas. This was not the intention of our foremothers and forefathers who originally proposed the idea of record keeping.

I will argue that clients or their families should not have free access to their mental health records, and that providing them with access could create (unforeseen) problems for them. I believe that clients' requests to examine or copy their records may have more to do with something going awry in the therapeutic relationship than with the legality of their access. Furthermore, issues of psychological damage to the client, practitioner's "knowing best," unsuitability of material for client to review, the NASW Code of Ethics guidelines, potential malingering, and the need to protect third-party confidentiality will be explored.

Unsuitability of Material for Clients to Review

Who is the worker writing the records for? If the records are written with the concern that clients might access them, it is clear that the utility of the notes are rendered suspect because of the possible noninclusion of important clinical information that a client might find derogatory in his or her treatment view. An example of this would be a narcissistic, sociopathic, or borderline client who discovers their diagnosis, only to become further enraged at the worker and begin to act out toward the worker/agency or to terminate therapy prematurely.

One must also consider the client's ability to understand that which is written in their mental health chart, because it is written in professional jargon. Misunderstandings could lead to a deterioration of the therapeutic relationship. Recently I consulted with a psychiatrist who asked me to provide a psychoeducational series of sessions to one of his clients who found her chart on his secretary's desk. In reading the chart, she discovered that he was considering electroconvulsive therapy (ECT) with her, a severely bipolar depressed client who had not responded to a series of psychopharmacological interventions. He had not verbalized the ECT consideration to her yet because he believed that she was not ready to discuss it as an option. The client interpreted the material with great paranoia (based in part on the movie *One Flew Over the Cuckoo's Nest*) and hopelessness (I will never get better), which led her into a suicidal panic.

The chart should be a place where struggles with problem-solving take place. Clients' access to their records takes away the right of the practitioner to think in written form. Without this critical material, progress notes simply become attendance records.

Psychological Damage to the Client

Another major concern is the client's readiness to deal with or accept information that may be included in the chart. An example of this would be a worker suspecting earlier trauma that the client is either consciously unaware of or is not ready to reveal. The professional's notes were not meant to be tactful, but therapy should be.

Potential Malingering

Patients may choose to manipulate treatment in such a way as to exaggerate (or pretend) mental illness to reap secondary gains of disability or insurance payments. Should the patient see his or her chart and find out that the worker does not assess them as being ill, this could create the possibility of the client going from provider to provider to achieve his or her goal.

NASW Code of Ethics

The NASW Code of Ethics states that "The social worker should afford clients with reasonable access to any unofficial social work records concerning them." (NASW Code of Ethics, II. H.3) The key word here is "reasonable." Do social workers in mental health settings disclose diagnoses directly to their clients? Using a biopsychosocial model, one should provide education regarding the diagnosis so as to outline together a treatment plan. The relationship, not the chart, should be where the material is used.

Protecting Third-Party Confidentiality

Those who drafted our Code of Ethics were mindful that many factors needed to be considered in determining the scope and nature of clients/families seeking access to their records. "When providing clients with access to records, the social worker should take due care to protect the confidences of others in those records." (NASW Code of Ethics, II.H.4) What do you do with the written material given to you about HIV+ status, relationship affairs, violent behavior, and addictive behaviors that the client has not shared, but a third party has? Given the increase in social workers providing systems (couples, family) therapy, third-party material is both important and useful. At the same time, it is essential to protect this third party's confidentiality.

Practitioners Know Best

Handling requests for access to mental health records by clients or their families requires skill. The Code of Ethics outlines affording clients "reasonable" access to their records, not carte blanche to all information. Several important steps must be taken to ensure that client access is in their clinical best interest. Decisions about what a client sees in his or her chart should be made foremost with clinical considerations in mind.

The Therapeutic Relationship

Frequently, the patient's desire to review their records does not reflect their true motivations. Often their motivations are driven by mystical thinking, fantasies, delusions, and other unresolved issues in the therapeutic arena. What motivates the client to request to see or copy the record? What is the client saying? Why now? What is known about the client that might shed light on the request being about fear, mistrust, suspicion, anxiety, a power struggle, or other concerns linked to the therapeutic process?

If the mental health worker and client are engaged in a productive therapeutic relationship, then the problems surrounding clients' access to their records most likely would not arise because the client would always be aware of the content in their "records." It is when there is an impasse in the relationship that problems get displaced onto the records.

The original reasons for keeping a chart were for providing continuity of care. The chart is meant to indicate clients' progress. Historically, records were not intended to be a mirror for the patient. Patients being allowed free access to their records is a poor compromise and substitute to psychotherapy, psychoeducation, and the opportunity to fully understand the relationship with the social worker beyond the written words in the chart.

REFERENCES

Richmond, M. (1925). Why the case records? *Family, 6,* 214–216.
National Association of Social Workers. (1990). *Code of ethics.* Silver Spring, MD.

Rejoinder to Professor Winchester-Vega   Sheldon Gelman

Although Dr. Winchester-Vega has articulated the pitfalls of client access, she has overly glamorized the therapeutic process and reinforced a one-sided and paternalistic view of helping. We need a better accounting of what professionals do, which can only be achieved by more accurate and appropriate records. The use or misuse of professional jargon within records merely serves to distance the parties in a relationship and reinforces what Dewar (1978) has characterized as the "premise of clienthood."

Social workers must be more attentive to what they write in client records and must take responsibility for the implications of information and judgments (Munday, 1987). As Bertha Reynolds noted some years ago, "Help must be connected with increase, not diminution, of self-respect, and it must imply the possibility of a reciprocal relationship of sharing, within a group to which both giver and receiver belong" (Reynolds, 1951).

Although I make the argument for access based on accountability and risk management concerns, clients' desire for access most often stems from curiosity about the contents of their record. Anger and dissatisfaction, which most often leads to filing litigation, occurs when clients are not treated with respect or as partners in the process. Appropriately implemented access policies, those that value the contribution of both clients and workers, can lead to the creation of more effective and efficient services. Workers and agencies that can commit themselves to partnership with clients can overcome much of the hostility that has traditionally been directed at the social service enterprise and create a truly accountable service delivery system.

REFERENCES

Dewar, T. R. (1978). The professionalization of the client. *Social Policy, 8*(1), 4–8.
Munday, B. (1987). Client access to personal social service records. *Eurosocial Reports* (No. 30). Vienna: European Centre for Social Welfare and Research.
Reynolds, B. C. (1951). *Social work and social living.* Washington, DC: National Association of Social Workers.

Is It Unethical for Professional Helpers to Encourage or Allow Clients to Become Dependent on Them?

EDITOR'S NOTE: Among social work educators and practitioners, dependency is almost always portrayed as a bad to be overcome, as something that gets in the way of all proper treatment objectives. Many probably could not even imagine a case for the opposite view. Here, along with a comprehensive, robust defense of the traditional position, the reader will find such an argument.

Jacinta Marschke, Ph.D., argues YES. She is Assistant Professor of Social Work at Fordham University Graduate School of Social Service. She co-authored with James Masterson, M.D., *From Borderline Adolescent to Functioning Adult: The Test of Time.*

Sharon Freedberg, DSW, argues the NO position. She is Associate Professor of Social Work at Lehman College, the City University of New York, and Adjunct Associate Professor at the Fordham University Graduate School of Social Service. She writes and teaches in the area of direct practice and is currently working on a book about Bertha Capen Reynolds and the social work profession.

YES

JACINTA MARSCHKE

Social work has always been committed to promoting client independence, fostering autonomy, encouraging client participation in treatment, promoting self-determination, and guarding against further loss of functioning. The encouragement of client dependency is inconsistent with these goals and therefore unethical.

Compton & Galaway (1995) differentiated between pathological/infantile and healthy/mature dependency. In pathological/infantile dependency, the relationship is need-gratifying, parasitic, and subordinate; in healthy/mature dependency, the relationship is reciprocal, mutually gratifying, and collaborative. One example of healthy/mature dependency is a client who seeks input from an "expert" because he or she lacks the knowledge or skills to master a new problem alone. Here the client receives help without relinquishing independence, which is enriched by his or her involvement with the worker.

More typical in social work practice are clients who are at risk to develop pathological/infantile dependency. Examples include clients who experience temporary but serious regression after transitional stress or trauma; clients who suffer with characterological or psychotic disorders; clients whose cognitive or physical disabilities have resulted in long-term physical dependency on others; clients who have been oppressed because of age, race, gender, culture, or economic status. Many of these same clients also manifest learned helplessness. This phenomenon occurs when, as a result of repeated failure to control their destiny, individuals integrate a hopeless and despairing orientation to life even in situations in which they could have some control. It is with these vulnerable populations that the worker must be wary about fostering dependency.

The worker who encourages dependency places clients at risk to regress and lose adaptive coping functions they employed previously; exacerbates the power differential between client and worker; establishes a hierarchical relationship that may undermine client participation in treatment; and focuses more on the clients' vulnerabilities than on their strengths. Although not mutually exclusive, these risks are discussed separately to elucidate why encouragement of client dependency is unethical from different perspectives.

Regression

Ego psychology, also known as psychoanalytic developmental theory, has dominated the field of social casework since the 1930s and provides a conceptual framework that is compatible with social work values. The theory is consonant with social work's focus on the "person in situation," recognizes the importance of intrapsychic, environmental, and interactive factors for development and behavior, appreciates the impact of early life experience on later development, and emphasizes the need to appeal to clients' strengths to achieve mastery. Ego psychology, together with social work values and goals and the related practice model, provide the foundation from which one can understand why it is unethical for workers to encourage clients to be dependent on them.

From an ego-psychological perspective, pathological dependency arises from developmental failures that occurred during the first three years of life. The over-gratification of the child's needs, emotional unavailability of the primary caretaker, or exposure to intense or ongoing trauma disrupts the "good enough" environment the child requires to develop normally. These early aberrations cause adult weaknesses in self-management skills, a lack of ability to establish and maintain reciprocal interpersonal relationships, conflicts about dependency and autonomy, and unstable identities.

When dependency is encouraged in these adult clients, the worker jeopardizes whatever fragile defenses and autonomy clients have achieved and may precipitate clients' recapitulation of early pathological parental relationships through transference. The return to more primitive functioning is also referred to as regression. The fostering of dependency also appeals to clients' unconscious wishes that the worker compensate for unmet infantile needs and disappointments. When this occurs, the client seeks a need-gratifying, caretaking relationship with the worker rather then striving for enhanced independence. By fostering independence, the worker spares the client additional frustration, because it would be impossible for the worker to gratify or compensate for the unmet infantile needs of the now-adult client and support and bolster the fragile self-nurturing skills the client has all ready mastered.

Power Differential Conflicts

Encouragement of client dependency highlights the discrepancy in competence between the worker and client and reinforces any negative cultural identity that may exist if the client is also a member of an oppressed population. In the latter, individuals are kept in subordinate positions on the basis of their race, gender, social class, religion, disability, or any other characteristic the dominant group chooses. Pinderhughes (1989) noted that power is a very definite factor in the clinical relationship. She stated: "It (power) is inherent in the roles of clinician and client respectively, where the helper is an expert who diagnoses, teaches and treats, while the client seeks assistance" (p. 110).

This power differential is intensified when the worker has authority to make decisions that will immediately impact the client's life. Examples of clinical situations in which workers carry enormous authority include child custody evaluations, adoption assessments, involuntary hospital admissions, and screenings for service eligibility. When the client is unavoidably dependent on the worker, it is critical that the worker help the client regain a sense of control. This can be accomplished if the worker is direct and specific about the limits of his own authority and the scope of the client's rights.

The power differential in the clinical relationship is further compounded for members of an oppressed population. For example, women constitute an oppressed population. In the mental health system, there is a gender bias in the system of classifying mental disorders (DSM I–IV) (Kaplan, 1983; Tavris, 1992) and in the standards related to healthy and normal female and male identity (Tavris, 1992). Characteristics associated with the healthy female include nurturance, dependence, passivity, and domesticity; those associated with the healthy male include competition, independence, strength, autonomy, and aggression. Women who overconform or underconform to the gender role are likely to be judged as unhealthy, or suffering from a self-defeating personality disorder or a dependent personality disorder. No equivalent diagnoses exist for the man who does not conform to the equivalent male role stereotype.

Tavris' (1992) highlights how the use of male standards to establish "normalcy" negatively influences the way women view themselves, how others view and relate to them, and how social institutions are structured to support the prevailing biases. Pervasive gender role stereotypes have resulted in a minimization of male dependency needs, a failure to support female needs for independence, a minimization of the healthy aspect of mutuality in female relationships, and a minimization of the deleterious consequences of exaggerated independence in males. Worker encouragement of dependency in female clients provides an example of how interventions can inadvertently reinforce cultural stereotypes and the oppression of nondominant groups.

Client Participation

The medical model of psychopathology, also referred to as the disease or the pathology model, has dominated psychiatric social work in spite of the fact that it does not conform to social work principles and undermines client involvement in the treatment process. Although not explicitly recommended, the underlying assumptions about psychopathology and treatment promote passive dependency in clients. The medical model attempts to conceptualize psychological disorders and behavioral disorders as analogous to organic illness. Although organic and psychological disorders are not comparable, the American Psychiatric Association has published four diagnostic classification manuals (DSM I-IV) similar to those averred for organic disorders, suggesting far more specificity and knowledge about distinct mental disorders than empirical research actually supports.

Kirk and Kutchins (1992) suggest that the most recent classification systems (DSM III and IV) are better examples of political and entrepreneurial endeavors than they are examples of scholarly and scientific inquiry. In spite of serious flaws, the DSMs and the field of mental health are still held in high regard by the general public because of their association with medicine. The adoption of language in mental health that is typically associated with organic diseases supports the continued association. Terms such as *psychopathology, disorder, disease, sick, illness, patient, treatment* and *diagnosis* are all adopted from medicine.

It is therefore not surprising that clients with emotional symptoms expect that if they report their symptoms the expert will "diagnose" the problem and "prescribe" the solution. Saleeby (1992) noted that this uneven distribution of control results in a hierarchy that elevates the power status of the expert and reinforces the subordinate position of the "disturbed" client. Because the client perceives himself or herself to be in a passive position, he or she is not apt to even consider playing an active collaborative role in the treatment. Client passivity is further encouraged by society when it permits people who are "sick" to be dependent. Because they are not expected to be accountable, passivity is encouraged, and dependency is indulged, clients are not likely to consider themselves active members of the intervention team.

Clients do much better when they actively participate with the worker in developing and carrying out plans. This process, referred to as contracting, requires that the client share responsibility with the worker for his or her own treatment. Unfortunately, this kind of client participation is less apt to occur in a mental health setting in which passivity and dependency are encouraged.

Too often clients who attend outpatient mental health clinics become "lifers." Mental health staff define "lifers" as clients who are diagnosed with chronic, "intractable," non–psychotic personality disorders, with poor prognoses. As long as the client keeps his or her appointments, shows his or her Medicaid card to ensure reimbursement, and causes no disruption, his or her exclusive dependency on the system is supported. These clients rely on their "illnesses" to explain their lack of autonomy and they become resigned to their bereft lifestyles. Their "disabilities" become their lives, and their investment in the mental health system a substitute for living. Professional social work values and ethics require that workers who practice in mental health settings guard against succumbing to any iatrogenic factors that undermine enhanced client autonomy.

Deficit Focus

Workers who encourage dependency risk further validating the negative and imbalanced view clients have of themselves. Instead of compounding this distorted view, workers should help clients to reclaim a more balanced and positive self-image. By fostering client dependency, or any weakness, the worker adds to clients' feelings of inadequacy.

Former clients, self-help groups, "consumer" and "survivor" groups, and organizations such as NAMI (National Alliance for the Mentally Ill) have repeatedly criticized the current mental health system for dehumanizing clients. They note that the almost exclusive emphasis on symptoms and dysfunction is destructive because it gives insufficient attention or balance to clients' achievements.

Saleeby (1992) defined a strengths-based intervention model that guards against "fostering or prolonging dependency" by marshaling clients' resources, teaching new coping skills, and offering concrete support. Because the assessment extends beyond client symptoms and dysfunctions, it helps workers appreciate the uniqueness and potential of the individual. Emphasis on understanding the context of the client's problem, balanced attention to assets and problems, and the collaborative nature of the worker/client relationship insures that optimal attention is given to fostering client independence.

Conclusion

Social work has never wavered in its commitment to fostering independence and autonomy among clients. The debate on the ethics of supporting client dependency derives from the adoption by some workers of theories and practice models that are incompatible with the profession's values and goals. Although the adoption of these incongruous theories may explain how workers justify the encouragement of client dependency, the risks to client autonomy and antagonism with social work principles make it unethical for workers to encourage or support increased dependency among their clients.

REFERENCES

Compton, B., & Galaway, B. (1995). *Social work processes.* Pacific Grove,CA: Brooks/Cole Publishing Co.

Kaplan, M. (July, 1983). A woman's view of DSM III. *American Psychologist,* pp. 786–792.

Kirk, S. & Kutchins, H. (1992). *The selling of DSM:The rhetoric of science in psychiatry.* New York: Aldine De Gruyter.

Pinderhughes, E. (1989). *Understanding race, ethnicity, and power: The key to efficacy in clinical practice.* New York: The Free Press.

Saleeby, D. (Ed.). (1992). *The strengths perspective in social work practice.* New York: Longman Press.

Tavris, C. (1992). *The mismeasure of woman.* New York: Simon & Shuster.

Rejoinder to Dr. Marschke
SHARON FREEDBERG

After pointing out two kinds of dependency, pathological/infantile, and healthy/mature, Dr. Marschke concedes that clients can legitimately depend on the worker for support and engage in a process that strengthens cognitive skills without relinquishing dependency. But she then proposes, without sufficient evidence, that most social work clients manifest pathological/infantile dependence related to faulty ego development, and consequently, would not benefit from a secure, ego-supportive dependent relationship.

Dependency is not inherently regressive, nor does it necessarily mean that clients will lose their adaptive coping mechanisms and autonomy. In fact, the clients Dr. Marschke describes as suffering from severe characterological or psychotic disorders most likely never had sophisticated coping strategies to lose in the first place. Inherent in all human beings is a striving for autonomy and competence, and the internal press toward growth is always more powerful than the wish to remain a dysfunctional child. There is a popular saying that children take two steps forward and one step backward in every developmental transition. The ebb is dependence, and the flow is progression and independence; both are necessary. The worker's emotional and physical availability (similar to those of a parent) allow progression to take place and a corrective emotional experience providing new opportunities for progression to occur.

Dr. Marschke's linear approach views dependency and autonomy as mutually exlusive rather than as interdependent. A client can be dependent on a worker for emotional support, information, coping skills, and still be independent, because the actual level of autonomy achieved or not achieved is more related to an early developmental process of differentiation of self. Conceptual paradigms by which society defines dependency need to change. When viewed from a feminist perspective, dependency can be seen as a phenomenon that exists within a relational context; it implies mutuality and reciprocity and is relative and dynamic rather than static and absolute.

Dr. Marschke is concerned that dependency widens the status differential between client and worker. The fact that the client has come to the worker seeking help confers a certain degree of power on the worker. Thus, the status differential between client and worker is inherent in the professional relationship and not on the worker's encouraging or supporting client dependency.

Dr. Marschke is correct in stating that when the worker is direct and specific about the limits of his or her own authority and the scope of clients' rights, clients can gain some control over their lives. Perhaps the real question is not whether dependency increases the power differential between client and worker, but how the worker uses his or her authority and to what degree the worker is comfortable with the client's competence and autonomy. As long as the worker is committed to following the NASW Code of Ethics, which demands that the worker's primary responsibility is to the client's needs and wants, allowing client dependency is ethical practice and not "bad" practice, as Dr. Marschke suggests.

Dr. Marschke also assumes that use of the medical model results in less client autonomy and increased control by the worker. This tautology leads her to conclude that the medical model of practice, which is associated with disease, pathology, and weakness, increases client dependency on the worker. Dr. Marschke throws the baby out with the bath water by dismissing the medical model rather than viewing it as a tool for classification. Diagnosis is one way in which social workers integrate scientific knowledge into the art of social work practice. It brings the traditionally viewed "male" sphere of social work into the "female" sphere rather than dichotomizing them. Using the medical model does not necessarily mean that clients are relinquishing autonomy or decisions about their own care.

Dependency shrouds a more insidious problem: the level of oppression, exploitation, and lack of available opportunities many clients confront in their lives. We must acknowledge the social and political realities as well as the worker's role in a society that maintains an inequitable socioeconomic system from which many clients see themselves as disenfranchised.

NO

SHARON FREEDBERG

Social work literature presents a bias against client dependence on the worker, an attitude that reflects the values of Western industrialized society. This attitude assumes that inviting dependency negates the value of self-determination, diminishes self-respect in the client, and excludes the client from participating actively in the problem-solving process. I argue that not only is it ethical to encourage or allow the client to be dependent on the worker, but that this dependence is necessary and essential for the client's continued growth and development, enhanced self-esteem, identity, and competence. For the purpose of this discussion, I assume that dependence refers to the client's reliance on the worker for a certain degree of emotional support, care, and nurturance.

The very act of coming for help involves some degree of dependency and the ability to trust. Stiver views dependency as a way of being able to trust another to get one's needs met, a process of counting on other people to provide help in coping physically and emotionally with the experience and tasks encountered in the world (Stiver,1991) According to Erikson (1963), this general state of trust implies that one has learned to rely on the sameness and continuity of other providers. This is the basic foundation for identity development and the healthy personality. The reestablishment of a state of trust has been found to be the basic requirement for a positive worker–client relationship without which growth and change cannot take place. Thus, some degree of dependence is a necessary and essential ingredient in the client–worker relationship.

Dependence is a dynamic phenomenon existing on a continuum from immature, absolute dependence with a midpoint of relative dependence to a point of complete independence. Few clients are so debilitated that they cannot function on their own, yet most need the security and comfort of the client–worker relationship for learning new skills and mobilizing coping capacities. The degree to which dependency is encouraged or allowed depends on the client's needs, the level of ego integration or personality organization they present, as well as the nature of the presenting problem.

In all cases it is important for the worker to determine the type and degree of dependency that clients need. The profession's bias against allowing for client dependency has prevented social workers from acknowledging differential needs for dependence in diverse client populations and from meeting those needs appropriately. As long as the dependency allowed or encouraged is focused on the needs of the client, and not on the worker, it is ethical.

Cultural Forces

Dependency is a value-free concept. Yet in Western culture the very word carries with it a pejorative connotation associated with weakness, vulnerability, and help-lessness. Where the male-constructed ethic of self-reliance, independence, and individualism has permeated our cultural ideals, men and women are encouraged to discard or conceal rather than to acknowledge feelings of dependency, or the need for caring and support. Psychoanalyst Michael Basch (1980) says that even in clinical practice, there is a cultural bias against dependence:

> We psychotherapists are creatures of the same milieu as our patients . . . a mi-lieu that looks askance at openly acknowledged dependence once childhood has passed . . . The old and the infirm often feel disreputable and blameworthy because they can no longer function independently. (Basch, 1980, p. 118)

Cultural influences are also reflected in gender role stereotypes regarding dependency. Feminist theorists such as Jean Baker Miller emphasize that the sense of self is a relational one, clarified and differentiated in relation to another (Miller, 1976). In the process of forming relationships, dependency is often mis-labeled as an expression of regressive needs. Other feminist thinkers, such as Carol Gilligan, have noted a cultural bias against allowing and encouraging dependence in relationships. In her classic feminist view of women and relation-ships, she demonstrates how dependence issues are experienced by women differently than men. For boys and men, separation and individuation are critically tied to gender identity, because separation from the mother is essential for the development of masculinity. For girls, issues of feminine identity do not depend on the achievement of separation from the mother or on the progress of differentiation. Because masculinity is defined through separation, male gender identity is threatened by intimacy, whereas female gender identity is threatened by differentiation (Gilligan, 1982).

Women's affiliative needs do not preclude their ability to function autono-mously or maintain a coherent self-identity. Nor do men's distant stance, as manifested in counterdependent maneuvers, preclude their need for connection. To compensate for cultural bias, the worker must respect the dependency needs of all clients and accept and regard these needs in a nonjudgmental way. People need help and assistance to be appropriately dependent; allowing this enables them to gain a clearer, fuller sense of self. Consequently, the worker can help both men and women gain a deeper understanding of their dependency needs in the context of a supportive client–worker relationship.

According to Willard Gaylin, from its inception, dependence is natural to the human condition and a universal aspect of human experience. As one matures, these dependency needs remain part of one's adaptive capacities and are transferred onto most meaningful relationships throughout life (Gaylin, Glasser, Marcus, & Rothman, 1978). A client's ability to depend on a worker for skills and knowledge is necessary to enhance the client's coping capacities and problemsolving abilities.

Psychological Theories

Although the values of individuation and separation have filtered into our clinical practice and theories as well as our cultural ideals, increasing attention has been given to clinical and developmental theories reflecting the importance of attachment and connection in which the worker struggles to create an empathic and responsive relational context. In clinical social work, the concept of dependency is based on the observation that an infant is helpless and requires care and feeding by his mother. As the infant learns that she satisfies his or her physical needs, the infant becomes reliant on and oriented to her. Despite the idealized state of oneness that an infant may feel with the mother, almost all individuals suffer some sense of deprivation in nurture, care, and support in childhood. These deficits result in a residue of unmet dependency needs that persist throughout life. In some cases, early trauma and developmental arrests have intensified the need for a consistent, gratifying object to facilitate growth.

The worker who is able to play the "maternal role" in understanding the client's subjective experience provides an opportunity for ego integration and hope (Van Sweden,1994). Thus, by encouraging and allowing dependence, the worker provides a corrective emotional experience so that the client can rework early developmental failures.

The degree of dependency fostered serves to encourage identification with the worker, thus strengthening the client's ego. This capacity for identification can serve an adaptive and maturational function in the construction of a personal identity. Thus, correct use of dependence in the change process can lead to an enhanced ability to engage in relationships and promote competence and self-esteem.

I have adopted Winnicott's (1965) term, "the holding environment," to further our understanding of how the use of dependency in the client–worker relationship is a necessary and constructive technique. Object relations theorists such as Winnicott recognize the importance of relational developments throughout a person's life; Winnicott believes that the earliest relationship and its affective quality informs and interacts with other relationships throughout one's development. All later relationships are based on a generalization of this early mother–child bond. If the mother is internalized as a stable object relation, the child's autonomous ego development leading to separation and object constancy is promoted. The infant comes to define aspects of himself or herself in relation to the internalized aspects of his or her mother, her strengths, and the quality of her care. Eventually, the enriched ego capacities allow the individual to function on his or her own. It is this internal process of identity development in the context of an important ego-enriching relationship that constitutes healthy growth and mastery, and mature dependence.

Winnicott's term "the holding environment" serves as a useful metaphor for the client–worker relationship in which the social worker acts as the "mother" in guiding the client on the journey to self-differentiation while maintaining the capacity for closeness and relatedness. The key feature of this holding environment is the mother's efforts to shape the environment around the child's wishes, to intuit what the child wants, and to provide it (Mitchell, 1988). The worker, through skilled use of empathic attunement, acceptance, and understanding, can create the proper facilitating environment in which his or her strengths as a good "self-object" are internalized by the client, thus bolstering the client's own adaptive functioning. This provides a secure foundation on which a healthy self develops.

Implicit in this kind of reparative work is the acceptance of client dependence; it provides an opportunity for ego integration, replacing futility with hope. Allowing client dependence is one of the healing forces of the "holding" environment and part of the worker's caretaking functions. A client who is forced into premature self-sufficiency does so by means of an illusion for which the ego pays a price (Modell, 1976).

Summary

The ability to acknowledge and express realistic dependency needs is an essential aspect of healthy psychological functioning. Unfortunately, the autonomous and self-sufficient adult has remained a psychological ideal in Western culture, influencing the practice of social work. As we learn more about early development, we see that an infant begins life with many capacities for relatedness, dependence, and interdependence. The social worker must support the client's ability to acknowledge and express the more adaptive aspects of dependency, including realistic fears, wishes to be cared for, and vulnerabilities. The struggle to achieve a healthy integration of passive–dependent longings and active autonomous strivings is a lifelong process. If dependence is seen as something to be avoided, something that precludes independence, the social worker may resist providing a secure base that the client needs in his or her journey toward self-direction and independence. Paradoxically, the truly self-reliant person has the capacity to trustingly depend on the other when the occasion demands and to know on whom it is appropriate to rely. The ethical social worker, in his or her ability to encourage and allow dependence, truly understands this.

REFERENCES

Basch, M. (1980). *Doing psychotherapy.* New York: Basic Books.

Erikson, E. (1963). *Childhood and society.* New York: W. W. Norton and Company.

Gaylin, W., Glasser, I., Marcus, S., & Rothman, D. (1978). *Doing good.* New York: Pantheon Books.

Gilligan, C. (1982). *In a different voice.* Cambridge, MA: Harvard University Press.

Lerner, H. (1983). Female dependency in context: Some theoretical and technical considerations. *American Journal of Orthopsychiatry, 53*(4), 698–705.

Miller, J. B. (1976). *Toward a new psychology of women.* Boston, MA: Beacon Press.

Mitchell, S. (1988). *Relational concepts in psychoanalysis.* Cambridge, MA: Harvard University Press.

Modell, A. (1976). The holding environment and the therapeutic action of psychoanalysis. *Journal of American Psychoanalytic Association, 24*(2), 285–307.

Stiver, I. (1991). The meaning of dependency in male-female relationships. In J. Jordan, A. Kaplan, J. Miller Baker, I. Stiver, & J. Surrey. *Women's growth in connection.* New York: Guilford Press.

Van Sweden, R. (1994). *Regression to dependence.* Northvale, NJ: Jason Aronson.

Winnicott, D. W.(1965). *The maturational processes and the facilitating environment.* New York: International Universities Press.

Rejoinder to Professor Freedberg JACINTA MARSCHKE

Dr. Freedberg's initial definition of dependency is very general: that is,"client's reliance on the worker for a certain degree of emotional support, care, and nurturance." Indeed, it is highly unlikely that any relationship would develop if the client did not experience the worker as supportive, nurturant, and caring. These attributes constitute basic ingredients of any therapeutic relationship. Clients' expectations of these qualities derive from their right to be served with respect and dignity, not from any underlying infantile dependency need.

Later in the document, Dr. Freedberg extends her practice definition of client dependency in a way that suggests that she agrees that the worker must be extremely cautious about encouraging client dependency. She notes that "the degree to which dependency is encouraged or allowed depends on . . . the level of ego integration, or personality organization they present, as well as the nature of the presenting problem." Additional references to ". . . realistic dependency needs," and "the need for the worker to support client's ability to . . . express the more adaptive aspects of dependency" suggest further that Dr. Freedberg is acutely aware that she appreciates the difference between a therapeutic alliance and dependency.

I disagree with her belief that the profession has integrated Western industrialized society's bias against dependency and has not acknowledged the need to attend to clients' dependency needs. My own clinical experience and review of the literature suggest just the opposite, that is, that social workers too often focus on clients' weaknesses instead of on their capabilities for autonomous functioning, and they believe that clients need longer-term treatment even when clients believe that they have achieved their goals. Perhaps this reflects the field's integration of another widely held cultural bias, that dependency is acceptable and encouraged as long as the client is perceived to be "sick."

Although both positions affirm the social work principle of client acceptance, they differ when the principle is applied to actual practice. Dr. Freedberg suggests that worker acceptance and encouragement of client dependency should compensate for societal biases and should sanction clients' pursuit of dependency need satisfaction throughout the entire life cycle. She also argues that this encouragement of dependency fosters a "corrective emotional experience" in which clients gratify previously frustrated infantile dependency needs, "rework early developmental failures," achieve self-differentiation, solidify ego integration, establish their identity, and function independently. To achieve the above, she suggests that worker acceptance must involve more than conveying a nonjudgmental appreciation of clients' strengths and weaknesses. In her view, worker acceptance should also include proactive interventions that reinforce the need-gratifying aspects of the therapeutic relationship. The application of this broad definition of acceptance and the "corrective emotional experience" perspective to social work practice raises some serious concerns. The orientation provides no guidelines from which to determine how much and for how long client dependency is required to complete the "reparative work." Neither is it clear when the encouragement of dependency become too much or destructive. One also wonders whether these therapeutic goals can ever be achieved in a social work relationship that usually involves no more than one session a week and, because of reality constraints, is usually time limited. These goals, as articulated by Dr. Freedberg, seem extremely ambitious when one considers that, relative to the client's life, the actual time the worker and client are together is minimal. Because the "reparative work" needed by these clients is so great and the availability of intervention so limited, one would think that clients' needs would be better served by maximizing their ability to self-nurture, minimizing their dependency on the "helping professional," and capitalizing on those need-gratifying resources in the community that are more immediately accessible when the client needs them.

Dr. Freedberg's observation that "women's affiliative needs do not preclude their ability to function autonomously or maintain a coherent self-identity" suggests a conceptualization and definition of dependency that may allow for client expression and gratification of dependency strivings without risking clients' autonomy, adaptive functioning, or self-determination. Although the concepts of dependence and independence have been viewed historically as mutually exclusive, the research on female development (Gilligan,1982) suggests that it is possible to depend on another and maintain one's autonomy, competence, and self-esteem. Motenko and Greenberg (1995) recently noted that aging individuals are more able to accept increased dependency when it occurs in a context that secures their autonomy. When familial relationships remain reciprocal, mutually gratifying, and functionally appropriate to each member's unique strengths and abilities, the aging individual can actually experience an increase in self-esteem and autonomy as he or she becomes more physically dependent. Bearing these concepts in mind, it would be possible for a worker to support client dependency as long as it posed no threat to autonomy and occurred within the context of a reciprocal relationship. There is even less of a risk that worker interventions will jeopardize client independence and existing adaptive functioning if the worker embraces social work's goals to foster client autonomy, self-determination, and client participation and then chooses to adopt only those additional views that are congruent with these aims.

REFERENCES

Gilligan, C. (1982). *In a different voice.* Cambridge, MA: Harvard University Press.

Motenko, A., & Greenberg, S. (1995). Reframing dependence in old age: A positive transition for families. *Social Work, 40*(3), 382–391.

Does Reliance on Diagnostic Labels Help Clients More Than It Hurts Them?

EDITOR'S NOTE: The new edition of the *Diagnostic and Statistical Manual* is thicker than ever, containing even more diagnostic labels. Diagnostic labeling has been eagerly embraced by many social workers. Does the use of such labels help clients more than it harms them? Is it useful in understanding clients' complaints and selecting effective service methods? Can clients be reliably categorized into particular diagnoses? Are the classifications suggested valid? Are social workers who use diagnostic labels ethically bound to inform clients about reliability and validity concerns? Are they ethically required to inform clients when they assign a diagnostic label to them or to their significant others? Social work scholars such as Stuart Kirk and Herb Kutchins have taken a leading role in reviewing the history and current methodological status of the DSM in their book *The Selling of DSM* (1992). The debates that follow should help readers to think critically about diagnostic labels.

Larry Icard, Ph.D., who argues the YES position, is Associate Professor, School of Social Work, University of Washington. He has authored several articles on the mental health of gay and lesbian African Americans and preventing AIDS among African Americans. He is the author of the forthcoming coming book titled *Social Work Practice with African American Men Who Have Sex with Men,* to be published by Haworth Press.

Sherri F. Seyfried, Ph.D., answers NO. She is Assistant Professor, School of Social Work, University of Washington, where she teaches cultural diversity and cross-cultural mental health practice. Having practiced clinical social work, her current research concerns the academic achievement of minority preadolescents, culturally competent research, and the development of a culturally relevant family environment instrument.

YES

LARRY ICARD

The function of diagnostic labels in practice has long been debated in the social work profession. The value of diagnostic labels for clients is of particular concern today given the importance diagnostic assessments hold for service reimbursement and fiscal accountability. A variety of diagnostic classification systems are available to practitioners; however, the *Diagnostic and Statistical Manual* or DSM and its most current version, DSM-IV, is the most widely used system in the field of mental health. Thus, my comments refer primarily to the use of the DSM.

In the question: "Does reliance on diagnostic labels help clients more than it hurts them?" the operative word is reliance. According to the *Random House Dictionary*, reliance is defined as confident or trustful dependence. Consequently the question can be interpreted as asking whether a practitioner's dependence on diagnostic labels is more beneficial than harmful to clients. I argue YES, and I present several benefits such labels offer to clients, such as: (1) conceptualizations for organizing information; (2) nomenclature for communicating ideas; (3) demystifying mental illness; (4) contributing to client empowerment; (5) reducing negative attitudes; (6) differentiation of severity; and (7) promoting efficient use of services.

Conceptualizations for Organizing Information

When clients seek help, practitioners frequently can be overwhelmed and unable to integrate the enormous amount of information that is related to the problem. Information that is significant for designing ways to resolve problems becomes confused with information that is not. Practitioners must have the ability to filter out unimportant information in order to structure relevant information in a coherent way that leads to optimal treatment planning. Conceptualizations and diagnostic classifications function as filters, allowing practitioners to create coherence out of the information clients present. Diagnostic categories thus serve as efficient summarizations of the practitioner's assessment of the client's problem.

Unfortunately, the important functions of filtering information and efficient summarizations can be compromised when diagnostic labels are applied in a shortsighted and inappropriate manner, for example, without proper knowledge or consideration for individual client circumstances. An example of the pitfalls in applying diagnostic labels in a shortsighted manner is offered by a therapist discussing treatment for a client diagnosed as borderline (Layton, 1995). The therapist describes how traditional interventions for treating borderline pathological conditions, for example setting boundaries and focusing on relationships to help the client experience connection and trust, were not working. Over the course of several sessions, the therapist realizes that the history of trauma in the client's life was being overlooked. As a child, the client had been severely abused, both physically and sexually. Modifying the treatment strategy to help the client deal with the trauma that she had experienced as a child, the therapist shifts attention from focusing on the character disorder to the context of social factors in which the character disorder became constructed.

It is important that we keep in mind that diagnostic classifications are a descriptive tool for categorizing psychopathology. They do not address the cause of the illness. Once the therapist realized the historical trauma underlying the client's dissociative behavior of a borderline pathological condition, the therapist was able to capitalize on the benefits that the diagnostic classification offered in facilitating an accurate assessment and appropriate treatment (Layton, 1995).

Facilitating Communication

Another way in which diagnostic labels benefit clients is that they enable communication and collaboration among practitioners from various disciplines. Social workers have become a major force in the mental health field. For this reason, as noted by Christ (1983), and more recently by Williams and Spitzer (1995), it is important that social work practitioners be able to communicate using common standards and indicators of severity that are deemed appropriate for practice in mental health.

Demystifying Mental Illness

Diagnostic labels help to demystify mental illnesses. Wasow (1978) describes the pain and discouragement she experienced as a mother of a son suffering from mental illness. For two years she hopelessly watched her sixteen-year-old son's emotional state deteriorate while receiving little information from mental health professionals as to what to call, much less how to explain, her son's idiosyncratic view of reality and puzzling behavior. It was not until a year later that a psychiatrist disclosed to her that he had early on diagnosed her son as suffering from schizophrenia. Wasow (1978) states:

> This fear of labeling occurs again and again in the mental health field. Labeling people is harmful, we are told. Certainly labeling has been abused, and it can be harmful. But it can also be useful. Refusal to give the disease a name will not help. (p. 136)

Quoting Siegler and Osmond, Wasow further notes:

> Even when there is no wholly satisfactory treatment for an illness, the doctor can make certain time-honored moves which will alleviate the suffering of the patient and his family. He can give the disease a name and thus reduce its mystery. (p. 137)

Client Empowerment

Diagnostic classifications are also important in contributing to the empowerment of clients. Fundamental to the values of the social work profession is the client's right to self-determination. Having a name for an illness permits the client to develop a general knowledge of his or her experience as well as what to expect in terms of services. Thus, the classification of an emotional illness helps clients gain some control over the type of care they receive. In those situations in which a client does not have the capacity to raise questions or understand the concepts and language being used to describe their problems, classification permits others do so. Classifications therefore provide information to help in advocating on behalf of clients.

Reducing Negative Attitudes

Historically, social attitudes in this country have been much more sympathetic to persons suffering from physical illnesses than to those with mental illnesses. In part, the often harsh attitudes about people experiencing a mental disorder is related to the evasiveness of the meaning of mental illness. Why is one child chronically depressed when the other children in the neighborhood are generally happy? Obviously, something must be wrong with the depressed child, or the child's family has done something to cause the depression. Such undiscerning attitudes on mental illness were prominent several years ago, and remain today in many parts of the country.

In the past, people experiencing a disabling emotional problem were often viewed as having some individual deficit. The classification of emotional disorders has helped to reduce such negative thinking. For example, before autism had its distinct classification as an emotional disorder, often the child as well as the parents were harshly criticized. Today, however, a better understanding exists largely as a result of its classification. The ability to diagnose and categorize emotional illnesses has therefore helped to further the general population's view of a mental illness as being somewhat similar to a physical illness. Classifying emotional disorders thus lent credence to mental illness.

Differentiation of Severity

Diagnostic classification helps establish a continuum that distinguishes chronic from mild illnesses. Classification of mental disorders by severity in turn contributes to making decisions about what type and under what set of conditions an emotional disorder becomes a public concern. Typically, when the severity and scope of a problem threaten the well-being of large numbers of people, society takes some responsibility for providing assistance. Diagnostic classifications therefore may be viewed as providing important information for making decisions regarding the allocating of public monies.

Promoting Efficient Use of Services

The federally mandated prospective payment system that was designed to control the health care costs for Medicare recipients—Diagnosis-Related Groups, commonly known as DRGs—cannot be applied to mental health care. Diagnostic classifications could potentially be employed along with other attributes for client services, such as level of social and physical functioning to delineate service costs, and serve as a tool for planners and administrators of mental health services in determining how to match resources to client needs. In great demand are better ways to predict costs for mental health services that can be accurately linked to the client's need for service. Such applications of diagnostic classifications, although at an early stage of development, could provide a welcome relief to the challenge we currently face in trying to contain escalating costs for health care.

Conclusion

In this essay, I have identified several benefits that diagnostic classifications offer our clients. Unfortunately, many writers on this topic are disposed to pointing out the costs rather than the rewards that diagnostic classifications hold for clients (Eysenck, Wakefield, & Friedman, 1983; Kutchins & Kirk, 1995; Wylie, 1995). Of primary concern is that diagnostic classifications are clinically viewed as defining that which is deemed normative and appropriate. Yet, as much as we are critical of diagnostic classifications, so too, I submit that we should require ourselves to recognize their benefits. To do otherwise would suggest a form of antiscientific thinking counter to the nature and meaning of professionalism. Yes, diagnostic classifications can and do benefit our clients. Practitioners, however, should guard against being overly reliant or dependent on diagnostic labels. To do so will result in negative consequences, including making narrow judgments and the reification of and use of concepts that do not accurately portray the client's problem. And, yes, diagnostic classifications are in need of continual refinement and modification to be most beneficial in responding to clients needs. Such is the ongoing challenge in attempting to respond to the ambiguities that characterize human behavior.

REFERENCES

Christ, G. H. (1983). A psychosocial assessment framework for cancer patients and their families. *Health and Social Work, 8*(1), 57–64.

Eysenck, H., Wakefield, J., & Friedman, A. (1983). Diagnosis and clinical assessment: The DSM-III. *Annual Review of Psychology, 34,* 167–193.

Kutchins, H., & Kirk, S. (1995). Response to Janet Williams and Robert Spitzer. *Social Work Education, 31*(2), 153–158.

Layton, M. (1995). The power of DSM-IV: Emerging from the shadows. *The Family Networker, 19*(3), 34–41.

Wasow, M. (1978). For my beloved son David Jonathan: A professional plea. *Health and Social Work, 3*(1), 126–146.

Williams, J. B. W., & Spitzer, R. L. (1995). Should DSM be the basis for teaching social work practice in mental health? Yes. *Social Work Education, 31*(2), 148–153.

Wylie, M. S. (1995). Diagnosing for dollars? *The Family Networker, 19*(3), 23–33.

Rejoinder to Professor Icard   Sherri F. Seyfried

The major difficulty that I have with Professor Icard's position is that the reader is led to believe that his argument will relate to issues specific to the DSM-IV. However, it is uncertain how his comments refer to the DSM. Most of his statements are general issues around the benefits of classification systems. As a result, the reader is left wondering, what is Icard's position regarding the DSM-IV? Does he really believe that social workers should rely on the clinical utility of the DSM-IV?

Classification systems are useful means for organizing information, and social workers should be familiar with the DSM. However, I have stated that the DSM is more politically expedient than it is clinically useful, and it appears that many social workers also share this sentiment. Kutchins and Kirk (1995) refer to a survey in which they found 33 percent of the social workers polled agreed that the DSM-III was useful, 48 percent disagreed, 19 percent were undecided, and 60 percent would not have used the DSM if they were not required to do so. Apparently many clinical social workers believe the DSM has limited clinical utility.

Icard suggests that critics of classification systems (presumably the DSM) should consider the benefits; "to do otherwise would suggest a form of antiscientific thinking counter to the nature and meaning of professionalism." Few would dispute that the DSM has certain political and economic benefits; however, for the most part, clients are not the recipients of those benefits. It is ironic that Icard refers to skeptics of the DSM as "unprofessional and unscientific." It has been documented that the validity and reliability of the DSM has been questionable for some time. Kirk and Kutchins (1994) state: "In fact, it appears that the reliability problem is much the same as it was 30 years ago. Only now, the current developers of DSM-IV have de-emphasized the reliability problem and claim to be scientifically solving other problems" (p. 83). Kirk and Kutchins further note: ". . . most reliability studies have been conducted in specialized research settings and may have little bearing on the actual use of DSM by clinicians in normal, uncontrolled clinical settings, where external bureaucratic demands, reimbursement probabilities and potential stigma influence their judgments" (p. 84). As noted earlier, Melvin Wilson (1993), in reference to the DSM-III and DSM-IV, believes the field of psychiatry may have narrowed its clinical scope in efforts to promote psychiatry's identity. How is it that individuals who question the clinical usefulness of the DSM become labeled as "antiscientific" or "unprofessional"?

Finally, Icard maintains that the primary concern of diagnostic classifications should be to determine "that which is deemed normative and appropriate." Normative and appropriate according to whose standards? The DSM is very "American" or "mainstream" in its focus on individual functioning. Dana (1995) warns us that ". . . the DSM III-R categories should be used with caution for individuals in the United States who do not have the dominant society's Anglo-American cultural orientation" (p. 63). Dana suggests the future addition of a cultural axis; however, he makes it clear that before this is done diagnostic procedures for cultural assessment must be established. To impose mainstream standards of behavior on clients would be antithetical to social work's mission, but most importantly, social workers would cause clients more harm than good.

REFERENCES

Dana, R. H. (1995). Impact of the use of standard psychological assessment on the diagnosis and treatment of ethnic minorities. In J. F. Aponte, R. Y. Rivers, & J. Wohl (Eds.), *Psychological Interventions and Cultural Diversity* (pp. 57–73). Boston: Allyn & Bacon.

Kirk, S. & Kutchins, H. (1994). The myth of the reliability of DSM. *The Journal of Mind and Behavior.* Winter and Spring 1994, Vol. 15, Numbers 1 and 2, 71–86.

Kutchins, H., & Kirk, S. (1995). Should DSM be the basis for teaching social work practice in mental health? NO! *Social Work Education,* 31(2), 159–165.

Wilson, M. (1993). DSM-III and the transformation of American psychiatry: A history. *American Journal of Psychiatry,* March, 399–410.

NO

SHERRI F. SEYFRIED

In the United States, mental health professionals are required to use the *Diagnostic and Statistical Manual of Mental Disorders* (DSM) for various administrative purposes and to submit diagnoses to insurers. As a result, the cultures of most mental health facilities are determined by the political and economical utility of the DSM. To what extent are mental health social workers influenced by the DSM? I argue that reliance on diagnostic labels will do clients more harm than good, for the following reasons: (1) the DSM restricts assessment and intervention, (2) the DSM is more politically expedient than clinically useful, (3) labeling creates negative effects, and (4) labeling reinforces biases and stereotypes.

The DSM Restricts Assessment and Intervention

Reliance on the DSM severely limits the social worker's ability to respect the uniqueness of the individual and the client's right to self-determination. At the point when clients come for help, they are often much less cognizant of their strengths than of their weaknesses. The DSM's emphasis on pathological behavior takes attention away from assessment of strengths, coping, and identification of supportive resources. Furthermore, with the emphasis on pathology, clinicians are merely treating symptoms of the problem and not the cause. Social workers who are part of a mental health team rarely find support for using a strengths perspective. As a result, they are encouraged to conform to a model that contradicts the profession's mission. How are clients to get well if clinicians are encouraged to emphasize pathology?

Moreover, the social worker is forced to fit the client's behavior into restrictive categories that may or may not accurately represent the client's situation. For example, followers of the medical model may provide a diagnosis of oppositional defiant disorder for the child who appears to be indifferent to authority figures and blames others for his mistakes. However, the clinician oriented to a person-in-environment perspective finds that the seemingly maladaptive behaviors are actually reactions to a hostile classroom environment.

Given that it is the social worker's ethical responsibility to respect the unique aspects of client functioning, and the structure of the DSM does not encourage assessment of individual differences, it is difficult to see how the DSM can usefully inform individual interventions. When clients are misdiagnosed and provided with inappropriate treatment interventions, they may develop less effective coping mechanisms or become resistant to treatment and eventually drop out. Social workers who rely on the DSM will seriously compromise the quality of service they provide their clients. Furthermore, they will risk the integrity of the profession because they do not uphold the fundamental values that are unique to social work.

Finally, in social work, individual-focused diagnostic labels do not allow for policy or social change initiatives. If the problem is inside the person (rather than in their living situation, life stressors, or socioeconomic resources), then policy change will have little impact. This is a consequence of a diagnostic system that does not take into account the environmental aspects of problems or solutions. This is another reason why the DSM and its use in mental health is antithetical to the basic value foundation of the social work profession.

The DSM Is More Politically Expedient Than Clinically Useful

A historical analysis of the DSM illustrates how its evolution had more to do with preserving psychiatry's professional identity than with enhancing clinical practice. Melvin Wilson (1993) provides a historical analysis of the DSM from its post World War II psychosocial orientation to the development of DSM-III (3rd ed.).

The psychosocial model of psychiatry was developed after World War II. This model combined the intrapsychic dynamics of Freudian thought and the environmentally oriented approach of Meyerian psychiatry. Karl Menniger (1948), a supporter of the psychosocial model, claimed that the World War II veteran's psychiatric experience clearly illustrated the "personality–environment struggle." This model came under attack in the '60s from critics both within and outside psychiatry. Critics outside the profession believed that if mental illness were caused by social problems such as racism, unemployment, and poverty, then mental illness had no medical basis. Psychiatrists argued that the psychosocial model did not lend itself to research; however a consensus was eventually reached that it was necessary to reevaluate the psychosocial model. This decision was largely influenced by public scrutiny of the model, restriction of public research funds, and private insurance reimbursements. The tide of opinion moved toward revision of the model. After some debate within psychiatry regarding what form the revised model should take or whether it was necessary to adopt another model, it was decided to return to the medical model or disease model, which considers the problem of emotional functioning to originate within the individual. It was thought that this model would be more compatible with medical research.

The development of the DSM-III heralded a return to the medical model of mental illness. The question remains whether the DSM-III and the current DSM-IV are reliable and valid. Wilson (1993) believes psychiatry, in attempts to regain its identity, may have narrowed its clinical scope. Kirk and Kutchins (1992) seriously question the reliability and validity of the DSM-IV. More specifically, they claim that the reliability studies for the DSM-IV were never intended to influence its development. If it is true that the major motivating force behind the development of the DSM was for professional reidentification, then we must view the DSM as a political medium. True, the DSM is part of the American mental health system, and social workers must use it for reimbursement even if it has unhelpful effects. Mental health professionals have to contend with the DSM; it is part of doing business in mental health services. But this mandatory use does not make it a clinically useful tool.

Labeling Creates Negative Effects

Szasz (1993) suggests that psychiatric diagnostic labels are used as a source of social control and that they serve no other purpose. More specifically, he claims that denying a person freedom (because of mental illness) is a political act and should not be interpreted as therapeutic intervention. Quite often clients are coerced to seek treatment against their will because family members and or mental health professionals perceive them to be mentally ill. The process of involuntary commitment is humiliating, degrading, and further reinforces the client's limited sense of self-worth.

Labeling of clients has negative, unintended effects that outweigh any positive benefits (Stuart, 1973). Stuart argues that labels are faulty because they are used as explanations of behavior rather than as descriptors (as they were intended). Labels reify the phenomena they are supposedly describing. For example, instead of saying the person is behaving in an antisocial way, the label takes on an explanatory power: the client is behaving that way because he or she has an antisocial disorder. As a result, labels influence social judgments about what people are capable of, and they influence self-concept, self-esteem, and self-efficacy.

Psychiatric diagnoses carry with them explanatory powers that influence how others will view clients. Rosenhan's study (1973) demonstrates this point. He found that professional mental health staff could not distinguish "insane" from "sane" patients. Rosenhan and his colleagues went to twelve different hospitals in five states, reporting to hear voices. After they were admitted, they stated they were no longer hearing voices. On discharge, they were given diagnoses of schizophrenia in remission. They were given this diagnosis only because they initially exhibited behaviors associated with schizophrenia. Their subsequent presentation of healthy behavior had no effect on the diagnosis. Labeling diminishes self-reliance and denies the client's right to self-determination. The reifying effects of labeling limit the client's free will to make decisions and negate the client's efforts toward self-discipline. Labeling encourages others to set limited expectations for the client's potential for recovery and self-efficacy.

Diagnostic Labels Reinforce Biases and Stereotypes

Culturally encapsulated diagnostic inventories such as the DSM have little regard for individual client characteristics such as age, ethnicity, gender, class, sexual orientation, or status. Consequently, it is inevitable that such inventories reinforce biases and stereotypes. Traditionally it has been the mission of social work to empower members of disenfranchised groups. Reliance on culturally insensitive diagnostic inventories is antithetical to this mission. But most importantly, reliance on such inventories will cause clients more harm than good.

The DSM is particularly "American" or "mainstream" in its focus on individual disorders as explanations for problems in living. As an afterthought, the DSM-IV (4th edition) did add a very brief section on "Culture Bound Formulation and a Glossary of Culture Bound Syndromes." However, this section is not incorporated into the multiaxial structure of the DSM-IV, and there is little instruction about its use. Furthermore, the glossary implies a very narrow and limited concept of culture that excludes the psychocultural adaptation and status of culturally different groups. It is the level of psychocultural adaptation and the power differential associated with status that affect the emotional well-being of culturally different individuals. It has been suggested that culturally competent assessment inventories should require the clinician to assess the psychocultural adaptation, coping mechanisms, of culturally different individuals. Assessing the level of psychocultural adaptation is particularly relevant when considering the emotional development of minority children (McLoyd, 1991; Powell, 1983). In this regard, the DSM has failed to acknowledge the coping strategies of culturally different populations. It has also been documented that the secondary status ascribed to ethnic minorities has an affect on their self-concepts and emotional well-being (Longres, 1991; Ogbu, 1991). Developers of diagnostic inventories, such as the DSM, impose the dominant standards of mainstream behavior; consequently, the clinical acumen of social workers will be severely limited by their reliance on the DSM.

In efforts to make the DSM more culturally relevant, some researchers have suggested the inclusion of culturally specific diagnoses. To enhance diagnostic practice with African American children, Johnson (1993) suggests that the DSM should incorporate a sixth axis that measures psychocultural adaptation. He also suggests additions to Axis I that include measures of racial trauma, the psychological experiences of racism. The culture-bound syndromes listed in the DSM-IV are not helpful in assessing the level of psychocultural adaptation or racial trauma. Psychological disorders related to male domination have not been part of the DSM nomenclature. Pantony and Caplan (1991) suggest that the diagnosis of delusional dominating personality be added to the DSM. They claim that some men experience rigid masculine socialization that results in serious psychological problems. With the increased reports of spousal abuse, namely, with women as the objects of the abuse, one would hope that Pantony and Caplan's suggestion be given serious consideration.

Authors such as Conrad and Scheider (1992), Lemert (1967), and Scheff (1984) argue that diagnostic labels are prescribed when behavior is considered to be out of the norm of mainstream society. What are the parameters that determine "normal" behavior, and whose standards are used to make this decision? Behavior that is perceived to be out of the "norm" is subject to discrimination. For example, before the DSM-III (third edition), homosexuality was considered to be an emotional disorder. After a strong protest from the gay community, the diagnosis was eliminated from the-DSM III. However, the discriminatory effects of diagnostic labeling are long lasting, and they encourage the prejudicial treatment of culturally different individuals.

In these increasingly conservative times, diagnostic labels are used as a means of social control (Szasz, 1993). The DSM is very American in its assessment of human behavior, and individuals that are not perceived to be part of mainstream society are punished and categorized as being atypical. It is in this sense that the DSM serves as a means of social control. Although social workers must use the DSM, this does not mean that it is designed to serve the client's best interest. In fact, social workers who rely on the DSM will do clients more harm than good, because the DSM fails to respect the uniqueness of the individual and diminishes the client's free will to make his or her own decisions.

REFERENCES

Conrad, P. & Schneider, J. W. (1992). *Deviance and medicalization: From badness to sickness.* Philadelphia, PA: Temple University Press.

Johnson, R. (1993). Clinical issues in the use of the DSM-III-R with African American children: A diagnostic paradigm. *The Journal of Black Psychology, 19(4), 447–460.*

Kirk, S. A. & Kutchins, H. (1992). *The selling of DSM: The rhetoric of science in psychiatry.* New York: Aldine de Gruyter.

Lemert, E. (1967). *Human deviance, social problems, and social control.* Englewood Cliffs, NJ: Prentice-Hall.

Longres, J. F. (1991). Toward a status model of ethnic sensitive practice. *Journal of Multicultural Social Work,* 1. 41–56.

McLoyd, V. C. (1991). What is the study of African American children the study of? In R. L. Jones (Ed.), Black Psychology (pp. 419–440). Berkeley, CA: Cobb and Henry.

Menninger, W. (1948). *Psychiatry in a Troubled World: Yesterday's War and Today's Challenge.* New York: Macmillan.

Ogbu, J. U. (1991). Immigrant and involuntary minorities in perspective. In M. A. Gibson & J. W. Ogbu (Eds.), *Minority Status and Schooling* (pp. 3–33). New York: Garland.

Pantony, K. L. & Caplan, P. J. (1991). Delusional dominating personality disorder: A modest proposal for identifying some consequences of rigid masculine socialization. *Canadian Psychology,* 32(2), 120–135.

Powell, G. J. (Ed.) (1983) *The psychosocial development of minority group children* New York: Brunner/Mazel

Rosenhan, D. L. (1973). On being sane in insane places. *Science, 179,* 250–257.

Scheff, T. (1984). *Labeling madness* (2nd Ed.). Englewood Cliffs, NJ: Prentice-Hall.

Stuart, R. B. (1973). *Trick or treatment: How and when psychotherapy fails.* Champaign, IL: Research Press.

Szasz, T. (1993). Curing, coercing, and claims-making: A reply to critics. *British Journal of Psychiatry, 162,* 797–800.

Wilson, M. (1993). DSM-III and the transformation of American psychiatry: A history. *American Journal of Psychiatry,* 399–410.

Rejoinder to Professor Seyfried   LARRY ICARD

In response to my colleague's argument that diagnostic labels restrict assessments and interventions, I submit that diagnostic criteria, in particular, the most recent DSM-IV, offer a system that classifies clinical presentations based on the quantification of attributes rather than the mere assignment of behavior to categories. Thus, it is the degree to which certain characteristics may be harmful and dysfunctions become pronounced that determines whether the summation of those attributes meets the conditions of a diagnostic category.

Similarly, the use of diagnostic classifications neither precludes, nor denies a practictioner's respect for and individualization of clients. Diagnostic classifications ultimately do require professionals to make distinctions based on standardized classifications; some standardization is necessary to facilitate practitioners' responses to clients' needs in an efficient and systematic fashion.

Dr. Seyfried also states that "individual-focused" diagnostic labels do not allow for policy or social change initiatives. As I point out in my statement, diagnostic classifications—contrary to the naive eye—do play an important role in shifting social attitudes from that of judgments on moral and individual inadequacies to a broader view of emotional illness as an issue affecting the welfare of our society. To say that diagnostic classifications of emotional illness restrict social policy because they focus on the individual is ludicrous. Clearly, physical illnesses such as diabetes, cancer, or acquired immune deficiency syndrome (AIDS) are in many ways individual illnesses. Still, the severity, magnitude, and scope of mental health problems, similar to these physical health problems, necessitates attention by public policies and monies and consequently require initiatives involving social change.

Closely related to her argument of individuality, Dr. Seyfried asserts that diagnostic classifications are indifferent to client diversity. Diagnostic classifications are in essence social constructions, and yes, they have all too often discounted the utility of certain behaviors of groups that are marginalized in our society. Homosexuals, women, and ethnic minorities have been and in many ways continue to be diagnosed by standards that do not recognize behavior that is a necessary response to chronic societal oppression. Yet, as knowledge, diagnostic classifications are evolving and must continually evolve. As pointed out in my colleague's statement, reflected in DSM-IV is the increasing attention that is being given to cultural as well as lifestyle nuances that have previously been neglected or unrecognized for their positive adaptive value. Thus, the challenge for social workers and other mental health professionals is to be aware of and sensitive to the consequences of the inherent social values and cultural biases of diagnostic classifications when assessing and responding to clients' needs.

Dr. Seyfried argues that diagnostic labels can conjure up negative images and thus stigmatize clients. Diagnostic labels are meant to serve as guidelines to be informed by clinical judgment rooted in specific individualized observation. The stigmatizing of clients that results from inappropriate use of DSM categories can be caused by a number of factors, including poor training and lack of professional behavior on the part of practitioners, in addition to negative societal bias in general toward people requiring mental health services. Better training and supervision and consumer groups and organizations such as the National Alliance for the Mentally Ill can help address the problem.

Although diagnostic labels can have adverse consequences for our clients, they also offer them benefits. As so poignantly illustrated by Wasow, whose comments I refer to in my statement, labels help to demystify mental illnesses.

Finally, implicit throughout Dr. Seyfried's statement is the notion that the use of diagnostic classifications is antithetical to the ethics of professional social work practice. I would like to reemphasize that to not use diagnostic classifications suggests a form of antiscientific thinking that runs counter to the nature and meaning of professionalism, and in particular, the social work profession.

Is the Use of Fringe Therapies—Those Lacking Substantial Theoretical or Scientific Merit—Unethical?

EDITOR'S NOTE: Chemistry, physics, and the other hard sciences advance in recognized, historically established ways: experimentation under highly controlled conditions leads to findings that are widely published and must be replicated by other scientists around the world before being accepted in the field's body of knowledge. This tight discipline has never characterized the mental health professions. Many would say that it cannot or even that it should not. Of particular concern is the treatment of clients using therapies that lack theoretical or evidentiary merit. Are such efforts an important way for the knowledge base of the field to advance, or do they lead down the path that risks abuse of clients and continuing ridicule of the profession?

Norman H. Cobb, Ph.D., argues YES. He received his Ph.D. in social welfare from the University of California at Berkeley in 1986. He is associate professor at the University of Texas at Arlington. He has written in the area of ethical behavior, students' appropriateness for the social work profession, and legal issues in social work education.

Catheleen Jordan, Ph.D., who presents the NO case, also received her doctorate in social welfare from the University of California at Berkeley in 1986. She is currently Professor of Social Work and Director of the Community Service Clinic at the University of Texas at Arlington. Her book, *Clinical Assessment for Social Workers: Quantitative and Qualitative Methods,* with Cynthia Franklin, was published by Lyceum Books of Chicago in January 1995. Also co-authored with Dr. Franklin, *Family Therapy: Innovations and Integrations,* is due out from Brooks/Cole in 1996.

YES

Norman H. Cobb

When reading the history of mental health services, everyone laughs at the absurdity of prior attempts to understand human beings, for example, phrenology (approximately 1834 to 1855), in which mental heath professionals adopted the latest "scientific" method to "read" the shapes of patients' heads to establish their personality characteristics. What is less funny and much closer to home are numerous examples of well-intended clinicians who propose innovative methods that will provide great humor for readers of future history texts. My favorite is the primal scream therapy of the 1970s. A few of my closest professional friends tromped off to Colorado to scream their lungs out and damage their vocal chords in the ill-founded, but "revolutionary," approach of relieving psychic distress. The end product was supposed to be freedom from past, painful, and unresolved events. In the end, they found neither freedom nor renewal. The empirical evaluation of primal therapy remains limited, negative, and critical of a fruitless intervention based on ill-founded theory. Other therapies based on clients' color preferences, muscle configurations, and untestable psychic constructs are also of questionable validity.

Also of concern are the interventions that have considerable length of service yet have similarly poor empirical evaluations. For example, a small number of workers with children in therapeutic settings still use the draw-a-picture technique to assess children's personalities and to facilitate discussions with the children. Research on the validity of draw-a-picture is very scarce and generally misleading.

Fringe and outmoded therapies were not proposed by charlatans, psychological deviants, or misfits. The clinicians were and are well-meaning helpers. Unfortunately, they lacked the interest, knowledge, or skills to evaluate the effectiveness of their methods, or they refused to see or accept the negative evaluations. Perhaps the desire to be helpful hinders their attention to effectiveness. Perhaps their successes with clients are attributable to other variables, which in turn cloud their ability to tease out the ineffective portions of their work. Perhaps some of the readers of this statement have stopped reading by now because I am underscoring the invalid nature of their trusted methods. They will swear to the effectiveness regardless of what the research says. They tend to operate like the parent who spanks his child for playing with the dials on the oven. When questioned by the caseworker, the parent most likely says either, (a) "That's the way I was raised and I didn't play with the oven ever again" or (b) while the child is diverted to the pain in her spanked bottom, the father says, "See, she's not playing with the stove." We tend to mistake the effectiveness of our methods, and we refuse to give up the methods we learned in the past.

Fringe therapies and some widely used methods equally lack the theoretical or scientific support to justify their use with social work clients. Their unethical use rests on four major premises: (1) Social work clients are vulnerable and unable to properly discern the validity, much less the ineffectiveness, of workers' methods. (2) The NASW Code of Ethics dictates that social workers use effective methods. (3) Effectiveness of treatment depends on research processes to measure effects and establish scientific confirmation. (4) In the absence of scientifically based validity, effectiveness may be inferred from highly validated theory.

Vulnerable Clients

Social workers' clients are vulnerable people. Like most citizens, most clients do not have the sophistication to discern if the services they receive are valid, reasonable, or effective. Frequently, if they have an expectation about the effectiveness of treatment, they anticipate that their experience will duplicate the help they have already experienced. For example, when they first had problems, they talked to family members, best friends, neighbors, clergy, or family physicians. If they had received sufficient help, they would not need the services of social workers. Although they may hope for success with the social work clinician, they certainly have significant feelings of apprehension. Ironically, in most cases, their last hope is to trust the clinician.

The judicial system has underscored this trust in the clinician. In courts of law, medical doctors, psychologists, and an increasing number of social workers have answered to an abdication of the fiduciary relationship: a break of trust between professional helper and client. The break in trust has typically taken the form of clinicians seducing clients, but the trust is also violated when clinicians do not keep adequate records, terminate clients who run out of money, and promise services or successes that they cannot deliver.

State legislatures have been quite interested in protecting clients who by their very vulnerability are dependent on the quality of services by social workers. State licensing or certification boards have developed in most states to monitor social workers' services and validate their knowledge. Unfortunately, the legal efforts were necessitated by citizens' reactions to documented examples of unethical and ineffective services. The profession of social work heartily supports such efforts to insure valid and ethical services. The National Association of Social Workers expects that all social workers conduct client services according to ethical standards.

Just as the Federal Drug Administration requires the validation of new drugs, the medical profession holds doctors accountable to established treatment protocols, and lawyers must conform to standards of judicial decorum. Social work professionals, particularly in mental health settings, must account for their services. If they cannot justify the validity of their services, they should return their state licenses or professional credentials, leave the trusted position of social work, and take up jobs (bartending, hair cutting, lemonade stand psychiatrists) and offer free advice. At least few people will take them seriously, and the ethical professionals who mold their valid and effective methods to meet particular clients needs will have the freedom to affect their vulnerable clients' mental health.

Code of Ethics

Social workers should be very nervous about using fringe and undocumented methods with their clients. The NASW Code of Ethics addresses social workers' responsibility to deliver valid and effective procedures and methods. In Section IV, L.:

1. The social worker should work to improve the employing agency's policies and procedures, and the efficiency and effectiveness of its services.
6. The social worker should provide clients with accurate and complete information regarding the extent and nature of the services available to them.
7. The social worker should apprise clients of their risks, rights, opportunities, and obligations associated with social service to them.

Improving, verifying, and communicating the effectiveness of services is difficult. When documented evidence exists for the effectiveness for interventions, it should be mentioned to clients or at least remembered in the minds of workers. When such information is absent, workers could be considered ethical if they built into their services a research component that monitored the progress and degree of change in the behavior of vulnerable clients. Through this process, workers could examine the effectiveness of their services and make suitable changes as needed.

Unfortunately, many workers are more interested in providing direct services than they are in conducting research. They characteristically work in settings where such research is made difficult by inadequate resources and a lack of encouragement to evaluate outcomes. Consequently, the huge task of seeing numerous clients with few professional resources results in the perpetuation of old outmoded methods and untested fringe therapies. Finally, add to this dilemma the fact that workers too frequently lack the skills to monitor effectiveness.

Scientific Validation of Effectiveness

Although all Schools of Social Work teach methods for evaluating programs and services, few workers in the field conduct such studies. Fewer Schools of Social Work teach methods for conducting single-subject research to monitor the progress of individual clients. Either the time constraints on workers or the lack of generalizability of research methods hamper the successful evaluation of fringe therapies or old methods. No discredit is intended for these graduates, because in reality effectiveness research is difficult. The time, setting, and expertise required to effectively conduct such research is sorely lacking in practice settings. The effectiveness research, therefore, needs to be in the hands of skilled researchers who have these resources. A good example is the recent funding by the National Institute of Mental Health to support effectiveness studies of interventions with impulsive children, angry and impulsive adults, and the chronically mentally ill. These efforts compliment the research conducted in various university-related centers across the United States. In these settings, clinicians have the expertise to evaluate innovative methods, safeguard the needs of voluntary and involuntary clients, and translate findings into educationally sound journal articles and classroom materials.

As a word of caution, our tendency to reuse what was taught to us is the justification for education; however, practitioners must continue to reeducate themselves about the effectiveness of interventions as new information documents levels of validity. The clinical research literature is quite clear that clients with thought disorders are likely to be harmed when clinicians use insight-oriented therapies. Most distressing is the fact that some clinicians continue to use these approaches with the wrong clients. The scientific support does document that action-oriented, behavioral interventions are most effective when coupled with medications and social clubs or activities. This example gives us a clear notice that specific practices that were acceptable in the past are no longer valid. We cannot continue to perpetuate theories and interventions that have proved to be of questionable value.

Few theories have sufficient empirical validation to support new interventions that lack sufficient scientific validation. Although behavioral theory may not have gained every social worker's allegiance, most master's and doctoral level workers have been exposed to the extensive empirical support for its principles and techniques. Behavioral methods are the cornerstone for interventions with children and adolescents. Even texts on couples and families that espouse various theoretical perspectives generally revert to basically behavioral methods to produce change. Additionally, various areas of cognitive theory have been supported by empirical evidence. The effects of perception on thinking is well documented; however, the less precise self-construct theories have received mixed reviews. Unfortunately, the previous resistance of psychodynamic theorists to empirical research is a continued boundary for its validation.

Theoretical Validation

In the education of social workers and other helping professionals, texts and faculty have taught traditional theories in the classroom when those theories have shown questionable validity. For example, most human behavior texts in social work, educational psychology, and so forth present Piaget as a leading model in cognitive development. Unfortunately faculty members teach Piaget's stages of cognitive development even though research documents the inadequacy of his model. Few faculty members supplement their human behavior lectures with information to qualify and clarify Piaget's classic information on cognitive development. In essence, we perpetuate the validity of the stages despite the evidence to the contrary.

In conclusion, everyone—clinician, educator, researcher—must accept some level of guilt over the lack of precision in our interventions and theories. Rather than call everyone unethical, we must at least take a position to oppose theories and interventions that are proved wrong and ask that ethical clinicians use approaches that have been shown to work with particular clients' problems. The validation and evidence continues to mount and establish interventions with ethical bases. We can shed the pseudoscientific preoccupation with our head size, preferred colors, psychic constructs, and primal screams. We have the budding scientific knowledge to address mental health problems and not make our vulnerable clients more vulnerable with poor services.

Rejoinder to Professor Cobb   CATHELEEN JORDAN

Dr. Cobb's position that social workers should not use therapies lacking empirical support is based on four arguments. I will address each of these.

Vulnerable Clients

I agree with Professor Cobb's contention that our clients are vulnerable and we must seek to protect them from unethical treatment. But in addition to protection of clients, we have a mission to help them to resolve their problems. If we limit our helping activities to only the few thoroughly validated interventions that exist, I doubt we would be dispensing very much help. Clients are individuals with highly individualized problems, needs, and ways of interacting with the world around them. Helping efforts must be molded to the unique needs and characteristics of the client. We do not yet know what works with whom under what conditions. So much is yet to be known. One piece of information we do know is that the client–therapist relationship is more important than the treatment modality. Conducting that relationship in an ethical manner, no matter what the treatment method, is the key to provision of ethical services.

Code of Ethics

My arguments for ethical use of fringe therapies using the practice as evaluation model follow the guidelines in the Code of Ethics. The Code calls for "providing clients with accurate and complete information regarding the extent and nature of the services" and "apprising clients of their risks, rights, opportunities, and obligations associated with social service to them." Nowhere did I read in the Code, "social workers must use only XXX treatment because of its clear superiority over everything else."

Scientific Validation of Effectiveness

Validation is wonderful, when it exists. The fact remains that social workers have not had the money for, and in some cases have not been oriented to, doing research. Although the climate in social work is changing toward a greater research emphasis, Professor Cobb's point that few social workers have the training to do clinical trials research is well taken. However, single-system evaluation is an ethical model for evaluation of practice that is easily implemented.

Professor Cobb cautions against perpetuation of invalid methods and mentions as examples of fringe therapies "primal scream" and "color analysis." Even though I am willing to recommend that fringe therapies not be eliminated wholesale, I am recommending that these therapies be used in the context of an ethical model of practice. The practice as evaluation model prescribes that problems be measured and data collected over the course of treatment and then analyzed. The implication is that the data then dictates continuance or discontinuance of the treatment. Also, use of this model does not excuse the ethical practitioner from being informed about the literature. No literature available on a therapy is not the same as literature indicating poor results. If a technique has been shown to be noneffective or even dangerous, then it should not be used.

Theoretical Validation

The same argument about "poor results" holds true for theoretical validation. If there is empirical evidence to suggest that the theory is incorrect or inaccurate, then it should be abandoned. However, in the absence of such empirical documentation, single-system evaluation may be used to monitor outcomes.

Summary

Single-system evaluation may be used in one's practice to build support for non–empirically supported theory and treatment methods, or what we have referred to as "fringe therapies." Single-system design is an ethical, easy-to-learn method for integrating practice and evaluation.

NO

CATHELEEN JORDAN

In an ideal world, we would know every detail about clients' problem behaviors and the specific treatments to "cure" them. The world is less than perfect, however, and even though we know what treatment works in some areas, much remains to be known. This treatise presents the rationale for use of fringe therapies and offers recommendations and guidelines for their use in an ethical manner.

Rationale for Use of Fringe Therapies

"Fringe therapies" are those treatments that have little or no research on the underlying theory or the efficacy of the model. The ethical dilemma is not whether to use fringe therapies, but rather how to use them in an ethical manner. Unfortunately, many social work methods do not have the underlying research support to avoid the label of fringe therapy. Psychosocial therapy, family therapy, and some cognitive behavioral methods, to name a few, are fringe therapies according to this definition. Bergin and Garfield (1994) reported the limitations of the research on these and other methods.

Serendipity

In some related fields, medicine being the classic example, treatment innovations come from either controlled research studies or serendipitous events. Serendipity is particularly relevant for a field such as social work, in which practitioners "start where the client is," try to "join" with the client during treatment sessions, and will try "anything that works" to help. Many new and valuable treatments are coined on the spot by a desperate social worker facing a resistant client. Rejecting all non–empirically supported therapies is to stifle the creativity of the field, the "art" of the artistic/scientific blend that is social work practice.

Few Resources for Funding Social Work Research

In medicine, new and innovative interventions are tested in controlled clinical efficacy trials before being made available to practitioners. Social work practice has not operated this way for a number of reasons, especially the lack of money. The NIMH sponsored report on Research (1991) indicated that social work researchers have not been funded as well as other disciplines by major funding sources such as the National Institute of Mental Health (NIMH). These findings led to a commitment to social work deans from NIMH to correct this oversight. NIMH, making good on its promise to support social work research, has funded three Social Work Development Centers at Schools of Social Work in St. Louis, Tennessee, and Michigan; several other proposals are under consideration. Additionally, NIMH is encouraging social workers, by providing workshops and mentoring opportunities, to submit proposals to fund social work research. Clinical efficacy studies are a major NIMH funding priority.

Changing Social Work Attitudes about Research

Lack of social workers' emphasis on research may revolve around an antiresearch philosophy that exists among some social workers (Jordan, in press). Simply stated, constructivist theorizing implies that we can never know others' objective reality; therefore, the scientific method is relatively irrelevant in describing clients' problems or social workers' attempts to solve them. Conversely, other forces, managed care for instance, demand accountability and call for greater validation of the therapeutic process. Social workers are being pushed as never before by the market to measure and evaluate client problems and outcomes.

Social workers are creative, are increasingly seeking funded research opportunities, and are "becoming" researchers, though they are in a transitional period toward accomplishing this end. I would like to recommend a social work "practice as evaluation" model as the solution to using fringe therapies in an ethical manner during this transitional time. Bloom, Fischer, and Orme (1995)have described this model quite effectively.

Solution: Social Work "Practice as Evaluation"

Whether practitioners are using fringe therapies or highly validated methods, they know very little about which specific techniques work best with particular types of clients or problems. The social work model described by Bloom and colleagues seeks to integrate evaluation and practice to individualize treatment and monitor treatment outcomes by use of single-system evaluation in practice. The characteristics of single-system evaluation are:

1. Specify the problem (or goal) of treatment
2. Measure the problem
3. Collect data in the baseline (before treatment) and treatment phases
4. Collect data repeatedly over the entire course of baseline and treatment phases
5. Operationalize the treatment
6. Analyze the data and decide on treatment modifications based on the findings (pp. 10–14)

This evaluation process is complementary, according to the authors, to practice:

1. Identify problem areas
2. Set long-term goals and short-term objectives
3. Specify contract
4. Assess client thoughts, feelings, behaviors, and environmental factors
5. Design treatment plan
6. Monitor progress
7. Analyze results of intervention (pp. 10–14)

The advantage of using single-system evaluation in practice, Bloom and colleagues continue, is to help the social worker practice more effectively and humanely. For example, single-system evaluation:

1. May be easily integrated into almost any practice situation
2. Provides graphs of objective information for use in decision-making
3. Is client focused because of its emphasis on individualized measurement and treatment
4. Is flexible to allow for changing conditions in the client's life
5. Clarifies information obtained in assessment that leads to selection of intervention
6. Allows for hypothesis (inference) testing
7. Is theory free and may be used with most methods used in clinical practice
8. Is easy to use and understand
9. Makes program evaluation by outside evaluators unnecessary
10. Provides a model for demonstrating social worker accountability and ethical practice to ourselves and others (pp. 21–22)

Guidelines for Ethical Clinical Practice

The social worker practice as evaluation model just recommended is important for its contribution to accountability of practice activities and to linking client assessment to intervention. Guidelines reviewed by Jordan and Franklin (1995) help the practitioner to achieve an ethical approach to practice.

Client Motivation

Clients' motivation to be involved in treatment and to make changes is an integral part of the therapeutic process. Clients' readiness may be recognized by their willingness to participate in treatment and in performing homework assignments, as well as their verbal indicators of readiness. Motivation may be increased by the social worker's selection of interventions that will lead to small, easily achieved successes for the client.

Client–Social Worker Relationship

The relationship between client and social worker is critical in the change process. "Considering the client's characteristics and preferences in selecting an intervention assumes that the client is an informed consumer who participates in selecting the treatment, consents to treatment, and has rights and choices in the therapy process" (Jordan & Franklin, 1995, p. 269). One way of protecting clients' rights when planning to use a treatment that has little or no empirical support is to share information about all treatment approaches that might be used, along with associated risks and benefits of each, so that the client may make an informed treatment choice. Additionally, Bergin and Garfield (1994) reported that no proof exists to assert that any method or orientation is more important to outcome than the therapist–client relationship.

Treatment Planning

Empirical support for the method is only one of many criteria recommended for evaluating interventions (Cormier & Cormier, 1991). Questions to ask to assess the viability of interventions are:

1. Is it easy to administer?
2. Does it match client characteristics and preferences?
3. Does it match problem characteristics?
4. Is it positive rather than punitive?
5. Does it encourage the development of client self-management skills?
6. Does it strengthen the client's expectations of self-efficacy?
7. Is it supported by the literature?
8. Is it feasible and practical to implement?
9. Does it avoid creating additional problems for the client?
10. Does it avoid burdening the client with too many things to do?
11. Does it avoid requiring unrealistic demands of the practitioner?
12. Does it avoid repeating or building on previous unsuccessful solutions?

Conclusions

In sum, many of the methods used by social workers may be called "fringe therapies" because of the lack of empirical literature supporting the underlying theory or the efficacy of the methods. The solution to ensuring that we provide ethical services to our clients is not in eliminating these methods from our repertoire, but in using them in the context of an ethically sound model. The practice as evaluation model fits this criterion.

References

Bergin, A., & Garfield, S. (1994). *Handbook of psychotherapy and behavior change.* New York: John Wiley.

Bloom, M., Fischer, J. & Orme, J. (1995). *Evaluating practice: Guidelines for the accountable professional* (2nd ed.). Englewood Cliffs, NJ: Prentice-Hall.

Cormier, W. H. & Cormier, L. S. (1991). *Interviewing strategies for helpers: Fundamental skills and cognitive-behavioral interventions* (3rd ed.). Pacific Grove, CA: Brooks/Cole.

Jordan, C. (in press). Does constructivist therapy offer anything new to social work practice? No. In Bruce Thyer (Ed.). *Controversial issues in social work practice.* Boston: Allyn & Bacon.

Jordan, C., & Franklin, C. (1995). Clinical assessment for social workers: Quantitative and qualitative methods. Chicago: Lyceum.

Report of the Task force on social work research. (1991). *Building social work knowledge for effective services and policies: A plan for research and development*. Austin TX. Capital Printing Co.

Rejoinder to Professor Jordan NORMAN H. COBB

Professor Jordan labels a significant portion of social work treatment as "fringe." In actuality, social work methods fall along a continuum from solid, verified interventions to the midrange methods with less or even mixed empirical support. At the far end, however, are approaches that we would both probably reject and label as "truly fringe." For example, the far end includes training spouses to hit each other with soft objects in some misguided effort to release tensions and divert "real" abuse. Unfortunately, similar stories are numerous and the ethics questionable.

Dr. Jordan is more accepting than I am of undocumented methods, however. She squarely places all treatment into a researcher practitioner mode and thereby avoids a broadside attack of her position. She asserts that all treatments, the fringe and not so fringe, must be monitored and verified. She contrasts serendipitous discoveries of new techniques with the efficacy studies of research centers. The implications of this contrast underscore my position that therapies with little or no empirical support should only be conducted in controlled conditions. Techniques with no validation are questionable in the one-to-one, uncontrolled world of most clinicians. As an off-handed comment, the presence of agency supervisors who watch over workers' clinical work is clearly not sufficient control for effective practice.

My colleague asserts that funding is the major stumbling block to researching effectiveness; however, the previous lack of resources in no excuse for perpetuating unfounded methods with vulnerable clients. Certainly, her recognition of NIMH's interest in social work research is a welcome development, but most importantly NIMH's assessment of treatment is to evaluate the efficacy of previously effective models of treatment. She is certainly correct in acknowledging the need to clarify what components of treatment work with which clients and who have particular types of problems. Bergin and Garfield (1994) do call for improved assessment of the effectiveness of theory and treatment; however, they are also quite complimentary of behavioral and cognitive methods. The efficacy of interventions must take the additional step to study methods in conjunction with specific types of problems. Fortunately, this is a far cry from endorsing fringe therapies.

Her response to the need for an ethical framework for monitoring treatment is the "practice as evaluation" model. By endorsing Bloom, Fischer, and Orme's model (1995), she emphasizes a highly promising and valid tool for clinicians. Unfortunately, too few schools of social work teach the model and require students to demonstrate their use and understanding of its effectiveness. I appreciate the fact that some researchers have followed graduates of programs that teach an empirical approach to practice. They found a significant number of graduates using the model for a good percentage of their clients.

Until this approach to practice is taught in social work education and employed by their graduates, social workers using fringe therapies run the risk of promising more than their tools can deliver. Graduate social workers who are concerned with ethical and effective practice should ask social work faculty to teach procedures and tools for evaluating practice. Through continuing educational programs, they should develop additional resources to safeguard the quality of their services. The result will be the testing of all therapies, the acceptance of effective methods, and the denunciation of ill-founded approaches.

In the final analysis, a careful assessment of treatment outcomes and the validation of theory are crucial to our clients, our professional competence, and the ethical standards of our profession. Given the infancy of our science of human behavior, however, we should expect to discard outmoded theories and practices. Our constituents should expect us to have the courage to assert that unfounded methods are unethical and must be discarded. We may have to say to our colleagues, students, interns, even some of the charismatic authors of social work literature, that invalidated methods and discounted theories are unethical and have no place in social work education.

Should Social Workers Enroll as Preferred Providers with For-Profit Managed Care Groups?

Editor's Note: The move toward managed care programs has increased apace. What should social workers' roles be in for-profit managed care programs? Does participation in such programs forward ethical values emphasized in the NASW Code of Ethics, such as service, social justice, integrity, and competence? Does this administrative format allow social workers to pursue these foundation values? Are managed care programs really any different from other care programs in their consequences for clients? Might not they protect clients from overly prolonged "services"? Do social workers have an important and appropriate role to play in such systems, and will they be left behind if they do not participate in these programs?

Robert Gorden, MSW, makes the YES case. He has been a practicing clinical social worker for fifteen years. He has established employee assistance programs (EAP) for a number of medical centers and home care agencies in Northern California. Currently he is head of Gorden & Associates, Oakland, California, a consulting and counseling practice that provides EAP, psychotherapy, management training and organizational development services.

Paul M. Kline, DSW, carries the NO side of the debate. He is Assistant Professor in the clinical sequence at the Boston College Graduate School of Social Work.

YES

ROBERT GORDEN

Social workers should enroll in for-profit managed care groups. The fact that there is a question about this, and that social workers will spend much time and energy deliberating the question, is a sign of the profession's strength and weakness. It is wonderful that social work has a body of ethics and a history and tradition of trying to help some of the poorest and neediest of our society. But this alignment with the poor ignores that people of all economic levels and groups can benefit from the technologies, practice, and knowledge base of the social work profession.

Other professions such as law have a tradition of providing pro bono work that helps the poor or disadvantaged have access to their services. However, there is not much debate that only poor people or disadvantaged persons deserve the time and attention of the legal profession. Physicians have their own tradition of allowing some of their patients to be seen for whatever they can pay. Some offer a half-day per week at a free clinic or other community service to enable uninsured patients access to health care.

I do not believe that there is a huge debate here on whether to accept payment from managed care. This does not mean that there is complete agreement about the potential conflicts that arise in these arrangements. Many people in the medical community have misgivings about managed care and the potentials for abuse and poor patient care that might arise.

Private Practice/"Fallen Angels"

Many social workers and some leaders of the profession believe that social work should only focus its energies on the poor and disadvantaged. There is also a suspicion of for-profit institutions. Some members of our profession see social workers who are in private practice as having deserted their mission. Other social workers may have a distrust of for-profit agencies, assuming that for-profit somehow is equated with uncaring or ruthlessness in the pursuit of the bottom line.

I have worked in both for-profit and nonprofit agencies, and I do not always see much of a difference between the two. Board decisions in the latter were often made by highly paid businesspeople who saw social work as something the workers would or should be willing to engage in for less than adequate wages. Some nonprofit agencies treat their staff and clients poorly, while offering services that are not always well designed or helpful to their clients. Certainly there is widespread agreement that many government-run programs put more obstacles in the way of helping the intended clients than trying to make their services accessible and pragmatic to the client's needs. Ultimately it is not "for profit" or "nonprofit" status that ensures that an agency, company, hospital, or insurance

company practices in an ethical or socially responsible ways. It is the actual behavior of the individuals or organization.

Managed Care

If social workers choose to not be part of managed care panels we will lose any
chance to influence care that is provided in this sphere. It is more important to
serve on these panels, and try to advocate for the proper level of treatment. This
will help clients who are caught in systems that may in fact be trying to suppress
use.

Conflicts will surely arise from some of these managed care arrangements.
If social workers are part of the system, we can observe abuses and educate clients and the public as to what issues and problems need to be addressed in legislation or public protest. It may be that some managed care plans try to exert
pressure to deny treatment to or undertreat patients while increasing their own
profits. But to encourage nonparticipation on the part of your most ethical or best
trained people would only leave less principled professionals to participate. If
they in turn are less effective as patient advocates or practitioners, how does this
help our clients or society?

Participation in and of itself does not guarantee ethical or unethical practice. This is true in any program that provides services, such as Medicaid or MediCal, or any number of agencies, public and private. Many doctors, therapists, and
professionals have defrauded patients and government programs by overbilling or
charging for services that were never delivered. It would seem self-defeating for
social workers to not participate in one of the main health care delivery systems.

Many counties are moving toward similar ways of providing medical care
and other services to their clients. Comparing the delivery of services in a nonprofit managed care plan with that of a for-profit managed care plan might help.
What difference is there between being a social worker providing services at
Kaiser psychiatry and a private practitioner seeing clients through their insurance
coverage through work? One is managed care through a not-for-profit health plan
that is under pressure to keep costs down. The other is also trying to be conservative with its approval of visits, for much the same reason.

My assessment and treatment should not be any different under either system. It may be that the insurance will deny further treatment before the end of the
recommended treatment plan. It may be that a particular Kaiser worker tells a client they need long-term therapy and that Kaiser does not provide this. Neither is
acting appropriately. Does this mean that social workers should not participate in
either system because abuses may occur? In fact, if the county can only provide
services to people who are acutely suicidal because of budget constraints, should
I as a social worker not participate because they are limiting who can get services
there?

Almost all mental health service providers would do well by themselves and their clients to look at the empirical literature to find out more about what is effective and what is not when treating various disorders. As it is, many providers have done work that is certainly economically advantageous to them or their agencies but not as useful to their clients as some other brief treatments that might have been applied. You could encourage a client to continue longer than needed, to help keep your agency's statistics high. To continue getting paid, a practitioner in an unmanaged care arrangement can keep coming up with reasons to continue with a client who came in with a short-term issue. You could convince the client and yourself that they need long-term therapy to work on structural personality changes. Here the question is not how you get reimbursed but what will most effectively help your clients. Perhaps we should worry less about who pays the bill and more about what really works with the problems we are asked and trusted by clients to help them with. A client is not better treated because the money came from a government program or from a major insurance carrier, a profit-making service or a not-for-profit agency.

"You Cannot Serve Your Patient's Needs in This Sort of Arrangement"

If I am sent a client from a managed care EAP and can see this person ten sessions at $60.00, which is less than my normal full fee, how am I not serving my client? For example, I have a client who has no job and lives in a drug halfway house. He is struggling to not use drugs, gain his family's trust again, and begin steady work after years of being drug addicted. He gets the benefit through his wife's employer. I am the first mental health practitioner to fully assess him for depression, skills deficits, and issues relating to sexual abuse. Keep in mind this person has been in and out of drug rehabilitation programs for 8 years, some lasting longer than one year.

Because I contract with his managed care insurance company, I am able to see this person and provide him with a base to get started in a new direction. I am paid more than an agency would pay me for my time. I then have the flexibility to offer him a low fee to continue with me after his visits are exhausted under the managed care system if he needs to continue. I have served the client, myself, and the managed care company without any conflict or diminution of my own professional integrity or standards. In fact, were I not a provider on this panel, he may have worked with a clinician who was not skilled in brief treatment therapies, or someone less willing to press for the maximum level of service for this individual. Also, as a social worker, I use a broader view of the individual's life context, which allows for a more comprehensive way of intervening and helping the individual. If social workers had not participated, this person may have received less competent treatment than he did at both private for-profit and nonprofit agencies.

By opting to not be part of the largest segment of the health care market in the coming years, social workers sideline themselves and lose opportunities for personal advancement. If we remove ourselves from professional activities that other professional groups are more than willing to provide, we trivialize our influence on this whole sphere of practice.

Rejoinder to Mr. Gorden PAUL M. KLINE

My colleague offers an argument in favor of social worker participation in for-profit managed care groups. In so doing, several points are raised that merit thoughtful consideration and response.

The first point suggests that social workers should actively participate in the for-profit managed care marketplace, with all of its limitations, inequities, and ethical traps, while simultaneously providing free or reduced-fee care to clients who are victimized by that system. To me, this argument proposes that the ethical compromises made by clinicians in the managed care world can be neutralized by noble acts of charity and self-sacrifice. In my opinion, these creative arrangements are made to ease the anxiety clinicians experience when they discover that they are trapped by a system of care that robs them of the freedom to act in the best interests of their clients. We create a mental ethical scorecard in which we hope ethical compromises are offset by acts of kindness. A profession that makes such a compromise to a ruthless system of health care betrays its values and its mission.

My colleague offers a compelling argument that social workers who participate in for-profit managed care arrangements can become agents of change in that system. However, to bring about change from within a system, the individual must have access to power and the opportunity to use that power so as to influence the system's behavior. Managed care companies rarely make room for social workers to hold such positions. Rather, the relationship between the social worker and the managed care company is unstable and one-sided. Social workers are offered positions that promote an anxious economic dependency and, consequently, the clinician has no meaningful opportunity to promote responsible change.

Finally, my colleague offers a series of observations and arguments that conclude with a statement that the profession cannot afford to be outside of this system of care. To me this conclusion has the feel of a surrender. It is a statement that betrays the demoralizing impact of powerful economic pressures that have severely tested the clinical skills and personal resilience of the social work practitioner. The profession cannot afford to leave its membership unprotected and unsupported in the face of such a crisis and should increase its efforts to advocate for a system of care that is just and fair for clients as well as practitioners.

NO

Paul M. Kline

"Loosely defined, managed care involves oversight by third party payers, or specialized fourth parties, to monitor the utilization of care (particularly inpatient care), and in so doing contain or reduce associated costs" (Mirin & Sederer, 1994; p. 164). The trend toward managed mental health care as the framework within which social work services are delivered is powerful and will likely continue to gain momentum. It is the premise of this essay that social workers should not enroll as mental health providers with for-profit managed care companies. I defend this position by focusing on three sources of ethical conflict frequently experienced by social workers who practice in the for-profit managed care environment. They are:

- The damaging effects of managed care on the client–worker relationship
- Ethical issues arising out of competing economic pressures
- Justifying inadequate care with simplistic clinical reasoning

The Damaging Effects on Client–Worker Relationship

In a recent address to members of the American Psychiatric Association concerning external threats to effective and ethical practice, outgoing president Lawrence Hartmann advocated a renewed dedication to values that have been the foundation of social work practice. "Humane values require us, in promoting mental health and fighting mental illness, to be aware of and care for and treat *whole people in context and over time* (1992; p. 1137). An orientation to clinical practice consistent with these values frees the social worker to respond to each client's complex psychosocial reality with an empathic appreciation for what desired changes might be realized through responsible and collaborative care.

However, clinical practice within a for-profit managed care environment often requires that the terms and conditions of the therapeutic relationship fall under the regulatory influence of the managed care company and its agent. The structure of the relationship can, in large part, be imposed on the client and the social worker, limiting the opportunity that clients have to reveal their complex psychosocial reality in their own time, at their own pace, and to the level of depth and complexity that they find necessary.

These regulatory conditions also compromise the social worker's ability to respond to the client's needs, goals, strengths, and vulnerabilities in a meaningfully empathic fashion. The social worker who alters clinical practice in response to these external regulations runs the risk of depriving clients of access to the full range of therapeutic resources that might otherwise be available in a more fully developed, authentic, and mutual therapeutic relationship (Brown, 1994; Meyer, 1993).

Competing Economic Pressures

We are witness to a dramatic shift in the ideological framework within which health care is provided. In his discussion of the evolution of Health Maintenance Organizations (HMOs), Bennett has observed that the original ideological backbone of the HMO as a resource for timely, comprehensive health care has been replaced by powerful entrepreneurial interests and motivations (1988). Social workers who enroll as preferred providers in for-profit managed care companies learn quickly that their economic well-being is, in large measure, tied to their ability to honor the company's for-profit objectives. These objectives are achieved by restricting access to mental health services, by funneling subscribers to approved providers friendly to the model of care imposed by the managed care company, and by dramatically reducing a client's length of time in treatment.

These efforts rarely involve direct negotiation between the managed care company and the individual patient or subscriber. Rather, social workers, by virtue of the agreements they make with managed care companies, are compelled to implement these restrictions in their clinical encounters with clients. Social workers become gatekeepers for managed care companies, making decisions about who has access to care and what level or degree of care is provided. The criteria for making these decisions are imposed on the social worker by the managed care company and are fueled primarily by a concern for the cost of care rather than the quality of care. These criteria are enforced by rigid administrative procedures and protocol that restrict the freedom that clinicians have to act, first and foremost, out of concern for the client's well-being. They regulate and interrupt the clinical process with one or more checks meant to insure that clinical decision making honors the for-profit objectives of the managed care company.

This struggle between responding to the complex treatment needs of the client while also working within the regulatory framework of the managed care company is made even more difficult when social workers simultaneously attempt to attend to their personal economic well-being. Failure to respect the company's administrative protocol can result in immediate financial penalty for the clinician. Conversely, the social worker who demonstrates the ability to implement the mandate of the agency (fiscal viability) is rewarded with more referrals and renewal of their provider contract.

Clinical practice in a for-profit managed care environment requires that clinicians protect their own financial security by sculpting treatment within the parameters laid down by the managed care company, which are established to protect its financial well-being. The result, too often, is that the client is then denied access to the full range of therapeutic resources, which, if applied, might otherwise alleviate suffering and improve psychosocial competence.

Justifying Inadequate Care with Simplistic Clinical Reasoning

How do managed care companies explain and justify their intrusion into the therapeutic relationship and their use of criteria for clinical decision making that honor economic objectives first? More importantly, how are they successful in recruiting social workers to provide care in an environment so filled with ethical land mines? This is achieved through a process of simplistic clinical reasoning that identifies and targets "treatable" symptoms, isolates them from the client's complex psychosocial reality, and equates "success" with some level of modification in the intensity, frequency, or disruptive effect of those symptoms on daily functioning.

Through a powerful process of indoctrination, social workers are taught how to think by managed care companies and their agents. They learn the unique language of the managed care company, a language that reflects a particular perspective on the varied forms of biopsychosocial suffering experienced by individuals, couples, families, and larger groups. Learning the language provides social workers with the means to justify efforts to secure proper care for clients or, conversely, to deny or restrict care. For example, children with behavioral and learning problems may be denied care through their health plan and instructed to seek out services from the local school system based on the determination that "educational" problems are not medical and therefore are not covered. Social workers are also taught which symptoms or strengths and resources are targeted by the managed care company as indicators of a client needing a less intense, less restrictive, or less comprehensive level of care than might otherwise be recommended or requested. Patients who need inpatient care, for example, may be forced to "fail" in "hospital diversion" programs before being approved for inpatient admission.

This policy of first using *all* less restrictive treatment resources before any patient is hospitalized, without a sensitive appreciation for the impact of such decisions on the patient and family, is often motivated by the need to cap costs rather than by a genuine concern for the client's well-being. The integrity of clinical practice can be threatened when we participate in a system of care where " . . . outsiders . . . push us and sometimes pay us to simplify" (Hartmann, 1992; p. 1138).

Conclusion

Social workers are experienced and effective practitioners when working within and against systems that fail to respond to the needs of our clients. Our effectiveness is, however, dependent on our holding the client's well-being as our paramount concern, freeing us to identify environmental threats to psychosocial competence and to advocate for social change. In the current economic and political climate, participation as a provider in for-profit managed care companies threatens effective and ethical social work practice by requiring social workers to serve two or more masters. Concern for client well-being is filtered through a series of questions and administrative restrictions that have little to do with the client's suffering and more to do with the economic security of the clinician and the managed care company. The cumulative effect of ethical conflicts resulting from countertherapeutic intrusion into the privileged client–worker relationship, competing economic pressures, and the encouragement to reduce complex biopsychosocial suffering to simplistic diagnostic labels and crude treatment planning threatens clinical process as well as the social worker's professional well-being and therefore cannot be tolerated.

References

Bennett, M. J. (1988). The greening of the HMO: Implications of prepaid psychiatry. *American Journal of Psychiatry, 145,* 1544–1549.

Brown, F. (1994). Resisting the pull of the health insurance tarbaby: An organizational model for surviving managed care. *Clinical Social Work Journal, 22;* 59–71.

Hartmann, L. (1992). Presidential address: Reflections on humane values and biopsychosocial integration. *American Journal of Psychiatry, 149,* 1135–1141.

Meyer, W. S. (1993). In defense of long-term treatment: On the vanishing holding environment. *Social Work, 38;* 571–578.

Mirin, S. M. & Sederer, L. I. (1994). Mental health care: Current realities, future directions. *Psychiatric Quarterly, 65,* 161–175.

Rejoinder to Professor Kline ROBERT GORDEN

Managed care does not dictate the relationship between clients and social workers. It is the social worker who defines the relationship in mutual negotiation with the client. Managed care does not force clinicians to create therapeutic relationships devoid of empathy, authenticity, depth, or complexity. These qualities, plus an appreciation of the client's complex psychosocial reality, are basic to the practice of professional clinical social work.

The argument that the "threat of external regulation" will alter clinical practice seems to ignore that every system of health care and social services has some regulation and influences on the care provided. If social workers were to avoid all outside regulations, they would not participate in any insurance plan, Medicare, or Medicaid. This would also eliminate practice in any federal, state, or nonprofit agency. External factors such as insurance, lack of income, increased county case loads, and state or federal regulations have always been a reality that have shaped service delivery. It is the social workers responsibility to assess the impact of these systems on their clients and then help them negotiate with the system. When the client is denied treatment that the social worker believes is necessary, they can advocate for more coverage. I have found that if I give sound clinical reasons for more care, it is usually approved. When it is not, then it is our professional obligation to help the client identify what other options exist.

Economic Pressures

The view that economics will dominate the social workers' decisions on how to practice or that they will become gatekeepers is inaccurate. Social workers who are providers on managed care panels are not the gatekeepers. They neither approve nor deny services. It is true that managed care companies do try to direct clients to providers who say they can work in a brief treatment mode, because usually the benefits under the plan are limited to twenty or fewer visits per year. Ethical conflicts are no more apparent in managed care than in those under fee for service. The conflict of interest created by the incentive to continue treatment longer or more intensively than actually needed was and is a problem in the field. Ethical conflicts do not stop at the door of nonprofit institutions or agencies. Providers in all areas of practice need to ensure that their ways of practicing are not unduly motivated by self-interest.

More Is Not Always Better

The argument that social workers not be involved in managed care also seems to imply that attempts to shorten the length, cost, or intensity of treatment is inherently wrong. The lack of access to the "whole range of treatments" is given as another reason to not become part of these plans. By ignoring outcome data social workers and others encouraged the growth of "regulators" to reduce what was seen as the wasting of resources and the need to control the escalation of costs. Managed care, DRGs, and capitated contracts were all responses to the excesses of all types of health care.

Outcome studies on depression have shown that cognitive behavioral, problem solving, and interpersonal therapies are more effective than longer traditional treatments. They were also equal to tricyclic medications (Bergin & Lambert, 1978). In a large National Institute of Mental Health study, short-term cognitive behavioral and interpersonal therapy were clearly the most effective treatment therapies for depressed outpatients, especially when combined with medication (Elkins et al, 1989). Therefore, more intensive, longer, or undirected therapies would not be better and could be seen as unethical if they prolong client suffering. Managed care requires most clients with chemical dependency coverage to first try an outpatient program. A review of all of the controlled studies of alcohol treatment showed inpatient and medical treatment of alcohol abuse to be no better than less expensive outpatient treatment (Miller & Hester, 1986). A review article (Holden, 1987) indicated that a large body of research has established that the intensity of treatment has no bearing on results.

In contrasting two uncontrolled studies of neurotic patients in the late 1950s, there was no evidence that longer, more intensive treatment was more beneficial. Behavior therapy had an 89.5 percent cured or much improved rate, averaging 30 sessions. The psychoanalytic therapy study showed a recovery rate of 60 percent and averaged 600 sessions (Brody 1962; Wolpe, 1958; Wolpe, 1964).

Reducing the client's symptoms and the disruptive effects they have on the client's daily life is in fact meaningful and is how clients measure success in therapy. "Symptomatic improvement is a necessary criterion for change in every case since it is the symptoms that bring the patient to treatment" (Wolpe, 1990, p. 335).

Finally, some managed care companies provide inadequate coverage, but this does not force providers to work against their clients. What does hurt our clients are clinicians who are uninformed, falsely biased, unethical, or too concerned about their own well-being before that of their clients. This can happen in managed care plans or in any other practice setting, regardless of who pays the bills.

REFERENCES

Bergin, A. E., & Lambert, M. J. (1978). The evaluation of therapeutic outcomes. In S. L. Garfield & A. E. Bergin (Eds.), *Handbook of psychotherapy and behavior change: An empirical analysis* (pp. 139–190) New York: Wiley.

Brody, M. W. (1962). Prognosis and results of psychoanalysis. In J. H. Nodine & Moyers (Eds.), *Psychosomatic Medicine.* Philadelphia: Lea and Febiger.

Elkins, S. T., Watkins, J. T., et al. (1989) National Institute of Mental Health treatment of depression collaborative research program, *Archives of General Psychotherapy, 46,* 971–982.

Holden, C., Is alcoholism treatment effective? *Science, 236,* 20–22.

Miller, W. R., & Hester, R. K. 1986. The effectiveness of alcoholism treatment: What research reveals. In W. R. Miller, N. H. Heather (Eds.): *Treating Addictive Behaviors: Processes of Change.* Plenum.

Wolpe, J. (1958). *Psychotherapy by reciprocal inhibition.* Stanford, CA: Stanford University Press.

Wolpe, J. (1964). The comparative clinical status of conditioning therapies and psychoanalysis. In J. Wolpe, A. Salter, L. J. Reyna. *The Conditioning Therapies.* New York: Holt, Reinhart & Winston.

Wolpe, J. (1990). *The Practice of Behavior Therapy.* New York: Pergamon Press.

Does the Goal of Preventing Suicide Justify Placing Suicidal Clients in Care?

EDITOR'S NOTE: Suicide is an emotional topic. Religious organizations view it as wrong, even sinful. Clients can be legally incarcerated against their will if professionals believe they are a threat to themselves. Consider the following quote from the 1995 draft of the NASW Code of Ethics: "Social workers may limit clients' right to self-determination when, in their professional judgment, clients' actions or potential actions pose a serious, foreseeable, and imminent risk to themselves or others." What are the ethical issues here? Who is to say that suicide is not a basic right? Can we predict suicide? If we cannot predict it, on what ethical grounds can we exercise undue influence or coerce people into unwanted "care"? Although both debaters agree that there is no evidence that suicide can be predicted (and thus prevented), they take quite different views about the role of professionals.

Andre Ivanoff, who argues the YES side, is Associate Professor of Social Work at the Columbia University School of Social Work. Recent publications include *Involuntary Clients in Social Work Practice* (with B. Blythe and T. Tripodi), and "Clinical Risk Factors Associated with Parasuicide in Prison" in the *International Journal of Offender Therapy and Comparative Criminology.*

Tomi Gomory presents the NO case. He is finishing his doctoral studies at the School of Social Welfare, University of California, Berkeley. His research activities include a critical review of outcome claims of well-accepted programs for the severely mentally ill and a conceptual and situational analysis of the historical changes in the public mental health system.

YES

ANDRE IVANOFF

The Issue and Assumptions

Involuntary care is acceptable when it may prevent the taking of human life. Is preventing suicide ethical? For practitioners who believe that it is not, the remainder of this argument is without meaning. When clients admit to acute suicidal ideation, verbalize suicidal intentions, or attempt suicide, the question of hospitalization may arise. Mental health professionals across disciplines must know where they personally stand on this issue before their clients become suicidal: the middle of a suicidal crisis is no time to begin sorting one's feelings on this critical topic (Ivanoff & Smyth, 1992; Linehan, 1993). To hold individuals behind locked doors against their will is a serious matter calling for a great deal of consideration in which the risks must be weighed against the benefits. Many suicidal crises do not require hospitalization if the practitioner can stay in close touch with the client, monitoring suicidal thinking and feelings; indeed, hospitalization may not offer the most effective treatment and may even promote barriers to treatment with some clients. The least restrictive treatment alternative and voluntary admission are always preferable options.

What constitutes providing care to a suicidal client? Suicide prevention often involves involuntary intervention, far short of inpatient hospitalization. When does action agreed to by a desperate, distressed individual technically become involuntary? Involuntary care ranges from seeing a clinician at the insistence of family members, taking medication because you are too depressed to argue against taking it, to confinement in various settings. Involuntary psychiatric hospitalization often represents only the final step in a hierarchy of involuntary intervention, not the first.

Does hospitalization prevent suicide? There is little research examining short-term suicide rates among those hospitalized or not hospitalized for suicide risk. The only randomized intervention trial (Waterhouse & Platt, 1990) assigned relatively low-risk parasuicides (suicide attempters) to either brief (24 hours or less) inpatient treatment or to ambulatory care and found no differences 1 and 16 weeks later on repeated parasuicide or other psychological measures. Most other research is based on long-term follow-up studies and is equivocal in outcome. The difficulty associated with constructing randomized intervention protocol for individuals at immediate or imminent suicide risk makes shorter-term studies less likely. The following sections detail the clinical, professional, and structural conditions that may necessitate involuntary care or hospitalization of a suicidal individual.

Clinically Necessitated Reasons

Even practitioners who believe strongly that involuntary hospitalization is unethical acknowledge they would not hesitate to place an actively suicidal patient into care during an acute psychotic episode (e.g., Linehan, 1993). Others make the case that hospitalization, regardless of level of suicide risk, and, whether voluntary or involuntary, is the immediate treatment of choice for severe phases of manic–depressive disorder, major depression, and psychotic presentations with delusions pertaining to death (Comstock, 1992; Litman, 1992). Psychotic thinking may be functional or organic in origin or the consequence of failed medication or failed medication compliance. The level of impulsiveness demonstrated or acknowledged by the client is also a factor in assessing whether hospitalization is necessary. History of highly impulsive behavior and the client's self-predicted responses to questions such as, "What do you think you would do if you left here now?" are often a useful gauge of impulsivity.

Clinically determined "failure to respond" to crisis intervention efforts is also frequently cited as a reason to consider involuntary hospitalization. Many suicidologists have written about the severe psychological pain that evokes suicide, viewing the role of clinician as one of persuading the client to cling to hope. This may be particularly difficult during critical periods in the life cycle (Yufit & Bongar, 1992). Whether the client or the practitioner is viewed as responsible for failing to attain hope or achieve a working therapeutic relationship, it is not possible to ensure the outcome of all interventions.

Professionally Necessitated Reasons

In cases in which the practitioner's professional well-being may be at stake, it is ethical to inform the client of this. For example, a practitioner may seek to place a suicidal client in care to avoid the threat of being sued or held liable if the client commits suicide (Linehan, 1993; Schutz, 1982). The practitioner may be aware that hospitalization reinforces suicidal behavior but may be afraid to take the risk of suicide if the client is not hospitalized. Clinicians should understand the relevant legal precedents and procedures necessary to admit a client into involuntary care in their locale (state or city).

Informal community norms and guidelines are also important to understand (Linehan, 1993; Schutz, 1982). The grounds under which personal philosophy against involuntary care or hospitalization may be violated must be spelled out to the client. The practitioner's position on involuntary care and probable response to threats of imminent suicide should be made very clear to the client at the beginning of treatment (Linehan, 1993). It is important to be clear and direct about the conditions under which interventions against the wishes of the client will be used. For instance, I was trained (and now train others) to always tell my clients that if they convinced me they were going to commit suicide, then I would actively intervene to stop them (Ivanoff & Smyth, 1992; Linehan, 1993).

Some practitioners are willing to take far fewer professional risks than others. Some agencies are less willing to let their practitioners take risks than others. Not all ethical interventions must be justified as designed to protect only the welfare of the client, independent of the practitioner's own welfare (Linehan, 1993). If the client has frightened the practitioner, this should be clarified, and the practitioner's right to maintain a comfortable existence should be explained (Linehan, 1993). Realistically, most practitioners have no intention of having their professional lives threatened because a client has committed suicide when it could have been prevented.

Suicide cannot be separated from its interpersonal context. When clients enter a therapeutic relationship, their subsequent behavior has consequences within that relationship and beyond: to pretend otherwise is both dishonest and a disservice (Bongar, 1992; Linehan, 1993; Maltsberger, 1986). Helping a client appreciate the intentions of those in the community who must respond to suicidal behavior can be a useful clinical focus (Bongar, 1992; Ivanoff & Smyth, 1992; Linehan, 1993).

Structurally Necessitated Reasons

Inadequate Community-Based Supports

Although the "ideal" suicidal client is one in, or with access to, ongoing intervention and a reasonably comfortable physical existence, the reality is that many multiproblem clients of social agencies may lack shelter, food, physical safety, and access to health and mental health services. "Exterior sustaining resources" (Maltsberger, 1986) may be fractured, lost, or unavailable. Whether the sustaining interpersonal support is a practitioner or significant other, the availability of substitute supports and the client's ability to use such supports are important: some clients are not capable of switching to available substitute supports. Often, no substitute sustaining supports, either formal or informal, are available.

Inadequately Trained Practitioners

A tragic irony in the U.S. mental health care delivery system is that the least trained mental health practitioners are responsible for care of the most distressed and disordered populations. Highly trained professionals are those least likely to be involved with the daily management of suicidal individuals. Judgments of clinical risk must take into account a multiplicity of individual psychological, social, and behavioral factors, including impulsivity, willingness to accept help, and empirical risk factors for suicide. Beyond these factors, however, it is widely acknowledged that accurate assessment of suicide risk requires a global, integrative assessment including these data plus clinical experience in dealing with other suicidal individuals (Comstock, 1992). Those legally or organizationally unable to exercise clinical judgment, (e.g., crisis line workers, line staff in residential facilities or correctional institutions), may be mandated to refer for involuntary hospitalization any client evidencing suicidal intent. Less restrictive alternatives to hospitalization may not exist, and organizations may be unwilling to risk liability for wrongful death.

Involuntary hospitalization should not be used because a mental health professional is incompetent; it is the responsibility of the practitioner to use all reasonable means to protect and ensure the safety of the client outside the constraints of involuntary hospitalization. However, given the autonomy assigned to less-trained practitioners, the complexity of variables involved in accurate risk assessment, and a significant lack of sustaining interpersonal or economic resources, few alternatives may exist.

Summary

Despite strong beliefs in client self-determination and least restrictive treatment alternatives, it is clear that there can be disadvantages to outpatient or ambulatory care. These disadvantages include the fact that the increased burden to the family or other caregivers may strain natural support networks beyond their capabilities, the practitioner's increased uncertainty about the safety of the client may weigh heavily, and the presence of actual (or judged) degree of immediate danger that exists in an outpatient setting. The family and friends of suicide victims (suicide "survivors") deserve assurance that due care and diligence are exercised to prevent suicide. They are also entitled to legally seek such assurance. In the presence of acute distress and suicidal intent, and the absence of sustaining psychosocial supports, involuntary care may be one of few ethical solutions.

There is no empirical evidence that inpatient psychiatric hospitalization has ever extended the life of a patient or prevented suicide. Despite the knowledge that it is increasingly only the most severely distressed and disordered individuals who fill inpatient beds, the high suicide rates in inpatient psychiatric facilities are cited circuitously as evidence that hospitalization may increase suicide risk. Given the ethical and other difficulties in conducting controlled studies on the efficacy of involuntary hospitalization, we may never have convincing data in this argument. However, there are convincing data on the associations between acute mental disorder and suicide: to *not* adequately protect an acutely suicidal individual violates the professional standards of the National Association of Social Workers, the American Psychological Association, and the American Medical Association, as well as community standards and expert opinion that support this intervention for the highest-risk patient (Litman, 1992). When we serve professionally in roles as health or mental health care providers, our obligation is to help safeguard the lives and well-being of others based on the best empirical and clinical knowledge available.

Case Example

S. was a 32-year-old woman with a 16-year history of major depressive episodes and repeated parasuicide (suicide attempts) of increasing lethality. After 9 months of moderate progress in treatment, S. began to experience delusions, incapacitating paranoia, and, not surprisingly, depression, suicidal ideation, and increasingly frequent suicidal urges. After two weeks of managing this in an outpatient setting, I suggested that S. admit herself for a brief inpatient stay to gain control over the delusions and paranoia (which I viewed as antecedent to the depression and suicidal urges). S. was adamantly opposed to this notion; forty-eight hours later, after multiple expressions of concern, explanations of my view of the current situation, and extended persuasion, S. went to the hospital.

A voluntary admission? Technically, yes. However, if our relationship had been less potent, or if S.'s paranoia or delusions had been slightly more severe, I would not have hesitated to have had her involuntarily admitted. Damaging to the therapeutic relationship? Perhaps, but I have faith in the capacity for reparation and repair in ongoing relationships. And I know that all forms of intervention are ineffective with dead clients.

REFERENCES

Dongas, B. (Ed.) 1992. *The assessment management treatment of suicide: Guidelines for practice.* New York: Oxford University Press.

Comstock, B. (1992). The decision to hospitalize and alternatives to hospitalization. In B. Bongar, (Ed.), *Suicide: Guidelines for assessment, management and treatment.* New York: Oxford University Press.

Ivanoff, A., & Smyth, N. J. (1992). Comprehensive treatment for suicidal clients. In K. Corcoran (Ed.). *Structuring change.* Chicago: Lyceum.

Linehan, M. M. (1993). *Cognitive-behavioral treatment of borderline personality disorder.* New York: Guilford Press.

Litman, R. E. (1992). Predicting and preventing hospital and clinic suicides. In R. W. Maris, A. L. Berman, J. T. Maltsberger, & R. I. Yufit (Eds.), *Assessment and prediction of suicide.* New York: Guilford Press.

Maltsberger, J. T. (1986). *Suicide risk: The formulation of clinical judgment.* New York: New York University Press.

Menninger, K. (1938). *Man against himself.* New York: Harcourt, Brace, & World.

Schutz, B. M. (1982). *Legal liability in psychotherapy: A practitioner's guide to risk management.* San Francisco: Jossey-Bass.

Waterhouse, J., & Platt, S. (1990). General hospital admission in the management of parasuicide: A randomised controlled trial. *British Journal of Psychiatry, 156,* 236–242.

Yufit, R. I., & Bongar, B. (1992). Suicide, stress, and coping with life cycle events. In R. W. Maris, A. L. Berman, J. T. Maltsberger, & R. I. Yufit (Eds.), *Assessment and prediction of suicide.* New York: Guilford Press.

Rejoiner to Professor Ivanoff   TOMI GOMORY

The good news is that Professor Ivanoff states that there is no disagreement between us about the efficacy of coercive treatment. It has none. "There is no empirical evidence that inpatient psychiatric hospitalization has ever extended the life of a patient or prevented suicide." The bad news is that Professor Ivanoff goes on to attempt to justify coercive interventions on what she calls ethical grounds. She does not explain, however, how an intervention that does not work can be "one of [the] few ethical solutions."

I will rebut Professor Ivanoff's assertions in order of their appearance in her essay. First, she asks, "When does action agreed to by a desperate, distressed individual technically become involuntary?" Professor Ivanoff seems to view this as a difficult problem. Let me reassure her it is not. It is any course of action that is not consented to by a person.

She next argues for "clinically necessitated reasons" compelling hospitalization. The three citations she supplies are assertions by authors without any meaningful argument and no empirical evidence. A clinician's so-called clinical assessment and intervention skills are practice folk myths or subjective beliefs about what works in the absence of well-tested outcome research. Ivanoff appears to be a believer.

"Professionally necessitated reasons" turn out to be exceptionally troubling under analysis. Professor Ivanoff suggests that a suicidal client may personally scare or professionally threaten the therapist and as a result may then ethically be involuntarily hospitalized. I believe that this is a completely misguided approach and, contra Ivanoff, professionally unethical. If a clinician is too frightened to hear a client's suicidal thoughts, ideas, or fantasies, then what is ethical on the part of that clinician is to choose not to work with suicidal clients.

Professor Ivanoff's statement, "if [clients] convinced me they were going to commit suicide, then I would actively intervene to stop them [presumably by involuntary hospitalization]" is remarkable in its naivete about the process of therapy. If she makes this statement at the beginning of her work with a client, she puts the client on notice as to what problems are not acceptable to talk about. Even if suicide is the key issue for that client, serious discussion about various aspects of suicide are not allowable, unless the client is willing to risk being imprisoned on a psychiatric ward. Furthermore, the decision to hospitalize is going to be made based on what intensity of suicidal feelings, ideas, desires is enough to "convince" Ivanoff of the client's determination to commit suicide. What is being tested in this situation is Ivanoff's capacity to tolerate discussion of suicide, not the client's suicidal intentions (which are unknowable).

The correct ethical stance is to firmly place the responsibility for seeking hospitalization or other treatment in the hands of the client, explaining up front that as a practitioner all I will do is talk with them. I must make clear that this dialogue may include any and all aspects of their concerns, including self-destructive feelings, along with potential options and choices the client may have. This clarifies and signals to the client what kind of treatment he or she can expect from me. Because I know from the available scientific research that I cannot prevent or predict whether the client in front of me will commit suicide, I do not take on the unrealistic burden of suicide prevention. By making this explicit at the beginning to my clients, I am allowing them to determine whether they want to work with me or would prefer a referral.

Her argument about "inadequate community-based support" because of the possible lack of shelter, food, physical safety, health, or mental health services for this group again is simply an assertion also true of many populations who are not suicidal. How the provision of such support prevents suicide is not discussed, probably because no empirical research corroborates this claim.

Under "inadequately trained practitioners," she states that the least trained practitioners work with the most "distressed and disordered populations." Professor Ivanoff completely ignores the fact that even a highly trained professional cannot predict or prevent a particular suicide. There are simply no such methods (see my NO essay). Paradoxically, she knows this to be the case.

She also claims that there is convincing evidence of the association between acute mental disorder and suicide, and consequently there is a duty to "adequately protect" (whatever that may mean) a suicidal patient. To not do this, she asserts, violates professional standards of several organizations, including the National Association of Social Workers. This is a curious statement from a university professor who I expect is familiar with statistics. Association by itself demonstrates nothing. Association, also known as correlation, can mean that a causes b, or b causes a, or a third variable c causes both a and b, or the association of a and b occurs simply by chance. I would respectfully disagree with Professor Ivanoff and assert that there cannot be any violation of professional or community standards based on associations of claimed entities because such associations tell us nothing of importance in and by themselves.

Of the case example Professor Ivanoff provides, the less said the better. Case examples of the sort included here serve little purpose beyond propaganda for any claims asserted. We have no way of evaluating the illustration or any of its claims. It is just a subjective description.

In conclusion, I believe that Professor Ivanoff, by agreeing with my contention that there is no empirical evidence corroborating that involuntary treatment is useful in preventing suicide, has conceded the essential point. The rest of her claims are without any well-tested evidence or are beside the point.

NO

Tomi Gomory

My response, in the negative, to the question up for debate is based on a very simple fact. There is not a shred of empirical evidence through unrefuted (Miller, 1994), controlled experimental research in more than 30 years of research by suicidologists (the alleged experts) showing either that suicide is preventable or that an individual suicide can be predicted (Hillard, 1995). This is so for all suicide prevention methods, coerced or consented.

Although I believe that the act of suicide is a moral and ethical, not a medical or psychiatric, issue, I have no problem with any treatment that is voluntarily requested by any troubled individual or is freely offered to such a person by any concerned professional. Such treatment may be for suicidal ideation (self-focused, scary, intense, angry thoughts) or any other minor or serious psychic pain. This seeking of help by an individual and the response by experts or others, whether they are called suicidologists, psychotherapists, clergy, relatives, or friends, is in the best tradition of what Thomas Szasz might describe as "ethical" psychotherapy (Szasz, 1965).

In this type of activity, there is a request for help from someone (the client) directed at someone (who may be a professional), who the client believes can be helpful in facing his or her problem(s). This help may be talk, medication, massage, or mahjong. Alternatively, a professional seeing that a person appears to be in some sort of difficulty, may offer his or her services for amelioration if he or she believes they are appropriate. Based on contractual consent, they work together on the problem or problems of the client until the problem has been resolved to the clients satisfaction or the participants mutually agree that the relationship has run its course. This type of therapeutic activity between consenting adults does not present any ethical difficulty. The issue becomes problematic when the alleged therapy is the confinement of so called suicidal adults in psychiatric facilities against their will or the coercive use of such treatments as electric shock, the prescribing of brain-damaging psychotropic medications (most such medications cause a high incidence of tardive dyskinesia), or various physical restraints. The debate is really about whether these coercive techniques are ever justifiable ethically or scientifically for the sake of suicide prevention (I exclude from my argument the involuntary treatment of "suicidal" children. Although a very important issue, by definition children as minors are under the coercive control of various adult authorities [parents, teachers, mental health professionals] and would require a separate argument).

I believe that the existing empirical research falsifies any claims of effective suicide prevention. Currently there are none (Hillard, 1995; Allard, Marshall, & Plante, 1992). There is only the personal decision by a "suicidal" individual to either not go ahead with the act, or if he or she is using the threat of suicide to manipulate the people around him or her, to learn to ask for what he or she needs differently. If there is no effective suicide prevention, then it follows tautologically that no targeted coercive treatments can be useful. Although people may be psychiatrically imprisoned against their will and can be forced to undergo electric shock or be medicated without their consent, this use of authority and power is not thereby a demonstration of any empirically well-tested concept of suicide prevention.

So what is left then to talk about? We might ask for example, how there can be almost 8,000 (7,989) articles in the University of California's psychology database on the subject of suicide covering more then 30 years (1963–1995) of research and theorizing? A cynic might suggest that mental health researchers have to make a living, some even at the expense of the dying. I would rather suggest that the act of suicide, which is claimed by the mental health field either to be a symptom of mental illness or to be itself mental illness, has suffered the same fate as the volitional behaviors that are asserted to embody the concept of mental illness.

Psychiatry long ago began to rename unwanted, disturbing, unpleasant, hard-to-understand purposeful human behavior and by the use of this semantic smoke screen convert acts to states of being or conditions indiscriminately called mental dysfunctions, diseases, syndromes, or illnesses. This psychiatric alchemy was necessitated by the alienists' (early institutional psychiatrists) desire to be baptized under the sacred authority of Medicine. By claiming to treat mental diseases rather than deviant behaviors, they gained in authority what they lost in truth telling.

Since the beginning of human social existence, there have been plenty of personally and socially unwanted behaviors to go around. The exercise of control over such behaviors and over the people manifesting them has varied. Before the late eighteenth century, mostly religious authorities were invested with this power. As science began to replace religion as the universal explanatory framework later in that century, medicine conformed more and more to good scientific practice, and by the mid to late nineteenth century, it could claim some explanatory power.

The prestige and authority of doctors grew as they were able to actually help physically sick people get better. Mimicking medicine, psychiatry claimed its right to control socially misbehaving people by asserting that these misbehaviors were diseases just like any others, and they (the psychiatrists) had cures for what ailed them (the deviants). Today, 150 years later, the psychiatric profession is still claiming that mental illnesses are just like any other illnesses and treating millions of people for them. Interestingly enough, we still have no unrefuted empirical evidence to corroborate this claim.

Such facts notwithstanding, suicidologists along with other members of the "helping" professions have argued that people wanting or planning to commit suicide are mentally ill. Consequently, they cannot make autonomous choices or at least are cognitively restricted from seeing the full extent of the alternatives open to them. The assumption of mental impairment articulated by the psychiatric mantra of "harm to self and others," which is invoked to justify involuntary hospitalization of anyone judged to be manifesting suicidal behavior, if taken seriously, would lead to absurd conclusions.

Involuntary hospitalization would have to be the "treatment of choice" for all people who are in danger of a lethal outcome based on many regular activities they pursue, well chosen or foolish. The habitual users of large quantities of cigarettes and liquor, for example, are far more numerous and more likely to die as a result of their behavior than are people talking about killing themselves. People undergoing any dangerous activity (construction jobs, walking the high wire, various sports, medical experiments, etc.) would have to be hospitalized if the phrase "danger to self" was meant literally by psychiatry. The absurdity is self-evident. Why then is this obviously arbitrary selection by psychiatry of just one particular dangerous, self-harming activity (suicide-related talk, planning, fantasizing, threatening,) for the label of mental illness so well accepted?

Medical doctors by their Hippocratic oath are committed to preserving life. People choosing to end theirs are a direct threat to the belief system of medicine (psychiatrists claim they are just like any other doctors). The institutional psychiatrist's defensive reaction, in the form of imprisoning or involuntarily medicating suicidal individuals, is "ego syntonic." Coercive efforts to keep people from harming themselves are justified by a belief system that assumes human life is always above any other ethical value. This notion is false and is refuted by the many heroes of humanity (Socrates, Jesus of Nazareth, Joan of Arc, Dietrich Bonhoeffer) who chose death over life for what they believed were more important values.

The last point I wish to make is that even in what we would ordinarily call suicidal behavior, there are those acts that are assumed to be "sick" behaviors and others that are accepted as justified (we understand the reasons for them). For example, self-starvation for a social or political cause (called a hunger strike) is seen as an admirable act, whereas self-starvation, by young women, for a personal cause (called anorexia nervosa) is seen as a mental disorder commonly requiring medication and hospitalization. What is the difference between the two acts? Nothing.

This confusion of autonomous action with apparent mental disorder can only occur when values, ethics, and science are confounded by both the controlling authorities and those controlled. The world as it exists entails tragedy. Life is problematic, and the choices to be made often invoke fear, anxiety, and pain. The human predicament consists of two conflicting desires. One is our desire for dependency. This consists of not wishing to be responsible, or wishing to be taken care of by some all-knowing authority—parents, the state, or God. The other is the desire for autonomy, to be self-possessed, self-reliant, free. This requires that we accept responsibility for our actions and be willing to live with the anxiety and ambiguity accompanying choice making. The decision of whether life under a certain set of circumstances is worth continuing is clearly a tragic human question, answerable only by the person living that life. By asserting that suicidal people are insane and that their choices are illnesses treatable by coercive psychiatric interventions, we diminish the humanity of the persons so labeled and cede authority to those who have no empirical or moral warrant for such a role.

REFERENCES

Allard, R., Marshall, M., & Plante, M. (1992). Intensive follow-up does not decrease the risk of repeat suicide attempts. *Suicide and Life-Threatening Behavior, 22*(3), 303–314.

Hillard, J. R. (1995). Predicting suicide. *Psychiatric Services, 46*(3), 223–225.

Miller, D. (1994). *Critical Rationalism: A Restatement and Defence*. Chicago: Open Court.

Szasz, T. S. (1965). *The Ethics of Psychoanalysis: The Theory and Method of Autonomous Psychotherapy*. New York: Basic Books.

Rejoinder to Mr. Gomory

ANDRE IVANOFF

My opponent argues that because psychological/psychiatric intervention has not been shown to be unequivocally effective, there is largely no ethical basis for voluntary or involuntary interventions to help distressed individuals. His secondary argument is that hospitalization of potentially suicidal individuals is not ethically justified because it has not been shown that hospitalization of those individuals reduces the likelihood of their self-harm.

This forum is not the place to argue the empirical effectiveness of psychological intervention, pharmacological therapy, and other psychiatric or residential treatments. Space and focus prevent discussion of how, and under what circumstances, practitioners use methods lacking demonstrated effectiveness; suffice it to say that almost all do. I share a strong bias for interventions with demonstrated effectiveness and can identify numerous psychological or psychiatric problems for which there are empirically based interventions. It is clear, however, that the society we live in popularly expects that individually or socially defined symptoms of aberrant behavior can be ameliorated by experts traditionally, using a medical model of treatment; in other words, we place ourselves in the hands of expert caregivers who define our pathology, know what is best, and prescribe relief. Regardless of preferred treatment models or theoretical orientation, while in roles as caregivers and mental health professionals, we are called on to support and protect life, sometimes even in cases when the client has lost all hope.

Suicide is not a simple personal act in our social structure, nor do I believe it should be treated as such. Suicide has significant social, as well as personal, repercussions. Contrary to Gomory's interpretation, I view the 8,000 articles on suicide found in his university's database as a testament to the profound impact suicide has on the living. I fail to understand how the act of suicide can be viewed only as an ethical exercise in free will by anyone who has witnessed the struggle against voices ordering self- (or other) destruction, alcohol- or drug-induced loss of contact with reality, or postpartum depression so severe that the risk affects both mother and child.

Do all such affected individuals request help or voluntarily accept it? Unfortunately not. The phrase "harm to self" when used to determine individuals needing care is stated more aptly as "imminent harm to self": it is absurd to suggest that habitual users of alcohol and cigarettes are at more imminent risk of harm to themselves than the distressed individual who plans, states full intention to carry out, and possesses the immediate means to carry out, suicide.

Suicide is a permanent, unretractable solution to what may be a temporarily unsolvable problem. The number of individuals who think seriously about suicide is far, far higher than the number who "attempt" suicide, which is far higher than the number who actually commit suicide. Most of those who engage in suicidal ideation verbalize suicidal intent, and even engage in self-harm labeled as attempted suicide, later change their minds. Are we so autonomous, so individually determined to deny this opportunity? Placing suicidal clients into care does not permanently deprive them of the right to suicide; at most, it defers a decision. Suicide is only an option for the living.

Does Coercion Have a Legitimate Place in the Treatment of Legally Competent Clients?

EDITOR'S NOTE: Most social workers work in public agencies, many of which involve implicit or explicit coercion, depending on certain actions or inactions of clients. Examples include child welfare agencies, protective services for the elderly, and mental health agencies (e.g., hospitalizing individuals against their will). Coercion conflicts with self-determination, a central value of the social work profession. Does coercion have a legitimate place in social work? If so, under what conditions?

Ray Liles, D.S.W., L.C.S.W., answers YES. He is in full-time private practice as a licensed clinical social worker in Colton and Crestline, California. At least half of his clients are sent to him by the court and other agents of social control. He is currently writing a paper tentatively entitled, "How Schools Become Toxic Environments for Children with Attention Deficit Hyperactivity Disorder."

Carol H. Meyer, D.S.W., who argues the NO position, is Ruth Harris Ottman Professor of Family and Child Welfare at the Columbia University School of Social Work. She has written extensively in that field and about social work practice theory. A former editor of *Social Work,* she is currently editor of *AFFILIA: The Journal of Women and Social Work.* Her most recent books are *Assessment in Social Work Practice* (Columbia University Press, 1995) and (co-editor) *Foundations of Social Work Practice* (NASW Press, 1995).

YES

RAY LILES

Social workers provide a variety of services to involuntary clients who are co-erced into coming to see us by various agents of social control. We also treat cli-ents who are driven to us by others who believe these clients need to change certain socially unacceptable behaviors. That we as a profession participate in this coercive process is a largely inescapable fact of professional life. We should be asking ourselves questions about the nature of the services we already provide to involuntary clients and the conditions under which those services are needed, eth-ical, appropriate, and useful. Furthermore, we need to ask ourselves hard ques-tions about how we can prevent the abuses of power that are an inherent risk in the delivery of services to involuntary clients.

We have responded to the needs of these involuntary clients since the begin-ning of our profession. The philosophical foundations of social work are twin pil-lars. We help our clients by attempting to support, educate, advocate for, and empower them in various ways, and yet at the same time we are often clearly agents of social control. The Charity Organization Societies were, in fact, set up at least in part to keep the needy from availing themselves of more than their fair share of goods and services being offered by participating agencies. To this day, in the minds of much of the American public, the term *social worker* evokes an image of a person who controls whether goods or services can be obtained (through means tests) or a person who comes snooping around to intrude into pri-vate family matters. Although members of our profession may protest mightily that this picture of social workers is neither current nor accurate, we are in many ways trying to change the course of a long-flowing river of impressions related to the provision of the coercive and involuntary services we have been associated with since the early days of our profession

Social workers use involuntary interventions in a variety of settings. These include: the "72-hour hold" common in many states (or other forms of involun-tary commitment) for mental patients who are seen as a danger to self, danger to others, or gravely disabled; clinical treatment or educational services within a drug diversion, alcohol diversion, or spousal abuse diversion program; anger management classes or clinical treatment for problem employees; clinical treat-ment as a condition of penal confinement; clinical treatment as a condition of pa-role or probation; and clinical treatment or educational services in relation to child welfare services offered in child abuse–related cases. And certainly we must ask ourselves about the level of coercion in all social work services "offered" to children who may or may not be capable of informed consent and may or may not be given any real choice when they are "offered" services.

To illustrate how and why coercion is used in the provision of social work services to essentially involuntary clients, I use the example of services provided to parents and children who have become involved in the juvenile court as the result of a child abuse problem. In many instances, child welfare services "offered" to families in which child abuse has occurred are backed up by the legal authority of the juvenile court. The court often says, in essence, "you will follow the terms of this reunification plan or your children will not be returned to you." Professionally trained social workers and others write these family reunification plans and act as monitors for the court in terms of client compliance with the plans. One could argue that, if clients accept services under these conditions, they have done so voluntarily because they could have refused services and abandoned their children to the child welfare system. Some parents do exactly that. Others accept services, some gladly, and many grudgingly and with obvious resentment and resistance. For the purpose of this argument, clients who are "offered" services and then advised of an averse consequence to them if they reject the services are "involuntary clients." They are, in fact, being coerced.

Child welfare social workers who "offer" these involuntary services often refer their clients to parenting classes and to individual and family therapy, services often provided by clinical social workers. They usually have a responsibility to report back to the child welfare social worker on the client's progress in treatment; they also can be subpoenaed to testify in court regarding their client's progress. Although the client may "voluntarily" sign a release of confidential information, the client knows this communication between professionals is part of the reunification plan. So the "do it if you want to get your children back" coercion is present even if the clinical social worker never uses those exact words when asking the client to voluntarily sign a release of confidential information.

Rationale for Coercion

So, how can the profession justify the coercive aspect of services we offer to persons who become our involuntary clients? How can we overcome the apparent violation of one of our profession's central values, that of "client self-determination"? On at least a philosophical level, most social workers probably recognize that clients have this "right" in the same way we all have the right to privacy and the right to free speech. We have those constitutional rights, but they are limited. As this argument usually goes, "your right to free speech ends where my nose begins." In other words, you have the right to express your opinions, but not in ways that hurt me physically.

It is conflict between the rights of various members of our society that provides the ethical rationale for the often coercive and involuntary treatment we offer our clients. For example, children have the right not to be physically or sexually abused or neglected. The simplest solution to child abuse problems is to offer abusive parents services that will effectively deal with the root causes of abuse. In an ideal world, services would be offered, parents would accept them, and the abuse would be stopped. In the real world, however, parents often refuse services or initially accept them and then fail to complete the course of treatment or education. In cases in which parents refuse to accept services on a voluntary basis, one could argue that we should just take children away and put them in foster care. Or perhaps we could put them into orphanages.

Parents of abused children might argue (and often do), however, that they have a right to the care, custody, and control of their children. These parents may say to those in authority that they made a mistake when the child was abused, but the problem can be dealt with and it will not happen again. They may argue that they believe they can simply stop abusing their children without availing themselves of any therapeutic, educational, or supportive services.

Children might also argue (and often do) that they have a right to live with their own parents. They do not want to be sent to live in foster homes or with other relatives (or to orphanages, for that matter). Children often know or believe that they are loved by their parents, even abusive ones, and given the choice, many children say they would rather stay with their own parents and have the abuse stopped.

Members of society might argue that society has a "right" to prevent child abuse through whatever method is needed because the social costs of this problem are so high. Many dysfunctional adults, such as convicted felons, have child abuse and neglect as a significant factor in their psychosocial histories. The social cost argument is, of course, not a new one when it comes to laws and regulations that infringe on persons' rights. It is often used to promote such things as the mandatory motorcycle rider hemet laws in various states. The argument is, "Yes, you should have the right to decide whether to wear a motorcycle hemet, but the costs to society are so large (hospital bills, rehabilitation, lost productivity) that we as a just society simply cannot allow you to exercise your right to choose in this instance."

So, how do we reconcile the rights of children to be protected from abuse with the rights of those same children to live with their own parents, the rights of the parents to have their children live with them, and the right of society to avoid the immense social and financial burden that can be directly or indirectly traced to the problem of child abuse?

The solution is obvious. We reconcile those rights by offering social work services to parents who have abused children. If the parents accept our services and if the services are effective and the family is able to stay together without future abuse, then we have solved the problem. Therein, however, lies the potential dilemma. What if parents who have abused their children exercise their right to client self-determination and refuse the services that have been offered to them? What if these parents initially accept services, but later exercise their right to client self-determination and stop using them before those services have had a chance to become effective? Social workers who are experienced in providing services to parents who have abused their children will tell you that the latter two questions are more than just theoretical possibilities. If parents who abuse their children refuse services in this instance, then we are immediately back to our dilemma. How do we reconcile all of these potentially conflicting rights?

We reconcile these rights by offering parents a deal we hope they will find hard to resist. We (the child welfare system, including the juvenile court) will offer you services specially designed to help you with the problem of child abuse. You will accept those services and we will give you back your children and get out of your life. This process is coercive and it creates a class of involuntary clients. Do the ends justify the means? Many social workers who have direct experience in child abuse intervention would argue yes.

Although in an ideal world we might not want to limit client self-determination and create any involuntary clients, we can see in this instance that we can effect a balance of all these conflicting rights. Given that the client accepts the services and that the services are effective, we have upheld the child's right to protection from abuse, reaffirmed the child's right to live with his or her own parents (by returning the child), reaffirmed the right of the parent to have care custody and control of his or her own child (same reason), and reaffirmed the right of society to avoid the immense social and financial burden of child abuse.

One might ask, "What happened to the right of client self-determination as all these other rights were being reaffirmed?" Although it may be difficult to see, the parents in the above example can exercise that right. They can refuse service. However, if they refuse service, there will be costs to them and to their children, and the costs may be severe and painful. We would sometimes like to think that rights can always be exercised without cost, but the reality is that in many instances they cannot. Society is replete with examples of the costs of exercising our individual and collective rights.

Conclusion

Social workers have always been involved in the implicit coercion of providing services to clients who not only come to us out of great pain, but are sent to us by other agents of social control. As a profession, we need to continue providing services to clients regardless of whether they come to us of their own free will or are sent to us by agencies troubled by their behavior. In certain instances, our clients' rights to self-determination will come in conflict with other equally important rights, such as a child's right to be free from parental abuse. We need to accept the reality of these conflicting rights and do several things. First, we need to make our highest priority the offering of effective services to voluntary clients in an effort to help them avoid becoming involuntary clients. Second, we need to create involuntary clients only as a last resort in cases in which the rights of others have been severely compromised by the client's behavior. Third, we, as a profession, need to provide effective ethical safeguards against the abuse of power by those social workers who provide services to involuntary clients.

Rejoinder to Dr. Liles

CAROL H. MEYER

Dr. Liles and I disagree on the use of coercion, even when it is conceded that we view the issues in the same way. I maintain that it is unethical for social workers to use coercion in their practice, not only because it conflicts with the Code of Ethics, but more importantly, because it denies to the (merely) involuntary client the legal right to justice that even criminals enjoy in this country. A judge, a jury, an attorney, rules of evidence, and so on provide protections that the client does not have (or is not told he or she has) in a social agency. Coercion cannot be rationalized as promoting self-determination, no matter how persuasively we try to convince the client that something is "good" for him or her, or that we "know better." The truth is that social workers have the power to coerce (in its many overt and disguised forms) without the proper constraints. Certainly, we can succeed if we exert that power skillfully, but does that make it ethical?

Unsatisfactory though it may be, the only ethical way to help involuntary clients is to be as clinically skillful as possible in framing the choices clients must make. At the end, where there is no "right" solution in a case, then the legal route is the most appropriate way to go, both because it will demand a solution and because it will offer the client the greatest protection of his or her rights. Perhaps when the legal process is seen as an outcome, social workers will be more able to sort out those cases that are actually in need of coercive action from those that are frustrating.

I am aware that this position may be anachronistic in these pragmatic days of accountability, welfare "reform," managed care, and demands for acceptable behavioral outcomes. But this debate was posed in an ethical and not a technical context. We are not considering how to best meet bureaucratic requirements, nor how to exert social control, even though social workers always have had to confront these matters. Social workers are not alone in their ethical quandaries. Issues of bureaucratic demands and social control face physicians, lawyers, teachers, and architects as well. If there is no ethical base beyond which we will not go, then we will have become technocrats and will have ceded our claim to being professionals. Physicians swear in their Hippocratic oath to "do no harm." Were social workers to take such an oath, could they swear to not deny self-determination to their clients?

NO

CAROL H. MEYER

This essay explores the implications of coercion in social work practice with nonvoluntary clients, saying "no" to it as a mode of influence, and considering alternate

ways of addressing behaviors that are variously called problematic, noncompli-
ant, antisocial, or deviant. The argument must rest on recognition of the implicit
and explicit power that social workers wield at all times—the power to provide or
withhold resources; the power to remove children, to restrict freedoms, and to influence clients through legal, clinical, or moral authority. This unequal distribution of power between client and practitioner makes it all the more necessary to
say "no" unambiguously to coercion because power is already stacked against the
client's self-determination by virtue of the fact that he or she has become a client
of a social work service. Saying "no" to coercion is required both on ethical and
clinical grounds.

Are expectations of the Code of Ethics universally accepted commitments,
or are there exceptions? If so, on what basis are these exceptions made? It is always easy to say "no" to coercion when a case presents benign problems and
when clients come voluntarily for help. It is when there are conflicting interests,
threats to well-being, or challenges to the "norm" that social workers might be
tempted to coerce "in the best interests of . . ." the client? his or her intimates? the
community? the agency? What are some examples of these difficult situations?
When caretakers abuse children? When men abuse women? When young women
choose to terminate a pregnancy? When people receiving public assistance confess to working secretively? When a homeless person refuses to go to a shelter?
When an aged person resists going into a nursing home? When a patient refuses a
recommended medical procedure? When a substance abuser will not attend a
treatment program? When a child refuses to go to school? When a person with
AIDS does not tell his partner about his illness? When a runaway youth will not
return home? When a troubled client chooses not to become a case? Is it the ethical thing to do to coerce clients to "do the right thing"?

Two Fundamental Questions

The first questions are: what is the standard for "the right thing," and where have
social workers gained sanction for coercing people to act "right"? In some of
these examples, the client might well be breaking a law and perhaps even acting
against a religious dictum, if not the social contract. Our analysis of the issue of
coercion should not suggest approval or disapproval of clients' behaviors; in fact,
their antisocial, illegal, self-destructive, or unethical behaviors, difficult as it may
be to accept them, can serve as the crux of our argument that it is never appropriate for a social worker to coerce a legally competent client, because the issue is so
clearly defined by the severe nature of their behaviors.

Of course, there are standards of behavior that govern in civilized societies,
although these are becoming difficult to determine in a multicultural society. Furthermore, all behaviors and choices of action are influenced by people's opportunity system. Do not personality structure; intelligence; education; family history;

other life experiences; peer relationships; community mores; racial; ethnic; gender; and age oppression; or poverty play a role in the choices people make? Social workers practice in this complex interplay of factors; they seldom have the luxury of defining an activity or an event in discrete ways; there is always a complicating factor to consider. (To consider is not to excuse, but to seek understanding so as to help and not coerce.) This is the chief reason that social workers are not welcome on juries, because they are notorious for looking beyond events, and thinking, "on the other hand . . ." or "from a different point of view. . . ." Social workers are not facile about defining things as good or bad, right or wrong, yes or no. It is a messy and unpredictable world out there, and social work may be the only profession that participates in multidimensional considerations. They are usually committed to viewing their client's world systemically, having to integrate many sides of events and therefore, many explanations for behaviors. This makes it very difficult to determine what is "right" in a given case. Right for whom? Under what conditions? Is it right to remove a child from an "abusing" parent who has grown up in a culture in which discipline meant beating a child? Is it right to force an aged person to enter a nursing home because her children want this? Is there an objective standard for either of these actions? Is there an absolute determinant for child abuse, or for when a nursing home is needed? And does not any determination change when resources are proffered or alternative behaviors are achieved? To justify social workers' coercion of clients, there would need to be an objective standard against which the client's behavior could be measured, and these are difficult to discern in cases defined in psychosocial or systemic terms.

The second question we want to address is, from where do social workers receive their sanction to coerce clients to do "right"? Police men and women are sanctioned by society to carry out the law, and the clergy are sanctioned by their religious communities to preach morality. Social workers are neither the police, nor ordained as clergy; they are charged by the public to provide social services. This becomes complicated when social workers are located in restrictive settings such as prisons or are placed in the position of coercing clients because of the agency's function with involuntary clients. True, social workers are asked (required?) to achieve outcomes that may be against the client's will; in fact, most of the time social workers are in the position of representing legal and social mandates. That is why practice is so difficult without the legal authority of the police or the moral force of the clergy. Every day, social workers confront young girls who have not faced what is entailed in having a baby, or battered women who do not want to leave their abusive partners, or aged people who would rather suffer isolation than enter a nursing home. It is safe to say that where social workers practice in social agencies, hospitals, clinics, etc. there are few if any clients who come for help voluntarily or who choose to change or be changed. Even when people want their life situations improved, they would rather have someone else do the changing; it is only human to ward off intrusion into one's life. When clients demonstrate severely destructive behavior, or when they are not perceived as being capable of non coercive help, then perhaps they should not be clients of social workers. Cases of severe violence in which there is no indication that the client has the capacity to reflect on his or her behavior may not be appropriate for social workers, because the coercion that is necessary is not a proper professional tactic (see Code of Ethics). Clients who are deemed to require coercion would be better (and more fairly) served in the justice system, where their rights would be protected by due process, informed consent, and privileged communication, if not by a judge and a jury.

Acting without Coercion

Where then does this leave social workers when police authority to coerce is removed as an interventive option and practitioners are left to rely on their professional Code of Ethics for guidance? It leaves practitioners exactly in the place for which they have been prepared through their professional education, with their clinical skills, which include the ability to engage resources in the environment. Social work practice that is guided by the Code of Ethics, professional purposes, and practice knowledge has a repertoire that is appropriate to the task of addressing the kinds of client problems and behaviors cited, although clinical methods might not always be effective at the end. (In the field of medicine we know that some diseases cannot be cured through medical treatment.) Clients always have the choice to act, even if the choice is narrowly defined, and social workers always have the option to confront clients with these choices, to help them find their own solutions. An example of this can be found in cases of child abuse, in which social workers are actually required to report such cases to child welfare authorities. The alleged child abuser has to be told of the necessity to report, but reporting is the beginning and not the end of the process. In fact, the reason for the report may actually serve as the entree to the case. What is the abuse about? Why did it happen? What needs to be fixed? If the caretaker/client does not want the child to be removed, the practitioner should inform the client about what is necessary to keep the placement from happening, and how he or she can help the client to avoid the placement. As experienced child welfare workers know all too well, helping families to prevent the placement of their children is a process that is strewn with obstacles. In addition to lack of resources and environmental alternatives, there is often client anger, avoidance of issues, distortions, and lies that may be called on to defend against the real authority of the social worker to remove the child. This kind of case is a test of clinical skills, not a reason to take the easier road of coercion.

Cases in which clients are nonvoluntary are often those in which clients are in trouble with the law or other social institutions or are threatening themselves or others through their behaviors. In such cases, whether because of the practitioner's frustration, concern for his or her client's welfare, interest in protecting others, or even pressures of time, coercion might be considered as the most effective intervention. These are surely among social workers' most difficult cases. In cases in which voluntary clients more readily participate in the helping process, even if they are complex and difficult to help, their behaviors are usually not as troublesome, so the practitioner would be less apt to feel the pressure to impose coercive methods on them. Nevertheless, the practice processes (not the substance) should be identical with both types of cases. Beginning with a clear contract and honest negotiation, in neither type of case is there ever justification for a corrupt contract. The desire to help, empathy, and support have to be present in all helping situations, even if the client is in prison. The requirement for exploration and assessment of the problems at hand remains constant, as does the phase of interventive planning. These familiar processes need not be equated with permissiveness; they are the necessary conditions for any social work intervention.

Finally, we come to the core of effective practice, which has to do with the client's willingness to "own" his or her situation. (This debate assumes the legal competence of the client, and thus the capacity to recognize his or her situation.) Without this "ownership," there is no engaged client, and it is safe to say that where the client is not a real participant in the process, there is no workable case. Coercion might be attempted so as to generate the client's compliance or obedience, but this can be done better through legal methods, and even then, such accomodating behavior would be at the least transient, and at the most, only present while the coercive threats were maintained. In other words, clinically speaking, coercion does not work. Once the client does participate in the process, the difficult issues we mentioned earlier in this essay all can be posed to the client in a framework of choices the practitioner can help the client to make. Here we return to client self-determination, and to the haven of the Code of Ethics.

Conclusion

We know that coercion is in widepread use, overtly, by policy, in departments of public assistance, and of course in restrictive settings such as prisons. Coercion is used as well in covert ways, not sanctioned by public policy, but disguised as seductive or manipulative clinical practices. Any covert practice that, without sanction, compels people to do things against their will is unethical as well as ineffective. When social work clients require controls and coercive methods, either because of their potential for destructive behavior or because of a legal mandate, they should receive the legal protections that accompany these controls, and social workers ought not be complicit in denying these in the name of what is "right." John Stuart Mill said it forcefully: ". . . the only purpose for which power can be rightfully exercised by any member of a civilized society against his will, is to prevent harm to others. His own good, either physical or moral, is not a sufficient warrant. Over himself, over his own body and mind, the individual is sovereign." (Mill, 1971).

REFERENCE

Mill, J. S. (1971). "On liberty." In S. Gorovitz (Ed.), *Mill: Utilitarianism.* Indianapolis: Bobbs-Merrill.

Rejoinder to Professor Meyer   RAY LILES

Carol Meyer's argument that coercion does not have a place in social work intervention is, to say the least, confusing. She points out, as I did, that social work ethics include the right of client self-determination. Then she goes on to say "that where social workers practice in social agencies, hospitals, clinics, etc., there are few if any clients who come for help voluntarily, or who choose to change or be changed." I make a similar point. It seems that we are both acknowledging that many of the clients social workers see are being coerced into accepting social work intervention. So, what are we to do? Refuse to see all clients who are being coerced into accepting our services? Unfortunately, Meyer comes very close to that argument when she goes on to say that "when clients demonstrate severely destructive behavior, or they are not perceived as being capable of noncoercive help, then perhaps they should not be clients of social workers." If we do not provide services to these clients, who will?

Meyer's argument is that these "destructive" clients "would be better (and more fairly) served in the justice system, where their rights would be protected by due process, informed consent, and privileged communication, if not by a judge and a jury". I find this part of her argument confusing as well. It is, in fact, the justice system that coerces clients into accepting social work services. The judge and the jury (through the agents of parole and probation) are the very ones who send us many of these "destructive" clients. The justice system "serves" them by punishing them (through confinement and fines) and by sending them to us. Social work intervention is sometimes a tool of the justice system. If we, by refusing to see coerced or involuntary clients, take away the tool of services, then we leave the justice system with only the tool of punishment.

I am not confused by, but I emphatically disagree with, Meyer's assertion that "clinically speaking, coercion does not work." Social workers have traditionally been trained to believe that clients have to want to change and have to accept services voluntarily to get better. Her assumption is not an uncommon one in our field. It is, however, wrong.

Social workers who have extensive experience providing treatment services to parents who have been sent to them by the juvenile or criminal court for child abuse–related problems report how the very same clients who arrived in their offices hostile, resentful, angry, and resistant often make major positive changes in their lives as the result of treatment. Many of these clients eventually come to see "the system" as really trying to help them, although this insight usually does not come easily or quickly.

It is not my contention that all involuntary clients, child abuse related or otherwise, get better as the result of services social workers provide to them. However, in at least one client population, (and I suspect others), "coerced" clients do get better, and their lives and the lives of their children are immeasurably enriched. When I was coordinating an interagency incest treatment program composed of largely "involuntary" clients, it was not unusual for a parent, at the end of his or her treatment, to say to the other parents in the program something like, "You know this may sound kind of strange, but having incest disclosed in our family and having to come to this program was the best thing that ever happened to us."

Is the Public Adequately Protected from Incompetent Practitioners through Licensing?

EDITOR'S NOTE: The successful practice of law, medicine, social work, and all other helping professions requires that clients place an extraordinary degree of trust in their helper, even if he or she is a stranger. In return, human service professionals are morally obliged to the public they serve to be competent practitioners. Although there is no disagreement about the existence of this obligation, there is an unending debate about how it is met. The debate below deals with what is the most common way social work undertakes to assure its public about the competence of its practitioners.

Joan E. Esser-Stuart and Paul H. Stuart argue YES. Joan E. Esser-Stuart is an Instructor in the School of Social Work and a Research Associate with the Institute for Social Science Research, the University of Alabama. She teaches courses in the social work practice sequence as well as social work research methods. She has published articles on family policy and evaluation research. Paul H. Stuart is a Professor in the School of Social Work, The University of Alabama. He is a social welfare historian and has published articles and books on the history of social welfare and social work.

Charles Atherton makes the NO case. He is Professor Emeritus of the School of Social Work at the University of Alabama. He has co-authored four books and authored or co-authored many articles, mostly on social welfare policy and social work education.

YES

JOAN E. ESSER-STUART
PAUL H. STUART

All states and territories now provide some form of legal regulation of social workers, most commonly in the form of licensing. The primary purpose is to protect the public from incompetent practitioners. State licensing laws accomplish this by imposing educational requirements for a license, by independently assessing the acquisition of minimal knowledge and skill required for competent practice, by requiring recertification, and by disciplining incompetent and unethical practitioners.

Educational Requirements

State licensing laws require that applicants show evidence that they have completed an appropriate professional education program, leading to a BSW or an MSW degree from a school that has been accredited by the Council on Social Work Education (CSWE).

The purpose of accreditation is to guarantee that social work education programs "prepare competent and effective social work professionals" (Frumkin & Lloyd, 1995, p. 2240). The CSWE's Curriculum Policy Statements (Edwards, 1995, pp. 2649–2659) prescribe the ways in which schools may achieve this purpose. By requiring that applicants for a license complete a professional education program, states ensure that applicants have met requirements imposed by social work education programs that conform to national standards promulgated by CSWE.

Independent Assessment of Professional Knowledge

The accreditation of professional education programs does not guarantee that graduates will know everything they need to know to practice competently. Nor does professional education ensure that the graduate will learn the self-discipline and habits of behavior that would cause him or her to search for and locate the information needed for competent practice. Therefore, something beyond receipt of a diploma is needed to establish the professional's competence.

A common mechanism for accomplishing this is the licensure examination. It is designed "to establish independently that the applicant is at least minimally competent to provide services to the public" (Shimberg, 1985, p. 2). Rather than guaranteeing that practitioners are highly competent, licensing laws are designed to ensure that practitioners have at least a minimal level of knowledge to carry out professional functions (Biggerstaff, 1995).

Most states require an acceptable or passing score on a credentialing examination. Different examinations are provided for the various educational and practice experience levels. For higher levels of licensure, usually designated "advanced," "certified," or "clinical," states require a period of supervised work experience after the professional degree before the applicant may take the examination (Biggerstaff, 1995). This insures that the applicant for this level of licensure has applied her or his professional knowledge and skills under supervision.

Most social work licensing examinations are four-option multiple-choice examinations derived from job analyses of practicing social workers. The examinations must meet requirements for occupational tests, which require that the items have content validity, that is, they must be "derived from job-related tasks performed by social workers" (Biggerstaff, 1995, p. 1621). These examinations have been found to be "a highly reliable and valid format for assessing knowledge relevant to clinical social work practice" (Biggerstaff, 1992, p. 185).

Although written examinations may adequately test for knowledge, they cannot test for skill in applying knowledge. Thus, two states, California and Virginia, require that applicants for the clinical social work license take an oral examination, in addition to the review of candidate qualifications and the written examination. Biggerstaff (1992) found the Virginia oral examination to be "a valid method of assessing competence for entry-level clinical social work practice" (p. 196).

Recertification

Once a practitioner has been licensed, for how long can the license be maintained? The issue of recertification is important, because it is not tenable to assume that "knowledge and skills once acquired are mastered for life;" nor are "social work knowledge and skills . . . static and [unchanging] over the worker's life" (Hardcastle, 1977, p. 16). Thus, social work licensure laws seek to protect the public from practitioners who may not seek opportunities for professional growth and development on their own. Most states mandate that social work licensees participate in approved continuing education activities to maintain the social work license.

These continuing education requirements seek to insure that social work professionals keep abreast of recent developments in the field. Participation in these continuing education opportunities helps practitioners to improve their knowledge and skills and thus practice more effectively. More comprehensive continuing education requirements for recertification may further safeguard the public.

Disciplinary Procedures

An additional avenue for protecting the public through social work licensure is the provision of disciplinary procedures. Some state laws incorporate codes of ethics for social work practice, and several other states have adopted the NASW Code of Ethics (Edwards, 1995, Vol. 3, pp. 2625–2629) to guide professional practice. The latter identifies competent practice as an ethical principle of the profession (in Section I, B).

Thus, state licensing boards have the power to discipline licensed professionals who are found to practice incompetently or unethically (Biggerstaff, 1995). Complaints of unethical or incompetent practice, brought by consumers or professional colleagues, are heard by the respective state social work licensing board. If either incompetent or unethical practice is confirmed, the board may impose sanctions. The board has broad discretionary power to determine the appropriate sanction. Sanctions may range from requiring additional continuing education to revocation of the license.

An Imperfect Guarantee

The requirements of educational preparation, a licensing examination, recertification, and disciplinary procedures are all designed to protect the public from incompetent practitioners. It is, however, an imperfect system. Some individuals who graduate from accredited social work programs may lack sufficient knowledge to practice. Some of these graduates may pass an imperfectly designed licensure examination, be recertified, and evade detection by colleagues or clients. In addition, neither professional education nor a licensure examination can eliminate unethical practice. Some individuals may stray from the ethical underpinnings of social work practice and fail to act appropriately.

Thus, licensing of professional social workers may not by itself guarantee protection of the public from incompetent practitioners. Nor do any of the other means employed to ensure competent practice—the accreditation of educational programs, peer review, an alert and vigorous professional association with a committee of inquiry, or professional supervision in accredited social agencies—by themselves guarantee competent practice. Just as professional educational programs may on occasion award degrees to individuals who have failed to master prescribed educational content, persons who lack requisite knowledge may pass imperfect licensing examinations and evade the systems set up by licensing boards, professional associations, and social agencies to ensure competent practice.

In the real world, a variety of mechanisms, all imperfect, are needed to protect the public from incompetent practitioners. Taken separately, each may be inadequate to the task of completely protecting the consumer of social work services. Even taken together, the system of protection will inevitably provide less than complete prophylaxis. However, less than adequate protection is far better than none at all.

The answer to protecting the public lies in improving licensing, not abandoning it. Thus, the experiences of state social work licensing boards with oral examinations promise to improve the ability of licensing laws to protect the public from incompetent practitioners because these oral examinations are better suited to assess the broad range of social work practice skills. The authors anticipate that the advocates of licensure will continue to be vigilant in pursuing additional mechanisms to further protect the public from incompetent social work practitioners.

REFERENCES

Biggerstaff, M. A. (1992). Evaluating the oral examination in Virginia's licensing of clinical social workers. *Research on Social Work Practice, 2*(2), 184–197.

Biggerstaff, M. A. (1995). Licensing, regulation, and certification. In R. L. Edwards (Ed.-in-Chief), *Encyclopedia of Social Work* (19th ed., Vol. 2, pp. 1616–1624). Washington, DC: NASW Press.

Edwards, R. L. (1995). *Encyclopedia of Social Work* (19th ed., Vol. 3). Washington, DC: NASW Press.

Frumkin, M., & Lloyd, G. A. (1995). Social work education. In R. L. Edwards (Ed.-in-Chief), *Encyclopedia of Social Work* (19th ed., Vol. 3, pp. 2238–2247). Washington, DC: NASW Press.

Hardcastle, D. A. (1977). Public regulation of social work. *Social Work, 22*(1), 14–20.

Shimberg, B. S. (1985). Overview of professional and occupational licensing. In J. C. Fortune (Ed.), *Understanding testing in occupational licensing.* San Francisco: Jossey-Bass.

Rejoinder to Professors Esser-Stuart and Stuart

CHARLES ATHERTON

My colleagues have taken the only line of defense possible: It is better to have a leaky umbrella than no cover against the rain at all. Although they argue that the protection of the public is the primary aim of licensing, they recognize that licensure also serves as a "turf protector." Our disagreement on the central issue hinges on the relative weight that each of us attaches to these two aims in practical terms.

If the protection of the public rests on "minimum education and knowledge requirements," it would appear that the public comes up short. The public is assured of minimal competence, while the licensee, on the other had, is rewarded with professional status and certainly more money in those instances when licensure leads to eligibility for third-party payments and fees from private practice. It certainly appears that the licensee gets the better part of the bargain.

Esser-Stuart and Stuart argue that continuing education and the discipline exercised by state licensing boards round out the protective effect of licensing laws. Space does not permit a discussion of licensing boards, but the analogy of hiring a fox to guard the chicken house comes to mind whenever one thinks of a regulatory body composed of people in the same trade or profession as those whom they regulate.

Continuing education, however, deserves a further look, because it would seem to have merit in ensuring that the minimum competence of the licensee will be upgraded. There are two related problems. First, licensing laws require only that a certain number of "contact" hours must be obtained. Nothing insures the quality of the offerings or their relevance to the needs of practitioners. Continuing education is one of the last bastions of the unfettered free market, in that what is offered is determined by what sells.

The second objection has to do with how continuing education works. One attends a conference or workshop provided by a professional organization, treatment facility, or school of social work, either separately or in some combination of sponsorship. One pays a stiff fee to spend two days or so listening to a panel of experts in a given area, and then collects her or his certificate, which is duly forwarded to the licensing board at the time of license renewal. Did anyone see the word "examination" in that description? A continuing education event might be highly relevant and of unquestioned quality, but because there is no examination there is not even a minimum guarantee that the participant has in fact learned anything. If there was anything other than a minimal standard of accountability, any sizable failure rate would surely discourage participation and thereby reduce the flow of customers.

The real problem with licensing, as I see it, is not that it is imperfect in protecting the public, but that licensing is regarded as a more powerful process than it actually is. I also remain convinced that licensing, in reality, is more important in protecting turf and income than in protecting the public, and that the consumer must judge practitioners by looking beyond the license on the wall and taking educational background, experience, and professional reputation into account.

NO

CHARLES ATHERTON

Although licensing is a lofty idea in principle, it primarily protects the status and income of the professional but provides little protection for the client or patient. Social workers have invested a lot of energy and time lobbying for licensure. As a result, all states now have some form of social work licensing. Proponents enlisted the rank and file in the cause by arguing that licensing would enhance the position of social work as a profession. As Iverson (1987) noted, however, the key rallying point was the enticing prospect of third-party payments that would support private practice.

More importance has been attributed to the notion of licensing than is justified. Years ago when licensing was being actively promoted, a large meeting of social workers was convened in one Midwestern state. A series of speakers argued for the advantages of licensing, citing the usual arguments: increased status, protection of the public from unqualified practictioners, and, of course, the vendorship potential. One speaker contended that social workers should be licensed because others, for example, nurses, physicians, and attorneys, were licensed. A voice from way in the back—not mine—added:

"But so are dogs!"

Too flip? Perhaps. But there is a serious point. We live in a time of professional overkill. The man who sprays insecticide around our house is a licensed professional. The woman who operates a carpet cleaning business advertises that her crews are all licensed professionals. This is not to say that these licenses are not legitimate, nor am I demeaning these jobs or the people who make their living by doing them. What I am saying is that nearly every trade, profession, or occupation now requires a license. But having a license does not guarantee that the public has any real protection against shoddy work or sleazy merchandise.

And why not? First of all, most licensing procedures require only minimal competence to meet the requirements. All states require a license to operate an automobile. Written examinations are elementary, and road tests will only screen out the most obviously bad drivers. If it were not easy to get a driver's license, there would be fewer licensed drivers. Would this protect the public? Not necessarily, because the outcome of stricter licensing laws simply might be that there would be more unlicensed drivers, not that there would be better drivers.

But is not the situation different in the licensing of professionals who work intimately with the health and welfare concerns of their clientele? Social workers should know better. Many of them have worked in settings in which they performed licensing functions. Foster care is a good example. To qualify for a foster home license, it is necessary to meet only minimum standards of physical and mental health and household safety. For example, in one state in which I used to work, it was mandatory to have the drinking water tested as part of the foster home licensing procedure. Rural wells rarely met the standard, so it was necessary to require the foster parents to sign an agreement to boil the ward's drinking water—water that the family had been drinking straight out of the tap for years. Was the water that the ward drank always boiled? I don't know, but I doubt it. I religiously conducted long, probing interviews with the applicants and their references before recommending a license. Did all the homes that I recommended meet licensing standards? I believe that they did. Did that license guarantee that the public (and the wards) were protected? Not necessarily, because all that was necessary was that the foster home meet a *minimum* standard, not even an optimum standard.

Social workers also license day care centers and children's institutions. Can it honestly be said that these licenses adequately protect the public from incompetent staff?

The skeptical reader may think that my examples are unfair because licensing of "real" professionals is different from licensing drivers, foster parents, day care centers, and children's institutions. To these skeptics, I reply that there is no difference in principle as long as licensing—in whatever frame of reference—is based on minimum standards of competence.

The naive faith that some social workers place in licensing is surprising because they are very familiar with various other licensed professionals with whom they have frequent contact and in whom they have little confidence. Social workers have all bitten their tongues when clients praised the services of licensed professionals about whom the social workers had grave reservations because of past experiences. In every community in which I worked, there was at least one psychiatrist known (off the record, of course) as "The Electrician" because he—it was never a she—used electric shock as the treatment of choice for nearly every condition. This was, of course, perfectly legal and it could not be said to be necessarily unethical. But I was never confident that the patient was getting up-to-date care.

Let me pick on the doctors for a bit more. Our press has carried stories of doctors who were stricken from the state's list of licensed physicians. Medical licenses are usually "lifted" because of sexual misconduct or some other form of illegal behavior, such as drug abuse. Rarely is professional knowledge or skill an issue. The doctor is still capable of passing a licensing examination and often reappears fully qualified and in practice in a different state. Is the situation in social work any different? I do not see how it can be.

Social work licensing laws in particular are highly suspect. First, many of them are basically title protection laws. They prohibit unlicensed persons from calling themselves social workers, but they do not prevent them from performing the functions commonly carried out by social workers as long as they do not use the title.

Second, in some states, many social workers are exempt from licensing if they are employed by the state. In this state, for example, social workers who are employed by the Department of Mental Health and Retardation do not have to be licensed as a condition of employment.

Third, licensing is accomplished primarily by passing a standardized paper and pencil test. These are not difficult, nor can they be because they can only reflect minimum standards of knowledge. Currently, all states use examinations provided by the American Association of State Social Work Boards. Thyer (1994) pointed out that there are no publically available analyses of the reliability or validity of the examinations. His own research raises serious questions about whether the examinations have any real value. Thyer suggests that the chief beneficiaries of licensing are not clients but those persons who profit from the licensing process, such as those who offer exam-preparation workshops.

Although references also may be required as part of the licensing process, rare is the person who can not find three people who will speak well of her or him. Furthermore, public disclosure laws, such as the so-called Buckley amendment, have rendered written references virtually useless in assessing character in applicants for jobs and licensing. Even writing true statements in a reference letter may subject the writer to a lawsuit and may threaten economic loss.

In summary, licensing laws may create a false sense of confidence on the part of the public. They may feed the vanity of the social worker who proudly displays her or his license, but they do not guarantee competence. Licensing reflects the overprofessionalization in our society and at best suggests that the licensee can pass a written examination that must be designed to permit most people who take it to pass. The main functions of licensing in social work, and in everything else, is to generate revenue for state government and to enhance the prestige and increase the income of the licensee. Any protection that licensing affords is a distant third place.

We will undoubtedly continue licensing of all kinds of trades, occupations, and professions. It is, I suppose, better than nothing, although if one is ill served by a professional, her or his remedy is better sought in the courts, rather than by appeals to a licensing board. Licensing in social work, as in anything else, does not negate the doctrine of caveat emptor.

REFERENCES

Iversen, R. R. (1987). Licensure: Help or hindrance to women social workers. *Social Casework, 68,* 229–233.

Thyer, B. T. (1994). Assessing competence for social work practice: The role of standardized tests. In R. G. Meinert, J. T. Pardeck, & W. P. Sullivan (Eds.), *Issues in Social Work.* Westport, CT: Auburn House.

Rejoinder to Professor Atherton

Joan E. Esser-Stuart
Paul H. Stuart

Many occupations, it is true, are licensed. So are dogs and automobile drivers. In each case, the justification for licensure is the protection of the public. Vaccination against rabies is required before a dog can be licensed, and automobile drivers must demonstrate that they know the rules of the road and can operate a motor vehicle to obtain a driver's license. In a similar manner, applicants for occupational licensure must demonstrate that they have obtained at least the minimum level of knowledge necessary to pass a licensure examination. In each case, protection of the public is the primary objective of licensure.

As Professor Atherton points out, licensing does not ensure that drivers will obey the laws or operate their vehicles competently. Nor is there any guarantee that professionals will use their knowledge appropriately when practicing—or that they will follow professional canons of ethics. Licensing professionals cannot guarantee complete protection of the public. It does, however, afford more protection than no licensure for occupations and professional practitioners.

Professor Atherton objects that "most licensing procedures require only minimal competence to meet the requirements." This is an interesting argument that must be viewed within a historical context. More than thirty years ago, a leading critic of occupational licensure complained that professions tend to set competence levels of professionals too high, requiring "a Cadillac standard" of every licensed professional, even if the result was that some people would go without professional services (Friedman, 1962, p. 153). We would argue that licensing standards should be set high enough that the licensed professional has the knowledge necessary to do the job, but not so high that the public is unable to secure needed professional services.

The licensing laws need to be improved, as well. Professor Atherton identifies three weaknesses of current social work licensing laws. First, many provide title protection only. That is, they do not prevent nonlicensed individuals from performing professional functions. Second, many state licensing laws exempt some state employees. Finally, in most states, the licensing examination uses only a standardized paper and pencil test. These are all valid criticisms. However, it bears repeating that the persons who take the licensing examination are required to have completed a course of study in an accredited social work educational program.

As we suggested earlier, improving the instruments used to measure the mastery of professional knowledge and skills should be a high priority for the social work profession. Without a doubt, the ability of the available measures to determine whether applicants for social work licenses have the needed knowledge and skills to perform professional functions could be improved. The reliability and validity of existing examinations should be examined. In addition, social work researchers should have access to these data. The oral examinations used in California and Virginia are innovations that provide the potential to ascertain the mastery of social work skills and methods of intervention. Improving measures of professional competence should be a major priority for social work practitioners, educators, and researchers.

We would also advocate for modifications in state licensing laws. These laws need to be amended to prevent nonprofessionals from performing professional functions. In addition, social work practitioners in state agencies should be held to the same standards as other social work practitioners. The issue of recertification is also important, because licensing laws protect the public from professionals who do not willingly pursue opportunities for professional growth and development.

At the end of his essay, Professor Atherton concludes that licensing is "better than nothing." We definitely agree and concede that "licensing in social work, as in anything else, does not negate the doctrine of caveat emptor." Licensing can do little to protect the public from unethical practitioners; it is designed to ensure that practitioners have a minimum level of competence, that necessary to perform professional functions. Improvements in the licensing examinations and state licensing laws are urgently needed to improve the protection afforded the public. Even absent such protection, licensing provides the public with the best available protection from incompetent practitioners.

REFERENCE

Friedman, M. (1962). *Capitalism and freedom.* Chicago: University of Chicago Press.

Should the Findings of Ethics Hearings Be Released to the Public?

EDITOR'S NOTE: Each year some professionals come before professional ethical boards of inquiry. Should the public have access to the findings of these hearings? Would this enhance ethical practice and discourage unethical behavior? Should the public as well as other professionals who make decisions about whom to refer clients to have access to this information so they can make informed choices?

William Butterfield, Ph.D., makes the YES case. He is Associate Professor at the George Warren Brown School of Social Work at Washington University in St. Louis. He is on the NASW National Committee on Inquiry, which is the ethics committee of the Association. He has chaired the Missouri NASW Committee on Inquiry and has served as a member of the NASW Legal Defense Fund.

Colleen Galambos, DSW, offers the NO argument. She is Assistant Professor in the social work department at Western Maryland College, where she teaches courses in practice, policy, human behavior, gerontology, and health care. She currently serves on the NASW National Committee on Inquiry. Dr. Galambos is a former board member of the NASW and a past president of the Maryland Chapter, NASW.

YES

WILLIAM BUTTERFIELD

Problems with the Confidentiality Policy

Confidentiality Procedures Limit the Effectiveness of the Association's Efforts to Protect the Public

The current adjudicatory process attempts to protect the public by requiring that social workers found to have acted unethically cease their unethical behavior and seek correction through activities such as supervision, counseling, and education. The policy assumes, if a social worker completes the rehabilitation process, that the social worker will have changed so that the public will be protected from further harm. It also protects the social worker from being permanently labeled as an unethical social worker. Here, the assumption appears to be that the rehabilitation effort will be uniformly successful so that the goal of preventing the permanent labeling of a social worker as unethical is not in conflict with the Association's obligation to protect the public.

Both assumptions can be challenged. The assumption of uniform rehabilitation lacks evidence. Thus, it is difficult to argue that full disclosure of the allegations and of the hearing panel's findings of fact and their conclusions is not in the public interest. Furthermore, the policy of confidentiality prevents the public from making independent judgments of the process or the likelihood of future unethical behavior. It also may discourage disclosure by other parties who become aware that their experience with the social worker was not unique. Finally, the prohibition on the publication of the findings makes it impossible for the public to determine if a social worker has a prior history of ethical misconduct. With one minor exception, (release of names of individuals who have been publicly sanctioned) anyone who asks NASW if a member has ever violated the Code of Ethics is told that such information is confidential.

Confidentiality Procedures Limit the Effectiveness of NASW Efforts to Protect Social Workers

NASW recognizes that, "It is not possible to control persons outside of NASW who are involved in the situation giving rise to the complaint; this situation is often known to a number of people when it occurs or before a complaint is filed. It is not always possible to maintain secrecy about the fact that a complaint has been filed." (NASW, 1991(a), p. 14) see also NASW, 1991(b). This puts the social worker at a distinct disadvantage. By NASW's own admission, there is some likelihood that others will learn that a complaint has been lodged against a member; for example, where the allegations have become widely known because of media coverage. As long as a formal complaint has not been filed, the social worker has the option of answering the allegations in the media and in other forums. However, once a complaint has been filed, a veil of confidentiality descends. The social worker is barred from acknowledging that the allegations are being investigated or from making public any evidence he or she might want to present to the hearing panel, or from releasing the conclusions of the panel. In other words, the social worker has no discretion or control over the process. This lack of control is further aggravated by the fact that when social workers join NASW they agree, unconditionally, to participate in any adjudication proceedings. The net result is that a skillful complainant or people associated with the complainant can manipulate the release of information to their advantage. This is because they are not barred from releasing information but only information of the fact that a complaint has been filed or of what happens during the processing and hearing of the complaint.

This process is all the more problematic when a complainant, or more often someone who should not even have knowledge that a complaint has been filed, disseminates information about the process that could only have been obtained from someone participating in the process. There are neither procedures nor authority to control nonmembers' behavior. The usual result is that the parties are warned to cease and desist but not much more. This can place a social work respondent at a distinct disadvantage because, even if the hearing panel finds most of the allegations to be without merit, the social worker is prohibited from releasing information that affirms the fact that *any part* of the complaint was found to be without merit. The Association has many tools to ensure that the social worker maintains confidentiality but very limited tools to ensure that others, not subject to it's jurisdiction, do likewise.

Confidentiality Procedures Limit the Effectiveness of NASW's Efforts to Protect and Promote the Values and Integrity of the Profession

In a limited sense, the current procedures do protect the integrity of the profession. Every year social workers alleged to have violated the standards of the profession are disciplined. In very serious cases, the Association publishes the sanctions in the *NASW News*. However, this procedure is deficient in two ways. First, it leaves hidden information about how the Association has acted in less serious cases. Second, and much more importantly, it deprives the public, the profession, and the members of the Association of a written compilation of the kinds of violations that occur and the Association's response to them. In law, such a compilation of findings is referred to as case law. Case law is often used as a precedent in deciding new cases that come before the courts. The lack of a historical public record denies state committees on inquiry the minimal means for learning how other similar cases have been decided or what sanctions were imposed, or what appeals were successful or not successful. With the exception of very broad and general guidelines supplied by the National Committee on Inquiry (NCOI), state Committee of Inquiry (COI) members are left to interpret the Code of Ethics and the other standards that can be applied solely on the basis of their personal experience. Their decisions are necessarily idiosyncratic. The NCOI and the National NASW Board's Executive Committee do have historical information available to them, but it is not organized to compare current cases with prior cases. The current system does not serve the profession well.

There Is a Better Way

An improved adjudicatory process hinges on how the needs of the public, the social worker, and the profession are balanced. These needs are not always congruent with each other. A ranking of priorities needs to be developed. The Code of Ethics clearly places service to the client at the top of its priority listing. Others have suggested different priorities. Loewenberg and Dolgoff (1992, p. 60), for example, rank five other principles above the right to confidentiality. Others place emphasis on the rights of the family and the community as well as of the client. (See, for example, the National Association of Black Social Workers Code of Ethics, Lowenberg & Dolgoff, 1992, p 211).

Possible levels of disclosure are shown in Table 9.1. Only three levels are in use by the Association. They are levels 2, 7, and 8, which are shaded in the table. Levels 7 and 8 are only used when violations are so serious that the Association publishes the violations and sanctions in the *NASW News*. NASW has also occasionally used published summaries of adjudicated violations (cell 2). For example, a recent NASW report (NASW, 1994), which was summarized in the *NASW News,* reported on the types of violations that had been adjudicated over the last ten years. NASW uses very few of the levels of disclosure available to it.

The ordering of the cells in Table 9.1 is based on how much information is made available to the public and to members of the profession. Others might believe that there should be a different ordering. These issues are matters for further discussion and do not change the purpose of the table, which is to provide a mechanism for discussing changes in the current confidentiality policies. To ensure fairness to the parties involved, disclosure at some levels would seem to require even higher levels of disclosure. For example, the publishing of allegations (cells 6 and 10) without later, or at the same time, publishing the hearing panel's conclusions, would seem to be unfair to the respondent in a case.

As one proceeds down and to the right in the table, more information is available to the public and to the members of the profession so that the Association's responsibility to protect the public is better served, as is its ability to ensure the integrity of the profession. Counterbalancing this good is the fact that full

TABLE 9.1 Level of Public Disclosure of the Adjudicatory Process

	Low (More Confidentiality)			High (Less Confidentiality)	
	I Without Identifying Information	II With Identifying Information	III With Supporting Documents	IV With Transcripts	V With Public Hearings
Publish acceptance of complaint with allegations	1	6	10	NA	NA
Publish conclusions	2	7	11	15	19
Publish sanctions	3	8	12	16	20
Publish corrective actions	4	8	13	17	21
Publish findings of fact	5	9	14	18	22

public disclosure may be less desirable from the point of view of the social worker or agency against whom the complaint has been filed.

If, for example, all the levels of disclosure contained in column I were implemented, the need of the profession to promulgate its values and to establish a body of precedent would be largely served with minimal harm to the confidentiality of the social worker or the agency against whom the complaint was filed. However, the public could not determine whether a particular agency or social worker had been a respondent in an adjudicatory hearing, nor could the public judge whether the corrective actions and sanctions taken were, in its judgment, appropriate. Thus, to protect the public, higher levels of disclosure are necessary even when painful to a social worker, an agency, or the profession. Maximum public protection would be afforded by disclosure of all aspects of the hearings, including opening the hearings to the public.

The ideal of full protection of the public must be tempered by the administrative overhead that higher levels of disclosure would require. The overhead costs involved in the maintenance and publication of materials could be reduced by the development of a database available on the Internet. In fact, publication on the Internet might be the major method for information dissemination. This would reduce the cost of maintaining the system as well as improve its accessibility. Overhead costs would be higher at higher levels of disclosure.

Greater disclosure would lead to more litigation. Hearing panels would have to be better trained and reports of the hearings better prepared. Both outcomes would improve the quality of the adjunctionary process and may encourage the Association to develop other mechanisms for conducting hearings, such as the hearing officer model that is now being tested by NASW. Stronger legislative direction might reduce the challenges to the Association's adjudicatory processes.

When the issues just discussed are considered, it seems to me, a good balance that is responsive to the needs of the public, the social worker, and the profession would be as follows:

1. When a complaint is accepted for adjudication, the Association should post to a public database the names of the complainant and the respondent and the allegations accepted for adjudication. Complaints not accepted would not be posted to the database.
2. After the approval of the hearing final report, the report would be posted to the public database. The final report would include the findings of fact, the conclusions, and the recommended actions and sanctions.

Other issues would also need to be considered, for example, whether there might be some rare circumstances in which disclosure should be limited. Also, the question of whether disclosure should be time limited and what procedures should be used for removing information from the public database would need to be examined.

Another issue that must be addressed is how to deal with breaches to the confidentiality of the hearing process. If the confidentiality rules are violated, then the party whose confidentiality has been compromised should have the option of disclosing whatever information they believe to be in their best interest even where it may be foolish to do so. This disclosure could be selective or more general, depending on the desires of the party requesting disclosure. Such a procedure would return some control to the party whose confidentiality has been abused.

In summary, the current confidentiality policies of NASW are tilted toward protecting the respondent in adjudicatory hearings. These policies do not serve the profession or the public very well. I have proposed revised policies that strike a more reasonable balance between the needs of the public, the profession, and those accused of violating the profession's standards and values.

REFERENCES

Loewenberg, F. M., & Dolgoff, R. (1992). *Ethical decisions for social work practice.* (4th Ed.) Itaska, IL: Peacock Publishers.

NASW. (1991a). *NASW chapter guide for the adjudication of grievances.* (Available from the National Association of Social Workers, 750 First St. NE, Washington, DC 20002–4241).

NASW. (1991b). *NASW procedures for the adjudication of grievances.* (Available from the National Association of Social Workers, 750 First St. NE, Washington, DC 20002–4241).

NASW. (1994). *Overview of a decade of adjudication.* (Available from the Adjudication Office of the National Association of Social Workers, 750 First St. NE, Washington, DC 20002–4241).

Rejoinder to Professor Butterfield   COLLEEN GALAMBOS

Dr. Butterfield correctly identifies inadequacies of the current NASW adjudication process, but his solution, presents more disclosure than is necessary. It does not adequately address problems with the current system, nor does it balance the rights of each party involved in the process. The three major goals identified by Dr. Butterfield—protection of the public, protection of the social worker, and protection of the values and integrity of the profession—will be considered along with the effects of public disclosure on these goals.

Protection of the Public

Butterfield asserts that public disclosure will (1) help detect patterns of unethical behavior, and (2) increase the reporting of ethics violations by repeat offenders through public awareness. This position makes the assumption that social workers who are involved in an ethics violation have previously engaged in this type of behavior. Adjudication history indicates otherwise. Most complaints filed against social workers have been first-time offenses. Only three cases have involved repeat offenses of persons who had been adjudicated previously (B. DuMetz, personal communication, September 8, 1995). Compromising the privacy of everyone to promote the disclosure of a few repeat offenses of misconduct does not serve the common good.

Public disclosure will act as a deterring factor for some individuals. Although I cannot locate adjudicatory-related statistics to back up my argument, an analogy can be found in crime reporting statistics. These indicate that only 39 percent of the crimes measured by The National Crime Victimization Survey are actually reported to police (Bastian, 1992, p. 5). In a study on violence among friends and relatives, reasons for police nonreporting were examined (U.S. Department of Justice, 1980). The belief that the incident was a private or personal matter was the highest response given for nonreporting (U.S. Department of Justice, 1980, p. 150).

The publicity attached to the disclosure of information related to ethics misconduct should be factored into any decision that involves a decrease in confidentiality. It would be unfortunate indeed if our disclosure policy deterred people from reporting offenses that may be embarrassing or humiliating for them.

Protection of Social Workers

The profession has an obligation to treat colleagues with respect, courtesy, fairness, and good faith (NASW, 1993, p. 7). Dr. Butterfield proposes that the acceptance of complaints with allegations is information appropriate for public disclosure. This damages the reputation of a colleague before an actual determination of unethical misconduct. Disclosure here does not accurately represent the actions of colleagues nor is it an extension of good faith. A preponderance of ethics complaints filed with NASW, when adjudged, are determined to be unfounded (B. Dumetz, personal communication, September 8, 1995). To promote this level of disclosure does not protect the rights of social workers and violates NASW's Code of Ethics.

Protection of the Profession

To promote public disclosure serves to weaken the professional value of confidentiality as defined by Bartlett (1970). The suggested public disclosure process essentially eliminates confidentiality of adjudication information. A new values ordering is used within this process that places protection of the public over professional confidentiality. This ordering conflicts with NASW's Code of Ethics and many state licensing laws. Confidentiality is waived over the protection of others only in the most serious of cases. Generally, these situations involve harm to self or others, such as cases of child abuse, homicide, or suicide. At the very least, if an adjudication disclosure policy is developed, it should include similar limitations.

In addition, two of the proposed methods to increase public disclosure; a case law system and the use of computer technology, may actually compromise the values and integrity of the profession. The use of case law within the judicial system does not necessarily guarantee that fairness and impartiality will occur in legal proceedings. Despite case law methods, trials are still influenced by local input and the personalities of the people involved in the process. Case law is also an inappropriate parallel to the adjudication process. To advocate for a system that treats professional social workers as criminals does not support professional integrity.

Caution must be used in developing a computerized database system. The use of an Internet structure may set up an elitist system in which some social workers, organizations, and public members have more access to information than others. The use of a public database suggests the availability of a certain amount of resources and computer knowledge. People and organizations with limited resources and access to those resources are disadvantaged in obtaining information related to the adjudication process. The lower class, persons who are not familiar with computer technology, individuals located in rural communities, and small grassroots organizations are some examples of groups of people who may not be able to easily access the Internet. Although organizations such as the NASW or State licensing Boards could mail adjudicatory information to these individuals, the burden is placed on those organizations to disseminate such information. This dependency contributes to unequal access. It is important that the profession of social work embrace technology, but it should be done with much consideration. It has been documented that the Internet has become increasingly commercial with limited public spaces (Hafner, July 24, 1995). For example, many rural areas are developing Internet services, but there are fees attached and time access is limited (Hafner, June 26, 1995). Part of the foundation of professional practice is to support social justice. The profession of social work must be careful that it does not contribute to the development of unequal systems. Adjudication of professional grievances and the disclosure process must strive for fairness and equity. To do less undermines the values and integrity of the profession.

Conclusion

Further consideration must be given to the rights of all parties involved in the grievance process. This process must be balanced, fair, and supportive of the values of the profession. Butterfield's proposed form of public disclosure creates incongruencies with individual rights, privacy rights, and professional values. Although there may be problematic areas within adjudication, many respondents and complainants have benefitted from a confidential process. If the adjudication process is revised, a disclosure process based on the severity of the complaint and the number of offenses offers a balanced approach to the dissemination of adjudicatory information. However, the incongruencies discussed in this response must be resolved before the profession exposes the adjudicatory process to public scrutiny.

REFERENCES

Bartlett, H. M. (1970). *The common base of social work practice.* Silver Spring, MD: NASW.
Bastian, L. D. (1992). *Criminal victimization, 1992.* Bureau of Justice Statistics Bulletin. Washington, DC: U.S. Department of Justice.
Hafner, K. (June 26, 1995). Wired in the woods. *Newsweek,* pp. 45–46.
Hafner, K. (July 24, 1995). The man with ideas. *Newsweek,* pp. 61–62.
National Association of Social Workers. (1993). *Code of Ethics of the National Association of Social Workers.* Washington, DC: NASW.

U.S. Department of Justice, Bureau of Justice Statistics, (1980). *Intimate victims: a study of violence among friends and relatives.* Washington, DC: U.S. Department of Justice.

NO

COLLEEN GALAMBOS

Ethics hearings involve a complainant, often a client or social worker, who alleges unethical conduct, and a respondent, or accused social worker who allegedly has committed an ethics violation. Because hearings are under the auspices of licensing boards or professional associations, they are considered to be a professional act between social work colleagues and a complainant. Hearings are facilitated by social workers who, in this role, are obligated to conduct themselves according to state and professional codes of ethics. These codes generally include provisions for maintaining confidentiality of professional information and transactions.

The publication or release of hearing findings is a violation of both client and collegial confidentiality. This information should be respected and held in strictest confidence. Support for this viewpoint can be found in the National Association of Social Workers (NASW) Code of Ethics: "The social worker should respect the privacy of clients and hold in confidence all information obtained in the course of professional service" (NASW, 1993, p. 6). This section refers to information shared by clients with professional social workers. According to this principle, information provided by complainants in hearing proceedings should be regarded as private. If findings of ethics hearings are released to the public, confidential information about the client and the situation is communicated with others. This is a violation of client confidentiality. The disclosure of information to the public may result in a reduction in reports or allegations of unethical conduct. Clients may be reluctant to pursue ethics complaints, knowing that the complaint will be open for public display in the future. This reluctance will be particularly strong in cases in which the client has been physically and emotionally victimized (e.g., sexual misconduct cases).

In ethics hearings, confidential information is also shared by the respondent or fellow social worker. The hearing itself is a professional transaction between designated social workers, the complainant, and the respondent. The NASW Code of Ethics provides guidance in this area: "The social worker should respect confidences shared by colleagues in the course of their professional relationships and transactions" (NASW, 1993, p. 6). This principle supports the argument that confidential information provided by the respondent or professional colleague should be regarded and treated as protected information.

The release of hearing findings provides confidential information to the public that was obtained within the professional transaction of the adjudication process. This action is a violation of collegial confidentiality, because private information is shared with others.

Respect for Colleagues

There is an operating assumption within the profession that social work colleagues have the right to be treated with fairness and respect. The NASW Code of Ethics addresses this area in Section III: "The Social Worker's Ethical Responsibility to Colleagues: The social worker should treat colleagues with respect, courtesy, fairness, and good faith" (NASW, 1993, p. 7).

Release of the findings of ethics hearings is said to be necessary to prevent new wrongdoing. This assumes that the colleague in question is unworthy and therefore unable to learn, change the behavior, and perform in a competent manner in the future. This assumption does not promote fairness and good faith. Conversely, conditions are created that restrict the social worker's liberty to determine his or her own destiny. Worthiness is questioned, and ultimately, disrespect is fostered through the publication of findings. Ideally, change should occur through a social work colleague's own efforts, not through the release of information to a public forum.

Fair Retribution

The act of holding an ethics hearing is a form of retribution or punishment. In an examination of retributive justice theory, two major principles are discussed. The first principle indicates that retribution is done in response to a wrong or harmful act. The second principle discusses the placement of limits on the amount of punishment, depending on the seriousness of the act (Solomon & Murphy, p. 281). The purpose of retribution is to morally improve the violator.

The application of these retributive justice concepts to ethics hearings and the social work profession provides justification for a graduated system of corrective actions and sanctions based on the type of misconduct. For certain ethics violations, fair retribution may be served through the actual hearing process and the actions or sanctions that are imposed on the accused social worker or respondent. To rule that the findings of every ethics hearing be published does not consider or allow the flexibility to adjust the punishment to fit the severity of the code violation. Should a social worker who was found to have poor bookkeeping practices be awarded the same punishment (i.e., publication) as the social worker who engaged in sexual relations with a client? In these two situations, the justification for publication appears to be uneven.

If publication of hearing findings is used as a sanction or form of punishment, it should be prescribed only in severe cases, such as serious boundary violations or sexual misconduct situations, where considerable harm has been inflicted on clients and society. In addition, corrective action or sanctions should be used only when a wrong or harmful act has occurred. Publication of findings should never be used in cases where the social worker is absolved of the allegations. In these cases, sanctions and punishment are unjustified, because harm to others is not proved, and the social worker is presumed innocent of charges. The reputation of the accused social worker should be protected through maintaining confidentiality of the charges and proceedings. There is also an inherent assumption that publication will somehow lead to moral improvement of the social worker. This sanction does not encourage moral change. In these situations, retribution takes the form of increased public awareness rather than a focus on improved professional conduct.

Potential for Harm or Maleficence to Colleagues

The release of hearing findings creates the potential for harm and harassment of colleagues. Although the parties involved in the hearing process are privy to expanded materials and information pertaining to the case, the general public does not have access to all pertinent information related to the ethics violation. The small amount of information that is permitted to be published to the public does not lend itself to a full understanding of the dynamics, factors, and issues operating within the case. The lack of adequate information leads to unjustly damaged professional reputations.

Additionally, public standards for ethical conduct may be different from professional standards, resulting in incongruity between public and professional opinion. Published information may be misconstrued and erroneous conclusions drawn from these misinterpretations. Because published information enters into a larger public domain, it is impossible for the profession of social work to perform damage control related to public misperception.

Considering these points, the publication of hearing findings does not fulfill a social worker's ethical responsibility to colleagues. It is a maleficent or harmful act if the profession does not weigh the damage inflicted from the publication of these findings on the social worker found to be unethical. There is the potential for misunderstanding, harassment, and prejudicial treatment of the social worker by the general public. It is the profession's responsibility to respond to this potential and monitor the severity of these sanctions.

The NASW Code of Ethics addresses the right of social workers to be represented in a fair manner: "The social worker should treat with respect and represent accurately and fairly the qualifications, views, and findings of colleagues and use appropriate channels to express judgments on these matters" (NASW, 1993, p. 7). Because accuracy and fairness cannot be guaranteed in publication or release, public display of information is not the appropriate communication channel to report misconduct of social workers. Communication of these matters should occur in professionally regulated and monitored forums such as hearing reports and letters sent to the involved parties. Using these methods, the flow of information can be better controlled, which serves to reduce public misperceptions and the potential for professional maleficence directed toward colleagues.

Conclusion

In conclusion, the publication or release of hearing findings to the public domain should not be confirmed by the profession of social work. Ethically responsible behavior between colleagues is not fostered through this type of policy. It violates client and collegial confidentiality, questions collegial worthiness, promotes unjust retribution, and creates the potential for professional maleficence between colleagues and the public. Only professionally controlled channels of communication should be permitted to convey information related to ethics hearings and unethical conduct by colleagues.

REFERENCES

National Association of Social Workers. (1993). *Code of Ethics of the National Association of Social Workers.* Washington, DC: NASW.

Solomon, R., & Murphy, M. C. (Eds.). (1990). *What is justice?* New York: Oxford University Press.

Rejoinder to Professor Galambos WILLIAM BUTTERFIELD

Galambos's response cites the Code of Ethics rules on confidentiality. She writes, "The publication or release of hearing findings is a violation of both client and collegial confidentiality." I do not think invoking the Code of Ethics as a guide to adjudicatory procedures is particularly useful. The issue is not, is confidentiality desirable and useful, but rather, how to balance the need for confidentiality for clients and social workers with the need to protect the public and the need to develop adjudicatory procedures that further the goals of the profession. Galambos clearly believes that confidentiality is a penultimate principal. I believe that there are legitimate reasons for breaching confidentiality.

Several of her arguments have to do with what she sees as the deleterious effects of public disclosure. She is concerned that: (1) "Clients may be reluctant to pursue ethics complaints, knowing that the complaint will be open for public display"; (2) "Publication of findings should never be used in cases in which the social worker is absolved of the allegations"; (3) Although publication will lead to increased public awareness, it will not improve professional conduct and may lead to "misunderstanding, harassment, and prejudicial treatment of the social worker by the general public"; and (4) "Because accuracy and fairness cannot be guaranteed in publication or release, public display of information is not the appropriate communication channel to report misconduct of social workers."

I think all of these concerns are debatable. Because we now prohibit disclosure, we cannot point to any empirical evidence that will help us to decide whether disclosure will make it less or more likely that clients will file complaints. My guess is that many clients would welcome disclosure. They are not reluctant to file civil lawsuits against social workers. The law suits are matters of public record. We also know from experience that clients have violated their pledges to not reveal the fact that adjudicatory proceeding are in process or the results of the hearings. Complainants often allege that the social worker is accused of violating the Code of Ethics or is a danger to the public or to other clients. Thus, from my perspective, I doubt that complainants would fear disclosure. Ultimately, the only way we will know is to see what happens if the procedures are changed. If the rate of complaints dramatically drops off, then Galambos's fears will be well founded. My guess is that they will not. Conversely, I think almost all respondents would prefer nondisclosure. There is a real possibility that their professional reputations will be damaged even if they are found to not have violated the Code of Ethics.

I have addressed these issues in my essay, and have tried to balance public and professional interests in disclosure with those who have a clear interest in non-disclosure. Galambos's arguments place much more emphasis on the protection of the social worker than on public and professional interests. As I have asserted in my essay, I believe maximum protection of the social worker does violence to other compelling interests. The reader will have to decide whether my arguments make sense.

Galambos's remaining arguments do introduce another view of the purpose of adjudicatory hearings. She says: (1) "The act of releasing hearing findings assumes that the colleague in question is unworthy and therefore unable to learn, change the behavior, and perform in a competent manner in the future"; (2) The hearing process is a mechanism for punishing social workers who have violated the Code of Ethics, and publication would increase the severity of the punishment; and (3) By implication, she also worries that disclosure will reduce the likelihood that errant social workers will comply with any requested actions that emerge out of the hearings. On this latter point, I fail to see why disclosure would alter the ability of the Association to impose sanctions that would compel compliance.

I think Galambos also is trying to say that if the social worker changes, there is no need to burden the social worker with a public record of past misdeeds, and to do so may change the process from a corrective to a punitive process. These are important points. As social workers, we are very aware of how such labels as "psychotic," "abuser," and the like, can and do gain a life of their own and that they can impact on people's lives many years afterwards. My guess is that "unethical" might be a similar label.

Certain types of disclosure (those listed in column I of Table 9-1) do not run this risk. If higher levels of disclosure are adopted, it may well be that new procedures will need to be developed that lead to a formal process for removing the label. Such procedures might range from publication of completion of corrective actions to formal expunction of the record. Similar concerns have been addressed in the criminal courts and could easily be adapted to the realm of adjudicatory hearings.

I have argued that more disclosure is needed to balance the needs of the public and the profession with the need to protect the interest of social workers who have been alleged or found to have violated the Code of Ethics. Additional disclosure is needed, and I believe it is time for the NASW to review its adjudication procedures. Such a review could lead to improved procedures that are responsive both to the needs of social workers accused of violating the code of Ethics and to the needs of other interested parties.

Is the NASW Code of Ethics an Effective Guide for Practitioners?

EDITOR'S NOTE: Does the NASW Code of Ethics provide an effective guide for practitioners? Does the Code provide guidelines for dealing with ethical dilemmas in which two or more values strain against each other (e.g., confidentiality and self-determination)? Does it help social workers to consider the possible conflicting interests of clients, significant others, the law, agency policy, public policy, personal values, and professional values?

Kathleen E. Murphy, Ph.D., carries the YES side of the debate. She is engaged in the private practice of clinical social work in Glenview, Illinois, specializing in work with chronically ill and disabled children. She was a member and former chair of the NASW Illinois Chapter Committee on Inquiry (1984–95), member and chair of the NASW National Committee on Inquiry (1994–97). She is a visiting lecturer at Loyola University School of Social Work and on the faculty of the Institute of Clinical Social Work, Chicago, Illinois.

Sandra Kopels, who argues NO, has both a law degree and an MSW. Before joining the School of Social Work at the University of Illinois at Urbana–Champaign, she practiced law, advocating for the rights of persons with disabilities. Her research is in the area of legal and ethical issues related to social work practice with vulnerable populations.

YES

KATHLEEN E. MURPHY

The Numbers

The simple answer to this question is YES and is self-evident based on circumstances of when social workers are found to be in violation of the code. The NASW Code of Ethics is a guide for practice, but it also is used as a basis of adjudication or peer review of circumstances in which the conduct of social workers is alleged to deviate from the standards expressed or implied by the code (NASW Code of Ethics, 1993, Preamble, p. v). There are approximately 150,000 members of the NASW, and since 1990 there have been, on average, 100 complaints annually of ethical misconduct (Dumez, personal communication, 1995). One can readily conclude that with fewer than .001% of the membership alleged to have violated the Code each year, the overwhelming majority of social workers are able to practice in an ethical manner according to the standards of the NASW Code of Ethics.

Similarly, in a study of malpractice claims against social workers filed with the NASW Insurance Trust between 1969 and 1990, it was found that of the 60,000 social workers covered by the trust, there were only 634 claims filed over the entire twenty-one years of the study. Even though not all claims were substantiated, this is an astoundingly small number of claims, over many years (Reamer, 1995). Although there is more to consider with regard to malpractice complaints than the NASW Code of Ethics, and even though one can assume an underreporting of viable complaints, certainly whether through peer review or litigation, it is not even a question as to whether, on the face of it, most social workers are able to practice in an ethical manner. Certainly it can legitimately be asked whether the NASW Code of Ethics is the cause of this numerically defined morality within the profession. However, as the most explicit and universally shared guide for ethical decision making, it must have some influence.

The Substance and Function of the Code

According to Gewirth (1978), people can and do guide their lives in many different ways. It is his position that among the various rules, ideals, and institutions that provide guidance, morality has a unique status because it establishes requirements of conduct that take precedence over all other actions, including self-interest. "Morality is a set of categorically obligatory requirements for action. . . ." (p. 1) The NASW Code of Ethics is just such an explication of moral obligations based on the fundamental values of the social work profession that include the worth, dignity, and uniqueness of all persons as well as their rights and opportunities. It is based on the nature of social work, which fosters conditions that promote these values (NASW Code of Ethics, 1993, p. v). However, the Code of Ethics is much maligned as being too aspirational and too general to be useful in actual practice. Yet this complaint misrepresents the purpose and function of the Code, which does not, cannot, and should not represent a set of rules that prescribe the behaviors of social workers. Social work as a profession is both a skill and an art, and it is the judicious and scrupulous use of moral judgment in situations of ethical implications that makes the Code an effective guide for the practice of ethical decision making. According to Levy (1976, pp. 23–24), "Social work ethics should not be confused with social work competence or the effectiveness of its application. As Begelman (1971) points out: "There is no necessary relationship between ethics and effectiveness in any treatment procedure. Effectiveness cannot be the sole criterion of whether the procedure is ethical" (p. 165).

The Function of the Social Worker in Ethical Reasoning

For the code of ethics to be useful, it needs to be used in a context of practice and within the context of the person of the social worker. That is, the social worker needs to be of good moral character, with the capacity to know and exercise good moral judgment. In point of fact, ethical decision making is entirely dependent on the concept of that which is moral. To be ethical means to be capable of making the distinction between right and wrong or good and bad in conduct and to be able to exercise this judgment to do that which is right or good and to avoid that which is wrong or bad. Ethics is moral philosophy relating to, dealing with, or capable of making the distinction between right and wrong in conduct. Therefore, one measure of ethical conduct in any profession is the congruence between what the practitioner is supposed to do and what he or she actually does. The more what the social worker is morally supposed to do coincides with what she or he actually does, the more ethical the practice. The problem, however, is that what the social worker is "supposed to do" is not always evident nor is it one-dimensional (Reamer, 1982). It is in the complexity of social work that the Code of Ethics stands out. Among professional codes and standards of practice, it is clearly a notable accomplishment as a statement of the abstract principles and values of social work and the relationship of those principles to the specifics of practice (Constable, 1989).

It is because ethical dilemmas exist at the interface of the application of ethical reasoning to clinical practice that there cannot be a binary formula or a "rule book" for resolving ethical dilemmas. Although certainly guidelines are needed if the structure and function of social work is to be carried out ethically, it is important to keep in mind that although all of the interests affected by an ethical issue in practice can not invariably be reconciled, ethical practice requires that they be satisfactorily reckoned with, not so much in quest of what may be considered a successful outcome, as in fulfillment of ethical responsibility. Competent practice is efficient; ethical practice is obligatory (Reamer, 1982). This requires not the mindless application of or adherence to the "rules" but, rather, the logically reasoned and adequately considered context of the ethical dilemma.

The Substance of the Social Worker

How we contend with ethical issues as members of society is not only a mark of our social and professional consciousness but also an indicator of our personal sense of morality. Personal morality, or what is often referred to as "virtue" or "moral character," consists of those traits within the individual that predispose the person to do what is right. Moral character is learned, cultivated, and practiced throughout one's developmental process but is most particularly formed within the first 12 years of life. Although the capacity for moral reasoning is intimately linked to cognitive development, one may develop cognitively far beyond what the capacity for morality may develop. Moral virtue is a character trait and as such is part of the psychic structure. Although there are some aspects of morality that may be taught, it is clear that in the deepest sense, moral virtue is part of the essence of the person.

According to Kohlberg's (1976) schema of moral development, at the highest developmental stage, the motivation for ethical reasoning is based on following certain ethical principles related to the given that there is an implied inalienable right to equality of human rights, dignity, and respect, just because people are people. In that context, it is rightfully argued by various professions that, with rare exception, certain rights belong to each person just because they exist, regardless of capacity or incapacity, not because there is a law but because there is a moral human right. The social worker functioning at this level of moral development, is motivated to do what is right as a personal commitment to the validity of these moral principles. At the other end of Kohlberg's theory is the lowest or preconventional stage of moral development. At this stage, the individual does what is "right" to avoid breaking the rules and in so doing to serve one's own interests and most importantly, recognizing the power of authority, to avoid punishment (Kohlberg, 1976). The social worker at this level of moral development does what is right, or avoids doing what is wrong, because there exists a rule and a likelihood of being punished if caught breaking the rule.

Although one can take issue with the nuances of Kohlberg's theory of moral development, the conceptualization of morality as a developmental process is clear across theories. This is particularly useful in considering the adequacy of the Code of Ethics. For example, it is interesting that the most frequently occurring substantiated area of violation of the Code is violation of II-F-5, the prohibition against sexual activity with clients (NASW, 1995). This is one area of the Code that is not vague or ambivalently stated; it is not "aspirational" nor unclear. In the previously cited study of malpractice claims, sexual impropriety was the second most frequently occurring complaint (n = 117 of 634) and by far the most costly (41% of dollars paid out in claims) (Reamer, 1995).

The prohibition against sex with clients is taught throughout schools of social work and is an area of malpractice that is addressed in many state laws. On the face of it, sex with clients is a well-known violation of ethics and, in many ways, one that should be the least subject to debate and a difference of opinion, yet it is a significant practice problem. For an issue that should not even be a question for social workers, I believe that violations of this nature occur specifically because it involves privacy and is hard to prove. Using Kohlberg's theory of moral development, sex with clients has nothing to do with any substantive moral reasoning or an attempt on the part of the ethical social worker to adhere to a higher moral road. Rather, it is moral reasoning at its most base, with the social worker meeting his or her own needs, in a situation in which the likelihood of being caught is minimal. Although sex with clients is an extreme example, I use it because there is no more clearly stated tenet of the Code nor more widely accepted standard of ethical practice, yet it is a standard that is clearly and knowingly violated. Another area of consistent ethical violation and malpractice is breach of confidentiality. Again, this is a well-articulated, well-taught standard of practice, yet a consistent problem in actual practice. Certainly one may periodically engage in inadvertent violations of confidentiality, but for the most part this also is a violation that is clearly and knowingly violated. In neither example, sexual impropriety nor confidentiality, is the violation a function of the code but rather of the inadequate thought, consideration, or application of ethical principles by the social worker. In violating confidentiality, it is often a function of doing what is expedient rather than malicious intent, but the point remains the same: ethical practice is more work and often considered not worth the extra time and effort because the likelihood of getting caught is minimal.

Conclusion

It is my position that although there are professional ethics and laws to which social workers must adhere, when we talk about the effectiveness of the Code to guide practice, what we are really talking about is that ethical practice is dependent on a greater motivation than standards of practice or legal mandates. In my opinion, there is a moral imperative that comes from within that is the essence of character. Although the Code can and should explicate the values of the profession, it cannot nor should it attempt to teach one to be of good moral character. Although with each revision, the NASW Code of Ethics gets longer and more detailed, it is my opinion that this is a sad commentary on our professional development because, without a substantive moral character and a commitment to the application of ethical principles to clinical practice, there is no rule book that will ever be detailed enough to impart moral consciousness. Social workers can and should discuss the values of the profession and debate the merits of our ethical duties and obligations, but the specific application of those values rests not with the Code but within the person of the social worker. Therefore, with a substantive moral character and a commitment to ethical practice in place, yes, the NASW Code of Ethics is an exquisite articulation of the values of social work and an effective guide for the practitioner.

REFERENCES

Begelman, D. A. (1971). The ethics of behavioral control and the new mythology. *Psychotherapy, Theory, Research and Practice, 8,* 165–169.

Constable, R. T. (1989). Relations and membership: Foundations for ethical thinking in social work. *Social Thought, xv*(3/4), 53–66.

Gewirth, A. (1978). *Reason and morality.* Chicago, IL: University of Chicago Press.

Kohlberg, L. (1976). Moral stages and moralization: The cognitive–developmental approach. In T. Lickona (Ed.), *Moral development and behavior.* New York: Holt, Rinehart and Winston.

Levy, C. (1976). *Social work ethics.* New York: Human Sciences Press.

National Association of Social Workers. (1993). *Code of Ethics* (1993, revised). Washington, DC: Author.

National Association of Social Workers. (1995). *Overview of a decade of adjudication.* Washington, DC: Author.

Reamer, F. G. (1982). *Ethical dilemmas in social service.* New York: Columbia University Press.

Reamer, F. G. (1995). Malpractice claims against social workers: First facts. *Social Work, 40* (5), 595–601.

Rejoinder to Dr. Murphy
SANDRA KOPELS

Dr. Murphy first argues that, based on the low number of ethical complaints and malpractice claims, it follows that the Code of Ethics enables social workers to practice in accordance with its standards. However, NASW's Delegate Assembly determined that the Code should be revised, among other reasons, because of the the number of allegations of code violations and the willingness of clients to pursue remedies. Similarly, Reamer's study of malpractice claims demonstrates a marked increase in the numbers of cases filed; from one claim in 1970, to 40 claims in 1980 and to 126 claims in 1990 (Reamer, 1995). Therefore, although the actual number of cases may be small, there is a growing tendency for clients to take action against their social workers. The planned revision of the Code recognizes the need to provide more specific guidance to social workers than currently exists.

Dr. Murphy's main argument is that the Code of Ethics is the explication of moral obligations and that it is the judicious and scrupulous use of moral judgments that makes the Code an effective guide for ethical decision making. In fact, she believes that ethical decision making is entirely dependent on the concept of morality, which she describes as the traits within the individual that predispose them to do what is right. She states that moral virtue is part of the essence of the person and cannot be readily taught.

If Dr. Murphy's argument is taken to its logical conclusion and moral virtue cannot be taught, then the Code cannot be an effective ethical guide. Only the individual's moral development matters. In her conclusion, Dr. Murphy states that the specific application of professional values rests not with the Code but within the person of the social worker. If a social worker's own morality is not congruent with the Code's provisions, then the Code is not the basis for that individual's practice. If subjective morality is the standard by which social workers practice, then Dr. Murphy's conclusion that the Code of Ethics provides sufficient guidance for ethical social work practice is not supported.

REFERENCE

Reamer, F. G. (1995). Malpractice claims against social Workers: First facts. *Social Work, 40* (5), 595–601.

NO

SANDRA KOPELS

The NASW Code of Ethics is:

> ...intended to serve as a guide to the everyday conduct of members of the social work profession and as a basis for the adjudication of issues in ethics when the conduct of social workers is alleged to deviate from the standards expressed or implied in this code (NASW, 1993, p. v).

The Code offers general principles to guide and evaluate conduct in situations that have ethical implications. To the extent that the Code expresses the fundamental values of the social work profession, it is a useful tool to set out NASW members' shared, ethical expectations. However, it is neither useful nor effective as a guide to the ethical decisions made by social workers. This results from the Code's failure to clearly delineate its standards, and by the lack of a mechanism to publish, disseminate, and educate NASW members about colleagues' actions that have been found to violate the Code.

The Code's Lack of Specificity

The current version of the Code contains 72 specific provisions categorized under six major principles that attempt to govern the social worker's conduct as it relates to clients, colleagues, employers, society, and the social work profession. Unfortunately, most of the Code's provisions contain broad, undefined terms, which renders them almost meaningless as a guide to behavior. For example, provision II.F.1 states, "The social worker should serve clients with devotion, loyalty, determination, and the maximum application of professional skill and competence" (p. 5). Are social workers who use *moderate* application of professional competence disloyal and undevoted to their clients? Similarly, other provisions merely set out general goals for social workers to strive to attain. For example, III.J.1 (p. 7) states that "The social worker should cooperate with colleagues to promote professional interests and concerns." Other than telling social workers that they should try to be good colleagues, the provision provides scant instruction as to ethical behavior. The problem is not simply the failure to define terms; it is also the fact that social workers can be sanctioned for not complying with these undefined provisions.

Social workers may find themselves subject to sanction, both legally and ethically, for doing what is unavoidable, viz., creating their own interpretations of too general Code provisions. For example, social workers understand that client confidentiality is an important ethical value that underlies the trust essential for the therapeutic relationship. The Code states that social workers ". . . should share with others confidences revealed by clients, without their consent, only for compelling professional reasons." (II.H.1, p. 6). However, what are the compelling reasons that warrant disclosing information without client consent? Because the Code does not define which reasons are compelling enough to justify sharing client confidences without consent, social workers must rely on their own sense of values and ethics to guide their decisions. Consequently, by relying on their own sense of values and ethics, the Code is not the guide. Yet, clients who do not believe that their social workers had "compelling reasons" for disclosure can lodge an ethics complaint based on the Code of Ethics.

As a result of the Tarasoff decision, when a client's behavior puts a third party at serious risk of physical harm, the social worker should use professional judgment to determine whether the third party should be informed of the risk (Tarasoff v. Board of Regents, 1976). In these situations, client information can be disclosed against the client's expressed wishes because of the perceived danger to the third party. However, are there limits on what is "compelling" to protect third parties? Is a pregnant client's drug use compelling enough to allow a social worker to disclose this fact to protect the fetus? Do compelling professional reasons include the duty to warn third parties of a client's HIV infection? The issue of warning about HIV infection is controversial and has been debated within the medical, psychological, and social work professions, and is included within this series of Controversial Issues in Social Work (Gelman, 1992; Reamer, 1992). Yet, do social workers who disclose their client's HIV infection to protect a spouse, sexual partners, or needle-sharing partner act ethically or unethically? Are they acting in accordance with or contrary to the ethical provisions of II.H.1? Regardless of the care devoted by the social worker to the decision making about sharing this information, the Code does not provide clear guidance to resolve this ethical dilemma.

The law complicates reliance on the Code when it prohibits or requires disclosure. For example, some states expressly prohibit disclosure of the identity or test results of AIDS-related information (AIDS Confidentiality Act, 1992). A social worker, relying solely on the Code, may believe that a client who refuses to divulge his or her HIV/AIDS status to a spouse or partner has created a situation sufficiently compelling to justify disclosure of this information. By disclosing, however, the social worker will have breached the legal duty created by the statute. Although the social worker may have acted ethically, he or she may not have acted legally.

To its credit, the Code does contain certain provisions that are very specific prohibitions on behavior. One entirely unequivocal provision is, "The social worker should under no circumstances engage in sexual activities with clients" (II.F.5, p. 5). Yet, from the years 1982 to 1992, almost 30 percent of all substantiated cases were violations of this Code provision, making it the most common ethical violation (NASW, 1995). Other studies have reported similar data (Reamer, 1995).

It may be argued that the Code provides sufficient guidance in this area but practitioners choose to violate this provision. Perhaps the problem exists because "sexual activity" is not defined. But if this Code provision, which is one of the most direct, specific, and clear statements in the Code, fails to adequately impart requirements or control behavior, then what guidance can be expected from the Code's many vague and undefined standards?

Lack of Knowledge or a Mechanism for Dissemination

Practitioners lack familiarity with the provisions of the Code. Munson (1986) found that, on the average, practitioners' knowledge of the Code was slightly under 60 percent accurate and that most had not read the Code for 3½ years. Berliner (1989) makes a similar argument. The failure to carefully teach ethical issues in the social work curriculum contributes to this lack of knowledge.

Once the National Committee on Inquiry adjudicates that an individual has violated the Code, NASW has no meaningful mechanism for disseminating this information. Instead, it keeps the proceedings confidential. If the facts about cases cannot be shared, then practitioners are not exposed to the specific situations, nor can they become familiar with the reasons social workers' actions violated the provisions of the code.

The legal system has methods for clarifying nonspecific provisions and disseminating decisions that interpret them. When certain legal provisions provide insufficient guidance for "reasonable persons" to know what conduct is expected of them, the laws can be struck down as being unconstitutionally vague. Additionally, court decisions are published in books that are readily available to those who desire access. In this way, a body of knowledge develops that helps elucidate terms and guides future behavior.

To illustrate, the acceptance of the duty to protect third parties from client harm developed from the legal decisions in Tarasoff and cases that relied on it. Subsequent decisions modified the duty to warn by broadening or narrowing its application and explicated situations in which practitioners found themselves subject to liability (Kopels & Kagle, 1993). The resulting interpretations guide decision making regarding the legal duty to protect. Social work has no comparable mechanisms.

The monthly *NASW News* reports persons who have been sanctioned for breaching the Code of Ethics. The listing provides only the individual's name and the state chapter to which he or she belonged; no information is provided as to why the individual has been sanctioned. For example, the November 1993 issue of *NASW News* reported sanctions levied against two individuals. The first case was a California social worker who violated code principles II.F.2, II.F.4., and II.F.5., which prohibit "exploiting clients, compromising clients' interests and engaging in sexual relations with clients." The second case was a Connecticut social worker who was "found to have violated ethics principles I.D.2., II.F.2. and II.F.4. by exploiting a professional relationship with a client for personal advantage and failing to avoid a relationship that conflicted with the client's interests" (Two Draw Sanctions, 1993). In both of these cases, no facts were provided about the cases. *NASW News* simply used the specific language of the particular Code of Ethics section violated. What actions did the social workers take in exploiting their clients? How did they take advantage of their clients? What relationships did the social workers and clients engage in that should have been avoided as conflicting with the clients' interests?

In contrast, the July 1992 issue of *NASW News* reported a South Carolina social worker who was found to have violated the Code's prohibition against engaging in "dishonesty, fraud, deceit, or misrepresentation" (Board Officers Act, 1992). This social worker failed to disclose her previous felony conviction when she applied for her South Carolina social work license. From this report readers learn that this type of nondisclosure constitutes "dishonesty, fraud, deceit or misrepresentation" and can use this knowledge to influence their own behavior. Unfortunately, very few of the items that appear in *NASW News* report the basis for the imposition of sanctions.

Conclusion

In 1993, NASW's Delegate Assembly determined that the Code of Ethics should be revised because of the increase in the number of allegations of code violations, the general litigiousness of society, and the growing sophistication of consumers. The planned revisions recognize the need for the Code to be much more specific. If the Code is ever expected to serve as a sufficient guide for social work practitioners, it must clearly and specifically delineate its standards and define its terms. Additionally, practitioners must be better educated about the Code's requirements. A method of disseminating peer-determined violations also must be developed and implemented.

REFERENCES

AIDS Confidentiality Act, 410 Illinois Compiled Statutes 305/1 et. seq. (1992).

Berliner, A. K. (1989). Misconduct in social work practice. *Social Work, 1,* 69–72.

Board officers act on sanctions cases. (July 1992). *NASW News,* p. 10.

Gelman, S. (1992). Is Tarasoff relevant to AIDS-related cases? In E. Gambrill & R. Pruger (Eds.), *Controversial issues in Social Work.* (pp. 350–354). Boston: Allyn & Bacon.

Kopels, S, & Kagle, J. D. (1993). Do social workers have a duty to warn? *Social Service Review, 67*(1), 101–126.

Munson, C. E. (1986). Editor's comments. *The Clinical Supervisor, 4*(3), 1–5.

National Association of Social Workers. (1993). *NASW code of ethics.* Washington, DC: Author.

National Association of Social Workers. (1995). *Overview of a decade of adjudication,* Washington, DC: Author.

Reamer, F. G. (1992). Is Tarasoff relevant to AIDS-related cases? In E. Gambrill & R. Pruger (Eds.), *Controversial issues in social work.* (pp. 342–349). Boston: Allyn & Bacon.

Reamer, F. G. (1995). Malpractice claims against social workers: First facts. *Social Work, 40*(5), 595–601.

Tarasoff v. Regents of University of California, 551 P.2d 334 (1976).

Two draw sanctions for code breaches. (November 1993). *NASW News,* p. 9.

Rejoinder to Professor Kopels   KATHLEEN E. MURPHY

Professor Kopels states that the lack of specificity and the lack of dissemination of information related to violations of the Code make it an ineffective guide for practice. As she noted, in the preamble of the Code it is stated that the Code is not intended to represent a set of rules that will prescribe behavior. Her analogy to the legal system is one that is commonly made and one that misrepresents the distinction made between the Code of Ethics and the law. Although both are an attempt to codify social values and social responsibility, the law is constructed reactively based on outcomes, whereas the Code is constructed proactively based on values. That is, the law is modified in substance and detail with every case and every decision; one knows how to think about legal matters because there are volumes that detail someone else's thinking. The Code states the values for the social worker to consider in any given ethical situation, but relies on the judgment of the social worker to make a reasoned decision given the details of a circumstance. The Code is intended to promote ethical practice, not to punish unethical practice.

The point that a social worker may act ethically while not acting legally is an important one. Clearly, all that is legal is not necessarily ethical, any more than all that is ethical is legal. The ethical social worker will often need to make decisions about what principles will guide one's practice and where to place one's moral loyalty. This is an important part of the social responsibility of being a social worker. This is not a failure of the system but is rather a positive aspect of the creative mission of the profession. The rule book proposed by Ms. Kopels would make practice "easier" in some ways but would not necessarily make it more effective nor more ethical. More importantly, a rule-oriented practice is a paint-by-numbers approach to the art of social work. I do not believe that as a profession we should aspire to achieve that rote and colorless application of the skill of social work.

As Professor Kopels notes, the lack of specificity and definition can lead social workers to reach different interpretations of the provisions of the Code. This is a positive, not a negative, in that reasonable and prudent social workers should be able to arrive ethically at different interpretations of the various tenets of the Code given different circumstances, with different clients and in different settings. The reasoned social worker, concerned about ethical practice and the definition of "devotion," "sexual activity," or "confidentiality" in any given situation, will consult with colleagues and figure out a definition that is consistent with the spirit of the Code and the circumstance.

Professor Kopels' point about the lack of dissemination of the Code as indicative of the ineffectiveness of the Code misrepresents the purpose of the Code. Familiarity with the Code, knowledge of ethical reasoning, and definition of concepts in the Code are the responsibility of the social workers who are expected to uphold the Code. In fact, I find the arguments about the lack of specificity and inadequate dissemination in support of why the Code is not an effective guide for practice, to be entirely consistent with my contention that it is the moral character of the social worker, not the Code, that can and should be held accountable for ethical practice.

Do the Ethical Standards of the Profession Carry a Higher Authority Than the Law?

EDITOR'S NOTE: The two authors here jointly wrote both sides of the argument . . . and then went on to prepare a single rebuttal challenging those two statements! No other procedure could have made so salient a key point; namely, that ideas are separate from the individual(s) who propose or present them.

Rufus Sylvester Lynch, DSW, LSW, and Jacquelyn Mitchell, JD, LCISW, argue both YES and NO. Drs. Lynch and Mitchell have served on the NASW National Committee on Inquiry, and have collaborated professionally for over two decades. Both have extensive practice experience and have jointly published and presented in the areas of ethics, justice system advocacy, and social work and the American justice system. They have recently completed a "Judicial Social Worker" practice model and have a manuscript on the model in press.

Dr. Lynch is a forensic social worker. He is on the faculty of the University of Pennsylvania School of Social Work, Cheyney University of Pennsylvania, and Lincoln University.

Dr. Mitchell is a social worker, an attorney licensed in Georgia, Pennsylvania, and the District of Columbia, and a certified mediator. She is an Assistant Professor in the Department of Sociology, Social Work & Anthropology, Christopher Newport University.

YES

Rufus Sylvester Lynch
Jacquelyn Mitchell

Who is best qualified to define ethical and professional practice in a particular professional endeavor? Professions have consistently and unequivocally responded to this query: Those professionally qualified in a field of professional endeavor are, of course, most qualified. When the subject is the social work profession, the response should be no different.

Professional Status

Status as a profession is the major prerequisite to practitioners self-regulating or using self-defined standards to evaluate practice. There is little dispute that social work meets the fundamental criteria that are characteristic of a profession and, therefore, has status as a profession. In the twentieth century, social work evolved from an occupation to a profession, joining an evolution of other professions that began as early as the Middle Ages, when standards and protections were developed for guilds (Schroeder, 1995). Essential in this evolution was the development of formalized training around a specialized body of knowledge, a professional association, and standards of practice.

Social work has met these criteria. Formalized professional training began in 1898, when the New York Charity Organization Society established the School of Applied Philanthropy, the precursor to Columbia University School of Social Work. The National Association of Social Workers (NASW), now recognized as the largest professional social work organization in the world, provides the requisite professional consortium for social workers. Standards of practice are provided by several different codes of ethics established by the various associations to which social workers belong, including the National Federation of Societies of Clinical Social Work, the International Federation of Social Workers, the National Association of Black Social Workers, and the National Organization for Forensic Social Work (Barker & Branson, 1992; Schroeder, 1995).

Undoubtedly, the NASW Code of Ethics is best known of the several codes used by social workers in the United States and represents the mission, goals, priorities, values, practice standards, and practice guides for social work, as defined by a representative body of more than 150,000 social work professionals throughout the world. Periodically reviewed and revised to insure currency with actual practice, the Code is currently under revision, with proposed revisions scheduled to be considered by the 1996 Delegate Assembly. Most importantly, these standards are actually used by social work professionals to guide ethical practice (Morales & Sheafor, 1995).

As with other professions, social workers tend to look to their Code of Ethics for guidance relative to standards of conduct and guidelines for resolution of competing professional obligations and duties (Reamer, 1995). Exhaustive research is yet to be done on the value of the Code relative to its usefulness to the practitioner attempting to reconcile his or her own operating values, or the extent to which the Code is or should be predominantly addressed to colleagues who need policing, rather than to the majority of social work professionals who are conscientious and therefore do not require policing (Caiden, 1981). However, the codes are generally accepted as a profession's current opinion about values, practice, and ethics.

Standards of Ethical Practice: The Contract with Society

That standards of practice essentially represent the profession's commitments to society relative to the practice of social work provides further support for the utilization of practice standards over the law in questions of ethics. Through the enunciation of standards, social workers define practice, delineate the values, establish standards of ethical behavior relative to clients, colleagues, employers, and other individuals and professionals, establish requirements for those having the status of "social worker," and provide a basis for handling ethical infractions committed by social workers.

Licensing statutes and boards further establish the profession's Contract With Society, as some licensing statutes incorporate the professionally established standards, thereby requiring adherence to the NASW Code as a condition of licensure. As of 1995, such statutes existed in all 50 states, the District of Columbia, the U.S. Virgin Islands, and Puerto Rico (Biggerstaff, 1995).

Indeed, the establishment of a social contract is one of the primary purposes of the creation of standards of professional conduct. Social work; other professions—including the American Psychological Association (1992), the American Medical Association (1992), and the American Psychiatric Association (1992)—have established such assurances to the public that practice will be held to established standards and that practice will be policed to insure compliance. For example, the preamble to the NASW Code of Ethics explicitly embraces the Contract, noting that the enunciated ethical standards apply over and above, and supplementary to, the requirements of regulatory boards (National Association of Social Workers, 1994).

As regards ethical issues, standards of practice provide superior consumer protection. Placing legal proscriptions in a position superior to that of practice standards has the effect of nullifying the Contract that the profession has generously entered with the public. Indeed, professionalism must mean more than compliance with the esoteric requirements established by the law, and require adherence to ethical codes, the generous protection provided by proscriptions established by those who know the "lay of the land."

The Authority of the Profession to Self-Police: Preservation of Professional Autonomy

Professional autonomy is the essence of professionalism and places the gatekeeping function in the hands of those most qualified for the task, the professionals with the knowledge of the area of practice and the collegial muscle. External regulation is less effective and, indeed, more costly (Constantinides, 1991). In the case of social workers, self-regulation of ethical practice is justified by at least four considerations: (1) the superior scope of practice standards; (2) the success of self-regulation; (3) judicial acceptance; and (4) the maintenance of the integrity of the social work profession.

Although the requirements emanating from standards and law are sometimes in agreement, the ethical proscriptions advanced by standards usually establish higher norms of behavior. Laws generally proscribe grossly negligent practice or actions that violate other criminal or civil statutes (Schroeder, 1995). The area of confidentiality is a notable example. The NASW Code of Ethics requires social workers to "hold in confidence all information obtained in the course of professional service" (National Association of Social Workers, 1994). However, under the law, a social worker can be compelled to testify as to confidential matters, although a client–social worker privilege is recognized in some states. Additionally, codes contain ethical commitments to social justice and against discrimination that might not be legally recognized.

Secondly, social workers have successfully regulated practice through mechanisms existing in professional associations and licensing boards. For example, NASW maintains an established peer adjudication process through which sanctions, such as censure and expulsion from the Association, have been imposed against social workers (National Association of Social Workers, 1991; Schroeder, 1995).

Thirdly and notably, courts have been hesitant to superimpose themselves over the regulatory authority established by professions to interpret professional ethical codes. This is especially so when the court restricts its deliberations to whether behavior is violative of an existing statute; in such instances, courts tend to leave the ethical decisions to association grievance procedures and licensing boards. The NASW procedure is among those self-regulation processes that have been upheld (Neumark v. National Association of Social Workers, Inc., 762 F.2d 993, 1985). Moreover, some courts use ethical codes to establish a standard of care that is owed by the professional (Constantinides, 1991).

Finally, insisting on the primacy of professionally defined standards of ethical conduct is an essential element in social work's status as a profession. Professional autonomy is as essential to social work as to other professions. As such, social work will survive and grow as a profession to the extent it is allowed to define and enforce ethical practice. Utilization of the standards of practice codified in the NASW Code and other codes is essential to recognition of the professional status of social work and should guide the response to any question regarding ethical social work practice. A contrary response undermines the professional autonomy of social work, the essence of professional status exemplified by the retention of the power to define practice and the efficacy of performance. This autonomy is protected through control of affiliation and license, creation of an ethics code, and a professional review mechanism (Constantinides, 1991). Fortunately, social work has those protections in place.

Conclusion

There is support internal and external to the profession for insisting that ethical social work practice be judged by the standards established by the collective knowledge of those who are, in fact, knowledgeable of social work practice. Therefore, when the issue is an ethical one, practice standards should take primacy over the dictates of the law. Social workers are as entitled to peer review as other professions.

REFERENCES

Biggerstaff, M. A. (1995). Licensing, regulation, and certification. In *Encyclopedia of social work* (19th ed.). Washington, DC: National Association of Social Workers.

Barker, R. L., & Branson, D. M. (1992). *Forensic social work: Legal aspects of professional practice.* New York: The Haworth Press.

Caiden, G. E. (1981). Ethics in the public service: Codification misses real target. *Public Personnel Management, 1,* 146–152.

Constantinides, C. (1991). Professional ethics codes in court: Redefining the social contract between the public and the professions. 25 *Georgia Law Review* 1327.

Morales, A. T., & Sheafor, B. W. (1995). *Social work: A profession of many faces* (7th ed.). Boston: Allyn & Bacon.

National Association of Social Workers. (1991). *NASW procedures for the adjudication of grievances* (rev. ed.). Washington, DC: Author.

National Association of Social Workers. (1994). *Code of Ethics: Professional Standards.* Washington, DC: Author.

Neumark v. National Association of Social Workers, Inc., 762 F.2d993 (1985).

Reamer, F. G. (1995). Ethics and values. In *Encyclopedia of social work* (19th ed.). Washington, DC: National Association of Social Workers.

Schroeder, L. O. (1995). *The legal environment of social work* (rev. ed.). Washington, DC: NASW Press.

NO

JACQUELYN MITCHELL
RUFUS SYLVESTER LYNCH

Although having total control over our personal and professional conduct is a seductive proposition, attempting to place standards of practice above the law is inherently dangerous to the status of social work as a profession, our status as individual social workers, the integrity of our standards of practice or ethics codes and, perhaps, our society as we know it. Therefore, in a "stand-off" between ethical standards and the law, we must "render unto Caesar" the position of primacy that it holds. The law is and must be preeminent.

Professional Status and Profession Protection

Under our system of government, it is the law that regulates conduct and defines the rights and responsibilities of all citizens. Similarly, the law imposes responsibilities and benefits on the social work profession. One of these benefits is professional status. It is the law that provides the authority by which social work is societally defined as a profession. As such, all standards of practice for social workers are derived from and protected by the broader societal imprimatur granted by the law (Barker & Branson, 1993).

How, then, can professional standards be greater than the authority from which they are derived? They cannot and should not. As with most professions, professional status requires social workers to recognize the ultimate authority of the law. The Model Rules of Professional Responsibility acknowledges such authority in the case of attorneys. The NASW procedures for the adjudication of grievances, based on its ethics code, significantly emphasizes the legal support for the process (National Association of Social Workers, 1991). Moreover, NASW's ethics code contains several references to the responsibility to be aware of or follow the law. For example, social workers are admonished against violation of the civil or legal rights of clients, to advocate for policy and legislative changes, and to protect the rights of those adjudged legally incompetent (National Association of Social Workers, 1994).

Obviously, licensing and title protection statutes existent in the fifty states, the District of Columbia, and the U.S. Virgin Islands represent legal regulation, that is, an exercise of the state's police power to protect consumers. However, these same statutes protect professional status. Through delegation of the state's authority to regulate practice, regulatory boards on which social workers usually sit can be established. Additionally and, perhaps, most importantly, through this same authority the profession is defined and the use of the term "social worker" may be restricted to individuals who have qualified under criteria determined by professional social workers (Saltzman & Proch, 1990). Like it or not, we require the law to enforce the status of the profession and our status as professionals.

Consumer Protection

All professions advance the protection of the public as a primary purpose of self-regulation. Professions argue that any benefit received from the internal policing of its members (prestige, fees, and the like) is outweighed by the benefits of protecting the consuming public and assisting the public with selecting qualified professionals. Although there is nothing inherently incredulous about such a position, such a social contract is only possible by virtue of the authority granted by the law.

The protection of the public and the profession flows from our "government of laws," established through a tripod form of government. In other words, the integrity of social work, social workers, and society is protected through the statutes, the courts, and the executive agencies. Through legislative action, the profession is defined, entry into practice is guarded, minimum standards are established, and a mechanism for the protection of the public is established. This force of law has been brought to bear in all fifty states, the District of Columbia, and the U.S. Virgin Islands (Lynch & Mitchell, 1995; Biggerstaff, 1995).

The judicial arm of the law is vested, under Article III, in the courts of our nation. Relative to social workers (See, for example, *Neumark v. National Association of Social Workers, Inc., 762* F.2d 993, 1985) and other professions, these courts have exercised their power to uphold determinations of ethical conduct by professional associations. Similarly, courts have intervened to consider criminal and civil sanctions for conduct that violated the law, as opposed to ethical standards (See, for example, *Steinberger v. District Court,* 596 P. 2d. 755, Colo. 1979; *DeShaney v. Winnebago County DSS,* 489 U.S. 189, (1989). Courts have also used ethical codes to establish duties owed by professionals, affording further credence to professional standards (Saltzman & Proch, 1990).

Executive level governmental entities, usually in the form of regulatory boards, provide another level of quality control for the public, the profession, and the professional. Because sanctions imposed can be severe (license revocation, for example), the impact on the professional can be substantial (Constantinides, 1991). Conversely, ethical codes only have real authority and impact when incorporated into standards adopted by such boards. Consider, for example, the NASW Code of Ethics and peer review process: only social workers who are members are subject to the requirements of the Code and then only on a voluntary basis. Sanctions imposed through the peer review process are generally limited to collegial, as opposed to sanctions of economic or even more severe impact (National Association of Social Workers, 1994).

Consequently, utilization of the Code by ethical boards broadens the impact beyond those who are members. Under the American system of government, the law provides social work and social workers the protections afforded to all of society—security from all of society's power being usurped by a few, to the potential detriment of us all. Because of this protection, a niche in the social service arena has been carved out for social work and social workers. The maintenance and recognition of this balanced power is essential to the preservation of American society, a society to which social workers have determined to owe duties and responsibilities and the society that provides the context within which we live and practice (Morales & Sheafor, 1995; National Association of Social Workers, 1994).

Finally, all facets of society, including social work, are subject to "reach" of the law—increasingly so. The law offers protection, opportunity, and dictates. No standards of conduct agreed on by a small group of individuals—whether or not the group has self-identified as a "profession—can be superior to the dictates defined by the society generally or offer the protection afforded by the law. We must, therefore, accept the protections and the proscriptions, as appropriate (Lynch & Mitchell, 1992).

Professional Autonomy and the Law

We should take some comfort in the legitimization of practice standards through the use of the legal system, because self-regulation is the heart of professional autonomy. Indeed, it is the power emanating from the law as delegated from the state that affords social workers the authority to evaluate practice against tenets in which social workers have faith and acceptance, when the question is one of ethical conduct. However, this grant of authority should be appropriately limited to accommodate the complementary protections the law bestows on social work and social workers. Indeed, there is good reason to subordinate the authority of practice standards to that of the law, including (1) the absence of a single mandatory set of standards; (2) the need for law's enforcement authority to protect the integrity of the profession; and (3) self- and professional preservation. Barker and Branson (1993) have identified the lack of a single set of standards to which all social workers must adhere, inconsistent state licensing statutes, and special certification with very little legal enforcement authority as weaknesses in established ethical standards for social workers. This deficiency could have the effect of undermining our professional autonomy.

At the same time, it is important to remember that the authority to self-regulate flows from a delegation from the state that retains the ultimate authority and responsibility to protect the public. Moreover, this delegation is premised on a contract with society to insure that practice will be adequately policed (Barker & Branson, 1992). Furthermore, acknowledgement of the primacy of the law and adherence to its dictates is required of all citizens, including social workers. Social workers who cast legal requirements aside in favor of practice standards court the danger of civil and criminal liability. This is especially true given the pervasiveness of the law in the lives of the social workers and the rest of society (Lynch & Mitchell, 1992; Saltzman & Proch, 1990).

Consideration of professional conduct from both ethical and legal perspectives is prudent for social workers. It is important to remember that conduct that may be ethically required may be illegal. Therefore, social workers who refuse to comply with a court order to release client information, who advocate for clients by violating a statute (such as the failure to report abuse or noncompliance, providing benefits to clients not qualified under the law, or holding themselves out as a "social worker" without a required license) may find themselves exposed to civil damages or conviction that, in turn, compromises the reputation of the entire profession (Dickson, 1995).

We must operate within the guidelines of the law, if we are to uphold the values and goals of the profession—protection of consumer, social work, and social workers. Only then does professional autonomy have real meaning.

Conclusion

Practice standards have a valuable function: establishing minimal standards relative to ethical practice. However, such standards do not, should not, and cannot replace the general societal standards, benefits, and duties that are established by the law. Practice standards do not have sufficient authority or applicability to protect social work and social workers in the torrents of the challenges of the twenty-first century and beyond. To take a contrary view is to court disaster. It is in the interest of the profession to give to "Caesar" that authority due, and retain the setting of ethical standards by our collective wisdom.

REFERENCES

Barker, R. L., & Branson, D. M. (1992). *Forensic social work: Legal aspects of professional practice*. New York: Haworth Press.

Biggerstaff, M. A. (1995). Licensing, regulation, and certification. In *Encyclopedia of social work* (19th ed.). Washington, DC: National Association of Social Workers.

Constantinides, C. (1991). Professional ethics codes in court: Redefining the social contract between the public and the professions. 25 Ga. L. Rev. 1327.

DeShaney v. Winnebago County DSS, 489 U.S. 189 (1989).

Dickson, D. T. (1995). *Law in the health and human services: A guide for social workers, psychologists, psychiatrists, and related professionals.* New York: The Free Press.

Lynch, R. S., & Mitchell, J. (1992). Institutionalizing the roles of court social workers. *Journal of Law & Social Work, 3,* 77–87.

Lynch, R. S., & Mitchell, J. (1995). Justice system advocacy: A must for NASW and the social work community. *Social Work, 40,* 9–12.

Morales, A. T., & Sheafor, B. W. (1995). *Social work: A profession of many faces* (7th ed.). Boston: Allyn & Bacon.

National Association of Social Workers. (1991). *NASW procedures for the adjudication of grievances* (rev. ed.). Washington, DC: Author.

National Association of Social Workers. (1994). *Code of ethics: Professional standards.* Washington, DC: Author.

Saltzman, A., & Proch, K. (1990). *Law in social work practice.* Chicago: Nelson-Hall.

Steinberger v. District Court, 596 P.2d.755 (Colo. 1979).

Rejoinder to Both Our YES and NO statements

We have had the advantage or disadvantage of arguing both sides of the issue. As with most issues, thoughtful consideration results in "yes, if," "no, if" responses. Such is the case here.

The query of which tenets should carry higher authority is somewhat of a red herring. Indeed, it would seem that what we should be seeking is universal professionalism among social workers. Such professionalism requires faithful adherence to both practice standards and the law. Our system of government and laws assigns roles for each source of dictates. To the extent that practice standards are used to determine ethical practice, the professional status of social work is safeguarded, social workers are protected, and the profession defines its Contract with Society. Undeniably, after years of sometimes contentious evolution, it is appropriate that we continue to support definition-by-the-profession, especially against expected twenty-first century challenges.

However, maintenance of professional autonomy is not without peril or limitation. One peril noted is the lack of universal standards or regulatory statutes, thereby compromising our ability to assure the public that there are uniform standards to which all social workers must adhere. Accordingly, perhaps one way in which we can best preserve professional autonomy is by at least thinking about the potential of establishing more universally accepted standards that are less aspirational, that more clearly provide ethical guidance for practice, and have applicability to all or most social workers.

At the same time, the pervasiveness of the law on all of society cannot be minimized. Social work is no exception. Like it or not, the law determines the who, what, when, how, and how much of social work practice. We receive benefit and headaches from these dictates; social workers are put to the task of serving multiple masters. We are admonished to conform our practice to the principles enunciated in ethical codes. At the same time, our licenses, jobs, and citizenship sometimes require contradictory conduct.

We and others have been encouraging the profession to heed the impact the law has on social work and social workers. We have called for inclusion of legally related courses in curricula, training for practitioners and the institutionalization of social workers in the justice system. This debate again emphasizes the pervasiveness of the law on social work practice. Although it is appropriate to look to professionally defined standards to determine whether practice is ethical, neither our Contract with Society nor our collegial contract ends there. Indeed, conduct that is illegal (murder, embezzlement, sexual misconduct, etc.) often harbors more potential harm for clients, colleagues, the profession, and society.

Therefore, we answer "Yes," practice standards should have greater authority when the issue is purely an ethical one. The courts would agree. However, when the issue is other than ethical, we answer "No!" The maintenance of the integrity of the profession, the professional and society requires acknowledgement of the preeminence of the law.

Is the Code of Ethics as Applicable to Agency Executives as It Is to Direct Service Providers?

EDITOR'S NOTE: The popular perception of all human service professions is that they are made up of direct service practitioners. Thus, the medical profession is perceived as being made up of doctors serving patients; teaching is made up of teachers lecturing to students; the vision of our own profession at work is of social workers helping clients. Certainly any reading of the NASW Code of Ethics conveys the impression that it was written with only the direct services worker in mind. And yet social work, as all other human service professions, has a much more complex division of labor than that. Social welfare executives, for example, may never see a client. This debate concerns the applicability of the Code to this segment of the professional workforce.

Elaine Congress, Ph.D., is the Director of the doctoral program at Fordham University Graduate School of Social Service and Chair of the Ethics Committee of the New York City chapter of the National Association of Social Workers. Much of her teaching and writing is concerned with professional ethics.

Burton Gummer, Ph.D., is a professor in the School of Social Welfare, Nelson A. Rockefeller College of Public Affairs & Policy, The State University of New York at Albany. He is the author of *The Politics of Social Administration* and numerous articles on social welfare administration and planning. His "Notes from the Management Literature" is a regular feature of *Administration in Social Work,* of which he is an associate editor.

YES

ELAINE CONGRESS

A recent report of NASW members indicates that 25 percent list management as their primary or secondary area of practice (Ginsberg, 1995). Therefore, it becomes increasingly important to study whether the NASW Code of Ethics is applicable to their practice.

Relevant Literature

Social work literature addresses the importance of ethical practice for the administrator. Levy indicates that "the principles and applications of social work ethics will vary in relation to the particular role and situation, although not in the fundamentals to which all social workers are bound in all their roles" (1993, p. 30). This suggests that the Code of Ethics, which is basic to ethical social work practice, applies to agency executives as well as to direct practitioners (See also Levy, 1982). Perlmutter explicitly states that the Code of Ethics is particularly important for social work managers who are faced with difficult ethical choices (Perlmutter, 1990). Reamer has stressed the increasing litigiousness of our society, which underscores even more the need for agency executives to adhere to a formal code, especially if they or their agencies may become defendants in malpractice or liability claims (Reamer, 1994). Lewis concludes that ethical management is not only possible but essential if a social work manager is to pursue his or her organizational goals (Lewis, 1989).

Greater Responsibility of Administrator

The agency administrator must simultaneously manage relationships at all levels of the service delivery system. Many of these responsibilities are explicitly spelled out in the NASW Code of Ethics. Because of the greater responsibility of the social work administrator in managing multiple, often conflicting responsibilities, especially in terms of financial and human resources, the need for a manager to have decisions guided by a formal code is even more evident.

Increasingly it has been noted that nonprofit administrators are not ethical (Gaul and Borowski, 1993). Unethical practice is frequently seen as failure to maintain appropriate focus on clients. Adherence to a code helps social work executives remain attuned to a fundamental value in social work practice, the primacy of clients and their needs. The concern about unethical administrative practice reinforces the importance of social work administrators applying the Code of Ethics to their practice decisions.

Code of Ethics

The first section of the NASW Code focuses on the conduct and comportment of the social worker. It clearly spells out the professional's duty to maintain competence and pursue ongoing professional development. Through the agency executive's ongoing concern about providing adequate services to clients, staff members learn professional behavior and skills needed for competent practice. Through his or her example, the agency executive also functions as a role model to staff members about appropriate professional behavior. The agency executive also sets the standard in the agency for professional development. The Code of Ethics provides the written justification for sending staff members to conferences and other educational seminars.

Paramount in the NASW Code of Ethics is the second section, which declares that the social worker's primary responsibility is to clients. The fact that social work administrators are often criticized for their failure to follow this principle suggests that the Code is frequently used to evaluate the practice of social work administrators. Because their primary responsibility is to clients, the ethical agency executive should first study the impact of any administrative decision on clients.

The social work executive has much power in determining how confidentiality, required by the Code, is interpreted and maintained in the agency. The agency executive makes decisions about the types of records that are kept, how they are stored, and what information is released to outside social and legal organizations. Also, if there is an alleged violation of confidentiality, recent court cases have named the agency executive, as well as the direct practitioner (Reamer, 1994). Increased litigation that involves social workers at all administrative levels suggests even more that the agency executive should adhere to the professional Code of Ethics as the standard for appropriate professional practice.

Section III of the Code enumerates the social worker's responsibility to colleagues in terms of treating the latter with respect, fairness, and courtesy. This refers to both supervisors for whom the agency executive has administrative responsibility and direct service workers within the organization. Because of the number of employees under the administration of the agency executive, as well as the role of the agency executive as a model of professional behavior, this part of the Code is especially applicable.

Section IV states that social workers have an ethical responsibility "to improve the employing agency's policies and procedures, and the efficiency and effectiveness of its services" (NASW, 1994, p. 8.) These objectives seem very related to the concerns of social work agency executives. Because of greater knowledge and control of resources, the agency executive is in an ideal position to monitor and improve the efficiency and effectiveness of agency services.

A provision of the Code of Ethics that appeared for the first time in the 1994 revision specifically relates to agency executives. Social workers are instructed to "not use a professional position vested with power such as that of employer to his or her advantage or to exploit others" (NASW, 1994, p. 8.). The agency executive who because of his or her control of salary, work assignments, and job responsibilities has much economic and social power over the worker is instructed not to use this greater power for personal gain or to harm others.

Also included in the most current Code of Ethics is the social worker's responsibility to colleagues who are impaired because of "personal problems, psychosocial distress, substance abuse, or mental health difficulties" (NASW, 1994, p. 8). The agency executive has always had a responsibility to intervene if the quality of services provided by an impaired staff member is inadequate. Agency executives have developed and encouraged participation in employee assistance programs (EAP) to help employees whose performance is detrimentally affected by substance abuse or other problems.

The Code of Ethics in section V stresses the social workers's ethical responsibility to the community. The agency executive has an important role in learning what services are available in the community, as well as in developing new services to benefit the community in which the agency is located.

The Code also relates to the professional responsibility to society. The most significant provisions in section VI state that the social worker should act to prevent discrimination, that the social worker "should act to ensure that all persons have access to the resources, services, and opportunities which they require." and that the social worker "should act to expand choice and opportunity for all persons, with special regard for disadvantaged oppressed groups" (NASW, 1994, p. 10). As agency executive, the social worker has the power to see that discrimination does not affect access, intake, or intervention services at the agency. The agency executive is obliged to offer services especially to the most disadvantaged.

Under this section, social workers are also encouraged to "advocate changes in policy and legislation to improve social conditions and to promote social justice" (NASW, 1994, p. 10). Agency executives are often in the best position to work toward achieving these objectives.

In summary, a review of the Code of Ethics indicates that this document applies to agency executives, as much as, if not more than to direct service workers. The fact that some have questioned if agency executives are ethical does not mean that the Code of Ethics does not apply to them. Situations in which the agency executive is considered to be unethical suggest that the Code of Ethics has been applied and the social work executive has been seen as not adhering to the principles set forth.

Non-NASW Agency Executives

A recent concern is that many social service agencies are not directed by professional social workers, but rather by those with a background in law, business administration, or public administration, who are not social workers and do not belong to NASW. Professionals from other disciplines are bound by the Codes of their respective disciplines. It should be acknowledged that the NASW Code of Ethics can only be enforced with agency executives who are NASW members. Even if the agency executive is a non-NASW, non–social worker, however, it is important for him or her to be familiar with the NASW Code as the professional social work staff he or she administrates will be bound by the NASW Code of Ethics. Furthermore, because of its focus on the primacy of clients, the Code of Ethics serves to set standards for practice within the social service agency, even though Code violations by non–social work administrators cannot be adjudicated by the State Licensing Board or NASW Committee of Inquiry.

Code of Ethics for Agency Executives

There is no Code of Ethics specifically for agency executives. Although the National Center for Nonprofit Boards has spoken about the importance of a Code of Ethics, a general Code of Ethics for all nonprofit organizations has yet to be developed (National Center for NonProfit Boards, 1994). Although there is a special section of NASW for Social Work Managers, this group has not produced a specific Code of Ethics. The National Association of Social Workers with 135,000 members represents the largest number of professional social workers and the NASW Code seems must known and used by professional social workers. Although other professional organizations to which social workers belong, such as the National Federation of the Societies for Clinical Social Workers and the National Association of Black Social Workers, have developed Codes of Ethics, these Codes are not as applicable to the role and multiple functions of the agency executive as the NASW Code of Ethics.

New Directions

Although a Code delineates current practice standards, it is not intended to be static and fixed for all time. The current Code can clearly be applied to the practice experience of agency executives, but a criticism of the current Code is that there is not a specific section on the ethical responsibilities of the administrator. The new proposed NASW Code of Ethics, which will be approved by the Delegate Assembly in 1996 and go into effect the following year, clearly addresses the duties of the agency executive. Also, the new Code makes more explicit a social worker's responsibilities when there are conflicting duties. These sections of the proposed revised Code will be even more helpful to the agency executive, who often must decide between two conflicting obligations.

REFERENCES

Fewell, C., King, G., & Weinstein, D. (1993). Alcohol and other drug abuse among colleagues and their families: Impact on practice. *Social Work, 38*(5), 565–570.

Gaul, G., & Borowski, N. (1993). *Free ride: The tax-exempt economy.* Kansas City, MO: Andrews and McNeal.

Ginsberg, L. (1995). *Social work almanac.* Washington, DC: NASW Press.

Levy, C. (1982). *Guide to ethical decisions and actions for social service administrators.* New York: Haworth Press.

Levy, C. (1993). *Social work ethics on the line.* New York: Haworth Press.

Lewis, H. (1989). Ethics and the private nonprofit human service organizations. *Administration in Social Work, 13*(2), 1–14.

National Center for Non-Profit Boards. (1994). Guidelines for developing a code of ethics. *Board Member* (Special edition—Accountability at the Crossroads).

National Association of Social Workers. (1994). *Code of ethics.* Washington, DC: NASW Press.

Perlmutter, F. (1990). *Changing hats: From social work practice to administration.* Silver Springs, MD: NASW Press.

Reamer, F. (1994). *Social work malpractice and liability.* New York: Columbia University Press.

Rejoinder to Professor Congress · Burton Gummer

The position I took in my paper was that the NASW Code of Ethics is not as applicable to social welfare administrators as it is to direct service workers. I went on to point out that it was not so much the Code's inapplicability as it was its *incompleteness.* In Congress's paper defending the applicability of the Code to social welfare administrators, she creates a straw argument by assuming that the ethical choices facing the administrator were either to follow the NASW Code exclusively, or to act unethically. Fortunately, there are other options available to the administrator concerned with the ethics of his or her practice.

I stated that the NASW Code spends an inordinate amount of time discussing the ethical dilemmas arising from the professional's relationships with clients and colleagues. These are important issues, but they are by no means the only or most important issues facing contemporary welfare administrators. The biggest issues in social welfare and the other human services have to do with the allocation of increasingly scarce resources. Often these decisions are taken out of the hands of administrators by the issuance of public policies that set guidelines for the allocation of resources. The Republican party's "Contract with America" seeks to restrict the level of support that an impoverished mother may receive for each of her children and most likely will stipulate that no case-specific considerations can override that policy. In most cases, however, the legislative body will shirk the responsibility for establishing guidelines and pass legislation that is vague on critical points, thus opening the door for the expansion of administrative discretion. Both the implementation of policies that go against the values and goals of the social work profession and the making of discretionary decisions in the case of vague policies present enormous ethical problems for administrators and workers alike, problems for which the NASW Code does not offer realistic guidelines.

The NASW Code is unrealistic as regards the ethics of policy issues because it does not deal with these issues in the proper context. This Code has the fallacy of "hypermoralism" in which ethics that are applicable to one context—the professional–client relationship—are imposed on activities that take place in another context—the making and implementing of public social policies. In my paper, I pointed to the kinds of ethical guidelines that would be appropriate for thinking about policy issues. Ultimately, the question comes down, as Hardin suggests, to whether professional ethics depend on what is possible: "As moral theorists of almost all stripes would say, ought implies can. If it is impossible for you to do something, it cannot be true that you ought to do it" (Hardin, 1990, p. 529).

The notion that the social agency is responsible primarily to clients is both unrealistic and undesirable. Social programs must serve a number of different and competing constituencies. To argue that the people footing the bill for these programs—the taxpayers—should not be allowed to put their mark on policies in terms of what they value is both unrealistic and undemocratic. This is but one instance of the need for social welfare administrators to mediate the claims of one stakeholder against the other. Similarly, the desire of professionally trained social workers to shape their caseloads in ways that concentrate on those clients who can make the best use of their services—even though this excludes other "less qualified" clients—is a legitimate right and must be dealt with.

Formal codes of ethics offer some help in addressing these issues, but they are by no means the final answer. The ultimate moral authority in these complex situations is the individual's own ethical code and his or her ability to articulate and stand by it. "The courage to act on one's own convictions arising from a sense of self-engendered authority is a necessary requisite for moral action" (Jacobson, 1993, p. 82).

References

Hardin, R. (1990). The artificial duties of contemporary professionals. *Social Service Review, 64*(4), 528–541.

Jacobson, K. H. (1993). Organization and the mother archetype: A Jungian analysis of adult development and self-identity within the organization. *Administration & Society, 25*(1), 60–84.

NO

BURTON GUMMER

This paper argues that the Code of Ethics of the National Association of Social Workers is not as applicable to social welfare managers as it is to direct service providers. I will argue that the Code presents problems for managers not so much in terms of its its being inapplicable, but in terms of its incompleteness. The Code has serious gaps for administrators (and line workers) in terms of its failure to provide ethical guidelines to deal with some of the most pressing problems that confront contemporary welfare professionals, particularly those that arise from the need to make decisions about how to allocate scarce welfare resources.

Evolution of Professional Codes

The first secular code of ethics was the Hippocratic Oath, introduced in the fifth century to govern the behavior of physicians. The fact that a need was felt for a code of ethics separate from the prevailing religious codes and societal mores reflected the unique role of the professions in medieval society, a role that has continued into present times. The uniqueness of the role is based on the independence that professionals—in this case physicians—claim as essential to the practice of their profession. This autonomy is needed in part because the special knowledge and training of physicians is such that their work can be evaluated only by other physicians. This argument still has some validity today, but it is not nearly as strong a case in knowledge-based modern industrial societies as it was in pre-industrial societies.

The second and more important basis for the professional's claim to independence from societal supervision is the nature of the professional–client relationship. This is, as physicians call it, a "sacred trust"; nothing should be allowed to interfere with the professional's ministrations to his or her patients or clients. Extraordinary rights are allotted to doctors and lawyers in the form of privileged communications, the exclusive authority to prescribe and dispense medications, and the like. In exchange for this grant of independence and special powers, the professions offered a code of ethics that would prevent abuses of their autonomy and prerogatives.

Since that time, a code of ethics has become one of the hallmarks of a profession. Nowadays, every group with claims to professional status has its own code of ethics; these include, in addition to the traditional fields of law and medicine, contemporary fields such as public administration, social work, accounting, city planning, and teaching. These codes also serve a synecdochic function, in which their existence presumes the existence of the other attributes of a profession such as the centrality of the service ethic, an advanced knowledge base, specialized training, and the need to make independent, discretionary decisions.

Professions: Private and Public

That assumption, however, is not always true, and therein lies the problem. Howe (1980) argues that all professions can be divided into two groups—the public and the private. The key issue is how autonomous professionals are in relation to the people they serve. The currently accepted model of professionalism is based mainly on the professions of law and medicine, which, historically, have been essentially private (although that is increasingly less so). All professions, Howe argues, aspire to the kind of socially granted, legitimate autonomy characteristic of a traditional profession like medicine,

> ... but such autonomy is most easily achieved when a profession is private, that is, when its members are primarily responsible to individual clients. However, a number of professions, including social work, urban planning, and public administration, provide collective services and involve economic externalities that affect the public at large. This makes them public professions in which control is retained by the public, and they are unlikely to achieve significant autonomy. (Howe, 1980, p. 179)

From its nineteenth century beginnings, the field of social work had built into it a conflict of responsibility between loyalty to its clientele and to the society at large. This dilemma is captured in Richard Titmuss's definition of social welfare as "all collective interventions to meet certain needs of the individual *and/or* to serve the wider interests of society" (Titmuss, 1959, p. 42; emphasis added).

The conflict between client and society was obscured, however, as social work—having moved from a voluntary to a paid activity—aspired to professional status. Social workers took medicine as their primary model of professionalism. It has serious shortcomings, however, when applied to professions such as social work that have a complex of public and private dimensions.

A major difference between private and public professions is how they are held accountable for their work. Private professions, such as medicine and law, are primarily responsible, at least in theory, to their clients, whereas public professions, such as public administration and urban planning, involve work that has consequences that go beyond their immediate clients and affect the public at large. Public administration and medicine are examples of professions at opposite ends of the public–private continuum. Social work historically has been conflicted over its appropriate place on this scale. Like doctors and attorneys, social workers profess a primary orientation to service to their clients. At the same time, social work services are not strictly a matter between the social worker and the client. Social service organizations produce *public goods,* or goods that have a mixed public and private character. Their services, Austin (1981, pp. 39–40) points out, "are assumed to have a collective or public benefit in addition to any benefits accruing to individual users or consumers. ... Because they produce outputs with a public goods element, human service organizations always involve some type of collective or public assessment of performance, in addition to or in place of individual user assessment."

All organized social work practice (private practice presents another set of ethical issues) deals with some conception of "social health." There is, moreover, no generally understood state of social health toward which all people strive. Much of the program of social work is to change behaviors in ways that are deemed socially beneficial. This raises, as Hardin (1990) points out,

> . . . value issues in determining what is good for clients. Doctors have been able to frame their task as much more nearly univocal, as the improvement of health. Lawyers look to a relatively single concern for their clients. There is inherently much more in dispute when a social worker decides what is best for a client . . . Every social worker involved in public welfare programs must often face the dilemma of serving as an agent of the state as well as of the client. This is a burden that doctors have only recently come to bear. (p. 536)

In the American political system, the existing political administration has been granted the authority by the electorate to establish what is socially beneficial. Moreover, it is the administrators of social agencies who have to deal directly with any conflicts between the values expressed in the policies of the current political administration, and the values and preferences of the social workers providing the service.

Ethics and Social Policy

The need to reconcile professional values with majority societal values is one area in which the Code of Ethics fails to offer guidance to the social worker, particularly the social welfare administrator. A second area has to do with how limited resources are to be used. The demand for social services has been growing while the supply has been dwindling. The same is true for medical services. Increasingly, the ethical dilemmas facing social workers and doctors have more to do with questions of triage and the distribution of losses than they have to do with the subtleties of professional–client relationships, which account for the bulk of the ethical guidelines in the NASW Code of Ethics.

Frameworks for evaluating the ethical behavior of public officials can be profitably applied to social work administrators, because both are responsible for the implementation of public social policies. Wilbern (1984), for example, identified six levels of public morality: basic honesty and conformity to law; conflicts of interest; service orientation and procedural fairness; the ethic of democratic responsibility; the ethic of public policy determination; and the ethic of compromise and social integration. The first three levels deal mainly with the administrator's personal morality, and the latter three address the ethics of the administrator's decisions or actions.

Many discussions of professional ethics begin and end with the issue of personal morality. Even in social work, in which 90 percent of the work takes place within complex organizations, the profession's Code of Ethics is mostly concerned with issues that arise between individual social workers and their clients. Administrators, however, have as great a need for ethical guidelines for actions that result from their organizational roles as they do for those that come out of their personal or professional beliefs.

One aspect of administrative work that creates a number of ethical concerns is the amount of discretion that is inherent in most administrative roles. Through administrative discretion, managers participate in the policy-making process for social agencies. This defines an ethical issue peculiar to one's organizational role, because most conceptions of the administrative function separate policy making from policy implementation. In the public sector, the responsibility for policy making is assumed to reside with elected representatives, executives, and their appointees, and in the private sector with an agency's board of directors.

This distinction between policy making and policy implementation has broken down, and administrators are generally recognized as active participants in the policy process. Although most administrators play an important role in determining what social programs will actually do, many do not admit to having this kind of power. They frequently resist the idea that they have an impact on policy making, which, in their eyes, can only be done by those bodies duly authorized to do so. This line of reasoning is usually based on the fallacy that if legislatures and boards of directors have much power, then administrators have none. Not only is this reasoning fallacious, Rohr (1978, p. 40) argued, it is dangerous as well, "for it is always dangerous when the powerful are unaware of their own power."

Although most administrators publicly acknowledge that their actions are determined by the voice of the people, in actual practice there is no way they can escape the responsibility to make ethical choices based on their own values. The voice will rarely be clear or univocal: "it will not be based on full knowledge, it will conflict in small or large degree with other persuasive and powerful normative considerations" (Wilbern, 1984, p. 105). The conflicts will be most severe when the popular will conflicts with the administrator's professional expertise and that of the agency staff. Administrators often rationalize actions that differ from legislative or board directives on the grounds that they are doing what their superiors would want done if they had the same information available to them.

No matter how persuasive or eloquent these arguments are, however, the use of administrative discretion to modify or change agency policies inevitably raises questions of disloyalty or underhanded practices. Administrators often try to avoid this dilemma by working to influence the content of policies while they are being developed. The change in the conception of administrators from value-neutral technicians to policy and program advocates who actively seek to invest the programs they manage with their own beliefs, values, and professional philosophies, raises important questions regarding the administrator's ethical responsibilities for policy development.

The ultimate ethical test of a social program is what it accomplishes. Did the program produce benefits for its clients? Were the beneficiaries those most in need of the service? How were the costs of the program distributed? The way in which a program is administered will account for some of the variation in the answers to these questions. However, the most important determinant of the questions of who benefits and who pays is the substance of the policies on which the program is based. This, in turn, raises what is for many the most crucial ethical issue for administrators, namely, their responsibility to play an active role in promoting the policies they believe are correct and opposing those they think are harmful. This role leads them into political arenas and necessitates the development of political skills. The ethics of social welfare administrators are, ultimately the ethics of people trying to promote their beliefs about the social good in an imperfect world.

References

Austin, D. M. (1981). The political economy of social benefit organizations: Redistributive services and merit goods. In H. D. Stein (Ed.), *Organization and the human services.* Philadelphia: Temple University Press.

Hardin, R. (1990). The artificial duties of contemporary professionals. *Social Service Review, 64*(4), 528–541.

Howe, E. (1980). Public professions and the private model of professionalism. *Social Work, 25*(3), 179–191.

Rohr, J. A. (1978). *Ethics for bureaucrats.* New York: Marcel Dekker.

Titmuss, R. M. (1959). The social division of welfare: Some reflections on the search for equity. In *Essays on The Welfare State.* New Haven, CT: Yale University Press.

Wilbern, Y. (1984). Types and levels of public morality. *Public Administration Review, 44*(2), 102–108.

Rejoinder to Professor Gummer   Elaine Congress

First, I would like to reiterate that my statement addresses the applicability of the Code of Ethics to agency executives, rather than what Dr. Gummer has reframed as the "incompleteness" of the Code of Ethics. Although I would agree with Dr. Gummer that the Code of Ethics does not represent a set of rules that will prescribe all the behaviors of social workers in all the complexities of professional life, this does not mean that the Code does not apply to social work managers. I would disagree that it does not offer guidelines about "how to allocate scarce welfare resources" and, furthermore, suggest that this is not the only aspect of the agency executive's responsibilities.

Although Dr. Gummer aptly describes the history of professional codes and responsibilities, he does not discuss the fiduciary relationship of the social worker in terms of the Code of Ethics. The nature of the social worker's relationship with clients has been defined as fiduciary, which implies that professionals, because of their greater power, have certain obligations to vulnerable clients with limited power (Kutchins, 1991, Lewis, 1972). Because the agency executive has even greater power than the direct service practitioner, there is a special need for a Code to guide their professional behavior.

As Dr. Gummer indicates, "a code of ethics has become one of the hallmarks of a profession." The Flexner Report of 1915 indicated that social work could not be considered a profession without a code of ethics, which led to the first development of a Code of Ethics for social workers. To say that the Code of Ethics is not applicable to social workers in administrative practice would seem to minimize their membership in the profession.

Dr. Gummer's division of professions into private (medicine and law) and public (social work) appears artificial, especially because social workers and other professions increasingly function in both private and public arenas. The Code of Ethics applies to the public agency executive as much as to the private practitioner. If there is concern that the Code of Ethics does not sufficiently cover an agency executive's responsibility to the public, it should be noted that the Code of Ethics in Section 6 specifically delineates the social worker's responsibility to society.

Dr. Gummer proposes that the Code of Ethics does not offer guidance to the social work administrator in terms of reconciling professional values with "majority societal values." I would agree that the Code does not do this and in fact would be very concerned if it proposed a method for doing so. The Code rightfully sets forth an operationalization of social work professional values. If there is a conflict with societal values, there is no question that the social work agency executive should follow professional values and the Code that supports this behavior.

I certainly agree with Dr. Gummer that administrative social workers increasingly must struggle with issues of limited resources. Management decisions about cutbacks should take into consideration the needs of the most vulnerable clients. A Code of Ethics that supports this perspective is certainly applicable to agency executives, because they make difficult decisions with limited resources.

Finally, Dr. Gummer argues that, contrary to what they claim, agency executives are increasingly involved in policy making as well as implementation. I would agree with this and reiterate that the role of agency executives in policy making reinforces even more the need for them to be guided by a professional code of ethics. If agency executives are no longer "value-neutral technicians but rather policy and program advocates who actively seek to invest the programs they manage with their own beliefs, values, and professional philosophies," the importance of having the Code of Ethics applicable to their practice is even greater. I interpret "professional philosophies" as those delineated by the Code. The alternative would not be desirable: agency executives directing agencies according to their own beliefs and values, which might differ significantly from the profession's commitment to vulnerable clients. Social work administrators' increasing involvement in policy development places them in an ideal position to promote programs that effectively incorporate social work values and ethical standards.

In terms of Dr. Gummer's last argument, I concur that agency executives need to have political skills to survive in the social welfare arena. I would be concerned, however, if they were only guided by a political agenda without regard to a social work value system as delineated in the NASW Code of Ethics.

References

Kutchins, H. (1991). The fiduciary relationship: The legal basis for social workers' responsibility to clients. *Social Work, 36*(2), 106–113.

Lewis, H. (1972). Morality and the politics of practice. *Social Casework, 53*(7), 404–417.

Are Professional Helpers Obligated to Talk to a Colleague about His or Her Unethical Behavior and, If That Is Ineffective, Report the Matter to Peers or a Higher Authority?

EDITOR'S NOTE: The revised edition of the NASW Code of Ethics (1995) calls on social workers to talk to a colleague about his or her unethical behavior and, if that is not effective, to take further steps. At first glance it may seem difficult to forward an argument for not following this advice. However, as the debate that follows indicates, such a position can be argued.

Frederic G. Reamer, Ph.D., is professor in the School of Social Work, Rhode Island College. His areas of interest include mental health and health care, criminal justice, and professional ethics. He is the author of numerous publications on social work ethics, including *Social Work Values and Ethics, Ethical Dilemmas in Social Service,* and *Social Work Malpractice and Liability,* all published by Columbia University Press. In 1994 to 1996 Reamer chaired the NASW Code of Ethics Revision Committee.

Max Siporin argues NO. He is Professor Emeritus, State University of New York at Albany, and currently resides in McAllen, Texas. He has published extensively on aspects of clinical social work and on social work moral/ethical philosophy. He is at work on a book concerning the aesthetics of social work practice.

YES

FREDERIC G. REAMER

First let me offer a glib answer to this question: Of course. Of course a social worker has an obligation to talk with a colleague about his or her unethical behavior and, if a reasonable resolution of the problem is not forthcoming, an obligation to move on to the next step (for example., reporting the matter to supervisors, the state licensing board, NASW Committee on Inquiry). After all, self-regulation is one of the well-accepted attributes of a profession. If social workers are not willing to approach colleagues about their misconduct and do what is necessary to confront unethical behavior, serious and legitimate questions could be raised about social work's status as a profession.

This message is reinforced by two explicit principles in the NASW Code of Ethics: "The social worker who has direct knowledge of a social work colleague's impairment due to personal problems, psychosocial distress, substance abuse, or mental health difficulties should consult with that colleague and assist the colleague to take remedial action." and "The social worker should take action through appropriate channels against unethical conduct by any other member of the profession."

But this sounds too easy. Life is much more complicated than this. For one thing, one might ask whether this is much ado about nothing, or about little. If only this were so. In fact, the number of ethics complaints and malpractice claims filed against social workers has generally increased over the years (Reamer, 1994, 1995).

Some of the ethics complaints involve fairly straightforward allegations of unethical behavior: for example, violation of a client's right to confidentiality; breaching a contract for service; or failure to obtain informed consent. In many instances, however, ethics complaints are coupled with allegations and evidence of practitioner impairment. Examples of this impairment, which often leads to unethical behavior, substandard care, and harm to clients, include mental health problems, severe burnout, and substance abuse. Although there are no precise estimates of the magnitude of social worker impairment, the problem is severe enough that in 1987 NASW published the *Impaired Social Worker Program Resource Book,* the introduction to which states:

Social workers, like other professionals, have within their ranks those who, because of substance abuse, chemical dependency, mental illness or stress, are unable to function effectively in their jobs. These are the impaired social workers.... The problem of impairment is compounded by the fact that the professionals who suffer from the effects of mental illness, stress or substance abuse are like anyone else; they are often the worst judges of their behavior, the last to recognize their problems and the least motivated to seek help. Not only are they able to hide or avoid confronting their behavior, they are often abetted by colleagues who find it difficult to accept that a professional could let his or her problem get out of hand. (p. 6)

Let us consider several real-life examples of social workers who have engaged in unethical behavior or who are impaired (identifying information has been altered).

Situation 1. Allan Smith, MSW, was a social worker in private practice. His client, Mary Jones, sought counseling from Mr. Smith to address some issues in her life. Ms. Jones told Mr. Smith that her marriage was strained and that she was feeling "depressed." Mr. Smith met with Ms. Jones once each week for 14 weeks. Toward the end of their professional–client relationship, Mr. Smith told Ms. Jones that he was attracted to her. Ms. Jones said that she was "flattered" and that she too was feeling "very close" to Mr. Smith. Mr. Smith told Ms. Jones that he thought it would help Ms. Jones's flagging self-esteem if they were to become involved sexually. "I want you to know how desirable and appealing you really are," Mr. Smith told Ms. Jones. The couple then began a sexual relationship that lasted two months. At that point, Ms. Jones began to feel very guilty and terminated both the personal and the professional relationship. Ms. Jones sought out a new social worker, Ms. Grey, and told Ms. Grey about her sexual relationship with Mr. Smith.

Situation 2. Rachel Barnes, BSW, was a child care worker in a residential program for adolescents with severe behavior problems. Ms. Barnes' primary responsibility was to supervise one of the program's units between 9:00 A.M. and 4:00 P.M. Ms. Barnes also provided informal counseling to residents and facilitated a discussion group twice each week. One day, one of Ms. Barnes's colleagues, Diane Milner, BSW, noticed that Ms. Barnes was behaving oddly. According to Ms. Milner, Ms. Barnes was unusually curt and abrasive with the unit's residents. Over time, Ms. Barnes's behavior worsened. Ms. Milner noticed that Ms. Barnes was showing up at work with the smell of alcohol on her breath.

Situation 3. Linda Holmes, MSW, was a clinical social worker at a community mental health center. Her caseload included clients who had been diagnosed with symptoms of schizophrenia and affective disorders. Linda Holmes's good friend and colleague, Bruce Janes, MSW, discovered that Ms. Holmes was inflating the number of overtime hours she worked and the amount of her reimbursable travel expenses. Mr. Janes was aware that Ms. Holmes was having some financial problems.

These three situations, all based on actual cases, illustrate the diverse range of circumstances that can yield unethical behavior. In the first case, a social worker violated boundaries and engaged in sexual misconduct. In the second case, a social worker verbally abused clients and, it appears, abused alcohol. In the third case, a social worker submitted fraudulent time sheets and travel expense vouchers. Clearly, in each situation the social worker who was aware of her or his colleague's problem and unethical behavior had an obligation to do something about it. That is the easy part.

The hard part concerns what that "something" ought to consist of. There are various options. One option is to talk with one's colleague, make him or her aware of one's concern, and explore possible remedies (let us call this first-degree effort). Another option is to share one's concerns with a supervisor, administrator, or members of an agency's board of directors (second-degree effort). A third option—a more drastic one—is to blow the whistle more formally, that is, by disclosing one's concerns outside of the agency or practice setting, to a state licensing board, NASW Committee on Inquiry, law enforcement authorities, the media, or some other official body that is charged with some kind of regulatory or oversight function (third-degree effort).

Let me be the first to say that it is often a mistake to pull out one's whistle and blow it shrilly and publicly whenever one discovers that a colleague has engaged in any form of unethical behavior. This impulsive response can be both shortsighted and counterproductive. Rather, social workers need to be circumspect and take more measured steps if they hope to address colleagues' unethical behavior constructively. How determined and assertive one ought to be depends on the circumstances involved. For instance, situations in which a colleague has inflicted, is inflicting, or is likely to inflict serious harm on clients (as in situations 1 and 2 above) call for much more ambitious attempts to address the problem than do situations in which a colleague's behavior is unethical but is not of the sort that is severely harmful (as in situation 3 above).

What criteria should social workers use to determine the degree to which they ought to confront colleagues' unethical or problematic behavior? First and foremost, social workers should consider the extent of the risk the colleague's behavior poses or is likely to pose to third parties, such as clients, clients' family members, the social worker's agency, the public at large, and so on. Obviously, the greater the risk, the greater the degree of effort warranted to address the social worker's conduct.

Second, social workers should consider the quality of the evidence on which their risk assessment is based. Solid, incontrovertible evidence is more compelling than flimsy or circumstantial evidence.

Third, social workers should consider the likelihood that confronting one's colleague or disclosing relevant details to third parties (such as licensing bodies, NASW, or law enforcement officials) will remedy the situation and minimize the risk of harm. If there is good reason to believe that such measures will succeed in taming the colleague's behavior and resolving the problem (either through constructive confrontation, rehabilitative efforts, or disciplinary action), higher degrees of effort are warranted.

Fourth, social workers should satisfy themselves that they have pursued all reasonable intermediate options before escalating to more aggressive measures. In general, social workers should avoid the more confrontational, contentious, provocative, and public avenues whenever there is reason to believe that less severe measures will suffice. If matters can be resolved relatively quietly but effectively, all the better.

In addition to these criteria, social workers should also take a close look at their own motives for addressing their colleague's conduct. Certainly there are many situations in which social workers have only the purest of motives for confronting colleagues or reporting them to professional organizations or law enforcement authorities. In most instances, social workers behave honorably and benevolently when they decide that colleagues' unethical behavior must be addressed.

But we also have to accept the fact that in some instances social workers' efforts to address, confront, or discipline colleagues are vindictive or sinister, motivated perhaps by long-standing personal animosity, professional jealousy, or political retribution. Motives matter, and social workers should be certain to confront colleagues' unethical behavior with a clean conscience.

Having said all this, it is important to acknowledge that social workers, and professionals in general, are notoriously reluctant to confront misbehaving colleagues directly or to take more ambitious steps to address colleagues' unethical behavior. There are various reasons for this. One is that social workers who are concerned about a colleague may worry, understandably, about destroying the colleague's career or introducing strain into their personal or working relationship. In addition, social workers may be concerned about damage that such confrontation might cause to a social service agency or human service organization's internal affairs and external reputation, or to the profession's reputation.

Social workers may also be concerned about how such confrontation might affect their own careers and reputations. Sadly, there have been many instances in which even the most conscientious whistle blowers have suffered mightily because of their willingness to expose unethical behavior and wrongdoing. As VandenBos and Duthie (1986) conclude after their survey of professionals' willingness to confront colleagues' unethical behavior and impairment:

> The fact that more than half of us have not confronted distressed colleagues even when we have recognized and acknowledged (at least to ourselves) the existence of their problems is, in part, a reflection of the difficulty in achieving a balance between concerned intervention and intrusiveness. As professionals, we value our own right to practice without interference, as long as we function within the boundaries of our professional expertise, meet professional standards for the provision of services, and behave in an ethical manner. We generally consider such expectations when we consider approaching a distressed colleague. Deciding when and how our concern about the well-being of a colleague (and our

ethical obligation) supersedes his or her right to personal privacy and professional autonomy is a ticklish matter. (p. 212)

When social workers become aware of a colleague's unethical behavior or impairment and believe that some kind of action is warranted, they should discuss their concern with their colleague directly. This is not only decent and honorable; it may also be an effective way to address the problem. Eventually, however, the social worker must decide whether to encourage and permit the colleague to address the problem voluntarily or to refer the matter to a supervisor, board of directors, licensing board, NASW, the media, or law enforcement authorities. These are not easy decisions.

There is no doubt that social workers have an obligation to confront colleagues' unethical behavior. This is part of what it means to be a professional.

REFERENCES

National Association of Social Workers. (1987). *Impaired social worker program resource book.* Silver Spring, MD: Author.

Reamer, F. G. (1994). *Social work malpractice and liability.* New York: Columbia University Press.

Reamer, F. G. (1995). *Social work values and ethics.* New York: Columbia University Press.

VandenBos, G. R., & Duthie, R. F. (1986). Confronting and supporting colleagues in distress. In R. R. Kilburg, P. E. Nathan, & R. W. Thoreson (Eds.), *Professionals in distress.* Washington, DC: American Psychological Association.

Rejoinder to Professor Reamer
MAX SIPORIN

We are in agreement that we are dealing with a serious moral/ethical dilemma. Fred Reamer's argument for this proposition is a very helpful discussion of the problematic complications involved in a social worker's effort to take action regarding to a colleague's unethical behavior. Yet his qualifications—about how the social worker should respond when talking with the colleague—is ineffective. It really represents a position against the acceptance of the proposition as stated. A principle that requires consideration of qualifying factors without explicit statement that this be done is not a valid principle. It is too general. The issue about the use of a higher authority also needs to be dealt with.

Reamer states that a "determined and assertive" response "depends on the circumstances involved." He also recognizes that a resort to an "aggressive" response may be interpreted as called for in the proposition as stated and that this may be counterproductive. He therefore counsels the use of "constructive confrontation" and the use of "reasonable intermediate options." He provides a set of very useful decision "criteria," which are guidelines for assessing the situation on which to base appropriate action. These criteria relate to the questions and qualifications that we have raised about generality and the use of authority. The suggestion for self-awareness about one's own motives is a good point.

Our discussion points to the need to revise the statement of his ethical practice principle. It should be stated so as to recognize that the social worker is facing a painful ethical dilemma. Other measures have been suggested. Taken together, the suggestions that Fred Reamer and I have offered should better enable a social worker to act directly and appropriately in fulfillment of a basic professional obligation.

NO

Max Siporin

At first glance, this proposition, as an ethical practice principle, seems very reasonable. But the more one considers it, serious questions arise. Two issues here merit discussion. One is the question as to why so many cases of unethical behavior by colleagues go unreported or are not met by corrective action by one's peers. The second issue concerns the meaning and the use of such terms as "unethical" and "higher authority" in taking confrontive and remedial action. Tackling these issues can help us modify the statement of the profession's ethical principles so that they may induce more acceptance, commitment, and implementation.

Why the Inaction with Regard to Unethical Conduct by Colleagues?

There is much evidence that social workers, other professionals, and people in general are reluctant to take action with regard to unethical behavior of a fellow-worker. I recall a situation, that occurred long ago, in which a fellow social worker in a mental hygiene clinic gained much positive recognition for working successfully with men patients who were suffering from impotence. She revealed to some of her colleagues, including me, that her success involved her getting these patients to accept her masturbating them to climax and counseling them to reinforce this desired consequence. She related this without any indication that she herself was deriving sexual pleasure from these experiences. Neither I nor my fellow workers raised any question with her, nor did any of us behave ethically by reporting this obviously unethical behavior to our supervisor or the director of the clinic. Actually I felt somewhat awed by her audacity and her ability to get away with such conduct. There was a rationalizing thought that her conduct was in the patient's interest and met the patient's need. Also, at that time, little was known about how to treat male sexual impotence successfully, and she was undoubtedly successful, as reported by a number of her patients, and by a lack of their complaints. So neither I nor my fellow workers did anything to confront this colleague or take steps to halt her practice.

One faces a painful moral dilemma when confronted with the behavior of a professional colleague who is negligent, abusive, exploitive, and otherwise harmful to clients, and also harmful to himself or herself. This is a more serious dilemma than many that are inherent in the practice of social work (See, for example, Loewenberg and Dolgoff, 1992; Reamer, 1990, 1995; Rhodes, 1986). Here, there is conflict between loyalty to the colleague and to the employing agency and community. There is conflict about interfering in a person's life and a person's right to self-determination. The colleague may be a friend or someone to whom one is indebted for past helpfulness, so there is an impulse to protect this valued relationship and the colleague as a person, in conflict with the obligation to protect the colleague's clients.

In reaction to such a dilemma, people distance themselves, deny the need for action, or rationalize their lack of intervention. They may fear the reactive anger or rejection, or punitive retribution or self-defeating consequences. They may be deterred by knowledge of incidents about whistle-blowers who are punished severely for their efforts, downgraded, or fired from their jobs. It is relatively easy to take the least costly way out of resolving ethical dilemmas and do nothing, rather than take on the tasks of analysis and decision, or seek expert consultation, or refer the case to administrative or legal authority.

The Libertarian Philosophical and Political Orientation of Many Social Workers

Another factor making for noncompliance with the ethical precept for intervention in cases of unethical behavior is related to a prevalent liberal philosophical and political orientation that is characteristic of many social workers (See: Siporin, 1982, 1992). Many are drawn into the profession because social work is a calling to help people who are poor, disadvantaged, discriminated-against casualties of our economic system. They are resolved to fight and reform the "oppressive, coercive, dehumanizing" institutional systems that create such casualties. Many, as Pearson (1975, pp. 138–139) observed, are dissidents and rebels, "social bandits," and "professional saboteurs," who tend to bend and break rules on behalf of clients. They are more tolerant of deviant behavior and tend to accept such behavior, including what may be considered clinically psychotic or psychopathic, as valid instances of different lifestyles or value preferences.

We can validly attribute social worker contributory influence, during the 1960s and through the 1980s, to the general trend that developed in our society with regard to deviant behavior. This is the trend, which Moynihan (1993) pointed out, of "defining deviancy down," in declaring much deviant behavior to be normal, and also the trend to "define deviancy up," as Krauthammer (1993) explained, in which certain normal behavior is redefined as deviant. As a result of the ideology represented by these changed definitions of deviant behavior, a substantial number of social workers are not fully committed to the standards for ethical behavior required of them by the profession or by the community.

The Proposition Is Too General

What is meant by the term "unethical" becomes a matter of varying or individual definition and may be subject to dispute. The use of sexist or racist language may or may not be unethical. Is all conduct in violation of the profession's Code of Ethics unethical? Many of the ethical directives stated in the Code are very general and subject to varied interpretations. They also seem to conflict with each other in certain situations, for example, with regard to protecting client welfare, and also loyalty to colleagues. The use of consultants, ethics commitees, and reasoned ethical decision-making procedures are one way of helping with these questions about specific meaning, as Reamer (1995, pp. 75–81) helpfully suggests. Yet, there is a need to clarify and specify what is meant by the term "unethical."

Also operating is the characteristic social work preference for a situational ethical perspective, so that moral/ethical judgments are made with regard for specific situational influences and contexts. A situational ethical perspective is one that is committed to a set of basic moral/ethical values, yet is made operational with a concern for situational contextual factors. I do not mean here a relativist moral/ethical point of view, to which some social workers do subscribe. Rather, there is a habitual, pragmatic approach to understanding human behavior from a more comprehensive viewpoint that emphasizes systemic and situational contexts for motivation, emotion, interpersonal relationships, and action, and that seeks to specify the actual behavior of people interacting with others in life circumstances. This problem-person-situation perspective leads social workers characteristically to be very aware of the moral complexities inherent in may of the social functioning problems with which they are asked to help. The basic social work value of being nonjudgmental to people as persons and respecting their inherent worth is associated with a distrust of grand ethical precepts or moralistic judgments about people and their behavior.

We can grant that a systemic, situational perspective that gives consideration to the multiplicity of factors operating in human living leads generally to an empathic, compassionate, and accepting kind of understanding of behavior as well as of people. This does, however, make for exceptions and allowances for deviant behavior, which also is understood theoretically as having potentially positive functions for social progress in society. Unfortunately, such acceptance may tend to excuse personal responsibility and accountability. It also fails to consider that not being fully or partially responsible for past action does not mean that one is absolved from responsibility for action to resolve a problem and to behave differently. There follows a belief that social, economic circumstances will somehow change, and as a result, the unethically behaving person will come to his or her senses and spontaneously reform.

The Problem with "Higher Authority"

The term *higher authority* in the given proposition also needs consideration. Although authority is understood to be present in some form in every helping relationship, (as Studt, 1959, well pointed out), and much effort has been made to help social workers make a more positive and constructive use of authority in helping clients (e.g. Hutchinson, 1986, Palmer, 1983), little attention has been given to the use of authority in remediation efforts with regard to social worker behavior. There continues to be a belief that authoritative prescriptions or commands may be coercive, restrictive, overcontrolling, dominating, and have negative destructive consequences for the people involved.

Also, there is the social worker's characteristic disinclination to use interventions with clients or with others that are based on overt, official, or especially legal authority. An example is Reamer's (1995, pp. 101 and 183) suggestion in favor of therapeutic and rehabilitation approaches to deviant social worker conduct, while accepting that disciplinary action may be necessary in some cases of social worker malpractice and misconduct. As indicated above, the libertarian, reformist orientation of social workers involves an innate stance that questions almost any kind of behavioral prescription, command, or directive, including a profession's code of ethical principles, and this may become a subject for reactive questioning, objection, and even disobedience.

Related to this point of view is a misconception of the very concept of morality as being authoritarian and moralistic, so that there has been a shying away from the use of a moral/ethical terminology. This view has been reinforced by the mental health and mental illness ideology and the primacy given to values of individualistic self-determination, autonomy, and self-fulfillment. The term "higher authority" thus has a connotation of possible negative judgment; of the imposition of limitations, coercive, restriction, and punishment; and of acting against the wishes and desires of another person. Its use should be avoided.

Some Suggestions

With a recognition of the influence of these factors that make for noncompliance to our given ethical principle, we can suggest some revisions. Unethical behavior needs to be defined more specifically as evidently or imminently harmful to the well-being of clients or others. The current efforts to help social work practitioners and students with the ethical dilemmas involved in practice need to be strengthened. Some means need to be developed to recognize and reward the action of a social worker who does well in following this principle.

The NASW Code of Ethics makes a helpful statement that disciplinary action should be taken with maximum provision for safeguarding the social worker's rights. It should also indicate that action on code violations are for the purposes of adjudication, consultation, and appropriate resolution, and that such action provides for a process of reasoned judgment and dialogue, expert consultation and advice, and the use of ethics committees.

Compliance with this principle needs to be understood as a legal and professional right and obligation to intervene. This right and obligation is part of the social contract that the individual social worker makes with the profession and with the community that licenses the practitioner to act for the common good. Such positive recognition would counteract some of the impediments to corrective action identified in this discussion and further the more effective implementation of the profession's Code of Ethics.

Also important is the need to define the interventive action with regard to deviant behavior of a colleague, as a moral act, as an act of moral/ethical choice and decision. Such an act helps realize our potential as an agent and as a person, humanly responsible, and responsive to the needs of fellow members of our profession, who thereby also are helped to realize their potentials as responsible agents and persons.

REFERENCES

Hutchinson, E. D. (1986) Use of authority in direct social work practice. *Social Service Review, 61;* 681–698.

Krauthammer, C. (1993). Defining deviancy up. *The New Republic, 209*(12), 20–25.

Loewenberg, F. M., & Dolgoff, R. (1992). *Ethical decisions for social work practice* (4th ed.). Itasca, IL: E. F. Peacock.

Moynihan, D. P. (1993). Defining deviancy down. *The American Scholar, 62,* 17–30.

National Association of Social Workers. (1994). *Code of ethics.* Silver Springs, MD: National Association of Social Workers.

Palmer, S. E. (1983). Authority: An essential part of practice. *Social Work, 28,* 120–135.

Pearson, G. (1975). *The deviant imagination.* London, England: Macmillan Press.

Reamer, F. G. (1990). *Ethical dilemmas in social service* (2nd ed.). New York: Columbia University Press.

Reamer, F. G. (1995). *Social work values and ethics.* New York: Columbia University Press.

Rhodes, M. L. (1986). *Ethical dilemmas in social work practice.* London, England: Routledge & Kegan Paul.

Siporin, M. (1982). Moral philosophy in social work today. *Social Service Review, 36,* 516–538.

Siporin, M. (1992). Strengthening the Moral Mission of Social Work. In Reid, P. N. & Popple, P. R. (Eds.), *The moral purposes of social work.* Chicago: Nelson-Hall, pp. 71–99.

Studt, E. (1959). Worker-client authority relationships in social work. *Social Work, 4*(1), 18–28.

Rejoinder to Professor Siporin

FREDERIC G. REAMER

Max Siporin offers eloquent commentary on the nature of social workers' obligation to talk with colleagues about their unethical behavior. Indeed, we agree on many points. Principal among these are Siporin's claims that social workers are reluctant to take action when they discover that a colleague has misbehaved; the term "unethical" is somewhat vague and what may seem to some to be a serious breach of professional ethics may seem rather trivial to others; social workers have paid relatively little attention to the ways in which authority may be used to confront professional misconduct; and current efforts to help social workers address ethical dilemmas need to be further strengthened. So where do we differ?

Siporin devotes much of his discussion to an explanation of the reasons why social workers hesitate to take action against colleagues' unethical behavior. These include social workers' inclination to protect colleagues and relationships with them, general tolerance of "deviant" behavior, and skepticism about the validity of broadly worded ethical precepts. Fine. I have no quarrel with this very reasonable line of speculation. But I do not see how this explanation of social workers' reluctance to take action against colleagues' unethical conduct (the premise) leads to the conclusion that social workers should not take action against colleagues' unethical conduct; after all, Siporin has taken the position against social workers' obligation to talk to a colleague about his or her unethical conduct, report the matter to peers, and so on. Parenthetically, it is hard for me to imagine that Siporin would not be horrified if in the context of today's ethical standards a social worker who witnessed the incident he described involving the colleague in a mental hygiene clinic—the one who had sexual contact with clients "long ago"—did not take some form of action concerning this breach of professional ethics. Norms change, and by today's standards social workers would clearly be remiss if they failed to take action in such circumstances (not to mention the liability risk they and the agency might incur by failing to address the problem).

I sense, in fact, that when all is said and done Siporin would agree that social workers do indeed have an obligation to confront unethical conduct in the way I describe, although he would insist (and I concur) that we need to be much clearer about what the term "unethical" means and where the line should be drawn between behavior that warrants collegial action or confrontation and behavior that does not. Siporin's own words seem to back up my claim:

> The NASW Code of Ethics . . . should also indicate that actions on code violations are for the purposes of adjudication, consultation, and appropriate resolution, and that such action provides for a process of reasoned judgment and dialogue, expert consultation and advice, and the use of ethics committees. Compliance with this principle needs to be understood *as a legal and professional right and obligation to intervene. This right and obligation is part of the social contract that the individual social worker makes with the profession and with the community that licenses the practitioner to act for the common good.* (emphasis added)

This is a compelling argument for social workers' obligation to take action when they discover that colleagues have engaged in some form of unethical conduct, no?

Does Professional Education Adequately Prepare Students to Resolve Ethical Problems of Practice?

EDITOR'S NOTE: Ideally, social work students would acquire key knowledge, skills, and values related to resolving ethical dilemmas during their education. Do they? Do bachelor's and master's degree programs do a good job of preparing students to resolve ethical problems of practice? If so, to what degree? Are there gaps? If so, what are they and how can we fill them? How much can be done during formal education programs compared with on-the-job learning?

Wendy Kugelman received her MSW from New York University School of Social Work in 1980. She was awarded her doctorate from Hunter College School of Social Work in 1990. She has practiced extensively in agencies and was on the faculty of University of Southern California from 1990 through 1995. Dr. Kugelman is currently engaged in private practice and agency consultation in Santa Monica, California.

Frederic G. Reamer is professor in the School of Social Work, Rhode Island College. His areas of interest include mental health and health care, criminal justice, and professional ethics. Reamer is the author of numerous publications on social work ethics, including *Social Work Values and Ethics, Ethical Dilemmas in Social Service,* and *Social Work Malpractice and Liability,* all published by Columbia University Press. In 1994 to 1996, Reamer chaired the NASW Code of Ethics Revision Committee.

YES

WENDY KUGELMAN

In considering the above question, we must first think about the role of professional education. We might agree that schools of social work prepare students to meet a complex web of social problems. Twenty years ago, Siporin (1975) described social work as:

> a social institutional method of helping people to prevent and resolve their social problems, to restore and enhance their social functioning... Social workers are professional helpers designated by society to aid people who are distressed, disadvantaged, disabled, deviant, defeated or dependent. They are also charged to help people lessen their chances of being poor, inept, neglected, abused, divorced, delinquent, criminal, alienated, or mad (p. 3–4).

Twenty years later, because of resource scarcity, the job is more complicated. Our professional roles are further inconvenienced by the ethical/moral commitments of our profession. I will borrow an argument from Richard Rorty (1986), an American philosopher, to clarify social workers' moral obligations. Rorty describes two moral tasks of liberal democracy, "agents of love and agents of justice." He states:

> ...Democracy employs and empowers both connoisseurs of diversity and guardians of universality. The former insist that there are people out there whom society has failed to notice. They make these candidates for admission visible by showing us how to explain their odd behavior in terms of coherent, if unfamiliar, set of beliefs and desires—as opposed to explaining this behavior with terms like stupidity, madness, baseness, or sin. The latter, the guardians of universality, make sure that once these people have been shepherded into the light by the connoisseurs of diversity, they are treated like everyone else. (p. 529)

Social workers function as society's moral arm. We are the agents of love and justice in our society. The point here is that social workers cannot divorce the ethical or moral aspects from the clinical aspects of our work. In our day-to-day practices, we become "connoisseurs of diversity and guardians of universality." That is what we do. Social work practitioners are always involved with ethical problems. In a discussion of social inequities, Lewis (1982) points out, "one cannot enter the stream of community life and remain dry: nor can one avoid some deflection of its flow" (p. 99). As we help society care for individuals and help individuals function within our society, we travel on moral territory.

We have to agree on a point before moving forward: After two years of full-time graduate education, students are prepared to practice competently. Educators do believe that students are being trained to deal with complicated practice problems (just sit in on any faculty meeting to find this out). My argument is simple. Ethics and clinical practice go hand in hand. If we are teaching students to fulfill the tasks outlined by Siporin—then by extension we are teaching them to be agents of love and justice—practice problems become entwined with ethical problems.

We know the following to be true. All students want a rule book to guide them in their practice decisions. We know this is true because we have all looked for and hoped for this very same book. A client steps into my office with a psychiatric disorder. He is having trouble on his job and is under terrible financial trouble. He wants to work on his marriage (and come in with his wife) but is involved in an extramarital relationship. He might be willing to stop the affair, but he does not really want to tell his wife. He also wants to work on his relationship with his children but cannot figure out how to spend time with them because he needs to work extra hours. In this brief presentation, both ethical and clinical issues are present. There are clear and present psychiatric problems that must be attended to. But what about the family? He wants to try to hold his family together Will he come apart as I try to help him hold his family together? Will he become destitute if he chooses not to work as many hours to spend time with his children? Will the cost of the treatment add further stress to this tenuous situation? I cannot separate the clinical and ethical problems in this case.

I would like to pull out my rule book and get a prescription for best helping this client. Unfortunately, I am stuck with my theories, skills, and wits. If such a rule book did exist, it would probably look something like a cookbook. It would have the ingredients, the right measurements, and baking instructions. It might even have appropriate substitutions. It would help me to decide how to focus on the ethical and clinical aspects of the case. Without this, we are forced to rely on practice principles. Students are always looking for that cookbook, the one recipe that will answer all the unanswered questions. Instead, we help them to think conceptually—to use analogies, to use principles. And if students can use this process to resolve practice problems, they can use the same process for ethical problems.

Social work educators agree we teach students a process rather then a "how-to formula." Even though we have not covered every ethnic variety and every type of social or personality problem in the curriculum, we still expect students and new social workers to be able to help a varied population. If we were teaching a "how-to formula" (from the rule book), faculty would say at the beginning of every semester, "If we have not discussed it in class, then consider yourself unprepared to help the client."

For example, a student presents a case. The case is of a poor woman from Belize. She has Tourette's syndrome and was recently diagnosed with lupus. She has three small children and no money. The county hospital has recently cut back services. Her husband, who is from San Salvador, is intermittently helpful. She has no family here. The family cat recently died of leukemia, and they have three other cats in the house. To move this student forward into action, we have to assure her (and ourselves) that we are teaching practice principles—that students learn through analogies. There is no rule book. Thus, if we are preparing students to deal with complicated practice problems, we are also preparing them to manage ethical problems.

In sum, if no rule book exists for practitioners, then no rule book exists for ethical problems. If we are teaching students to manage the "distressed, disadvantaged, disabled, deviant, defeated, or dependent," then, by extension, we must be teaching them to use practice principles. Furthermore, we must be teaching them analytical skills and how to use ethical principles. Neither practice principles or ethical principles contain formulations for the actions. Actions necessary to put principles to fruition in practice must emerge from the professional self of the practitioner and must take place in the context of the service situation.

References

Lewis, H. (1982). *The intellectual base of social work practice.* New York: Haworth Press, p. 10.

Rorty, R. (Summer, 1986). On ethnocentrism: A reply to Clifford Geertz. *Michigan Quarterly Review, 25,* 525–534.

Siporin, M. (1975). *Introduction to social work.* New York: Macmillan.

Rejoinder to Professor Kugelman   Frederic G. Reamer

I must confess that I do not know whether Kugelman has answered the question, "Does professional education adequately prepare students to resolve ethical problems in practice?" with a "yes" or a "no." What does seem clear is that Kugelman is skeptical of attempts to teach students how to address ethical dilemmas. I find this response puzzling. Consider one of Kugelman's own examples, the one concerning her client who is experiencing some sort of psychiatric difficulty, job and financial problems, marital stress, and who is involved in an extramarital affair. According to Kugelman, "in this brief presentation both ethical and clinical issues are present. . . . I cannot separate the clinical and ethical problems in this case."

I could not agree more. Clearly this case poses significant clinical challenges (the fellow's psychiatric symptoms and overwhelming stress) and ethical challenges (the moral issues raised by the extramarital affair) and, perhaps, issues of confidentiality and the social worker's duty to respect the client's right to self-determination. But, Kugelman seems to argue that one cannot teach practitioners how to handle these sorts of ethical issues because "no rule book" exists.

Frankly, I am confused. Since when does one need (or want, for that matter) a rule book to teach anything in social work? To my knowledge, no rule book exists in any of the profession's domains, whether they concern clinical work, community organizing, administration, social policy, or research and evaluation. Any seasoned educator knows that the principal goal of education is to acquaint students with key concepts and theories, and a wide variety of cognitive and practice skills, to enable them to work with a daunting range of complex situations in practice. Much of what we teach is designed to enhance students' ability to generalize to new and novel circumstances—no rule book required or supplied.

Now, I trust that Kugelman would not be comfortable assigning someone who has no clinical education to the case she presented. I gather that Kugelman would argue that it would be unwise for someone to help her client if that individual has no familiarity with concepts such as assessment, diagnosis, relationship building, intervention, termination, and evaluation. Practitioners need to have a firm grasp of core, time-honored concepts. Moreover, I suspect that Kugelman would not be surprised to learn that even the most experienced and well-educated practitioners might disagree about the best way to approach this case. These are givens in the real world. Although we cannot expect complete consensus regarding the most appropriate ways to intervene in clients' lives— because there is no "rule book" to generate such consensus—we do believe that there are conceptual tools and practice principles that social workers can master to help them think through systematically how best to intervene. This is what and how we teach.

Is there any reason not to extend this same framework to ethical issues encountered in practice? I cannot imagine that social workers will ever reach consensus on complicated ethical issues, no more than I expect social workers to reach consensus on complicated clinical (or any other practice) issue. What I can imagine is a profession that takes seriously its responsibility to educate students and practitioners about the ethics-related concepts, intellectual tools, and theoretical frameworks (along the lines I described in my commentary) to help them think more rigorously and deliberately about these compelling issues. Rule books are irrelevant in ethics, just as they are in all other areas of social work practice. To argue that the absence of an ethics rule book implies that social workers cannot be taught about ways to address ethical issues is to wrestle with a straw man (person). Furthermore, to argue, as Kugelman seems to, that teaching social workers to be "agents of love and justice" constitutes an adequate education related to professional ethics is akin to arguing that teaching social workers to be "compassionate and helpful" constitutes an adequate education related to clinical skills. I dare say there is much more to it.

NO

FREDERIC G. REAMER

Every social worker encounters ethical challenges throughout her or his career. They may not appear frequently in every career, but they do appear. Under what circumstances is it permissible to breach a client's right to confidentiality to protect a third party from harm? Is it appropriate to interfere with a client's right to self-determination if the client is clearly engaging in some kind of self-destructive, but not life-threatening, behavior? Should clients always be told the truth, even if the truth is likely to be hurtful? Must a mandatory reporting law concerning child abuse always be obeyed, even if doing so is likely to lead to more harm than good? How should a social work administrator allocate scarce resources, such as agency funds, so that everyone involved is treated fairly? The list goes on . . . and on.

How well equipped are social workers to deal with these sorts of ethical dilemmas that arise in practice? Not very, I am afraid. Certainly, in recent years we have made considerable progress in our attempts to educate social workers about ethical dilemmas in practice. But social work has a long way to go before we can say with confidence that all, or even most, practitioners have the skills needed to recognize ethical dilemmas when they appear, sort out the ethical issues embedded in them, and engage in rigorous conceptual analysis of competing points of view about these issues.

What evidence is there, you might ask, to back up this strong claim? First, social work's literature on social work ethics is just beginning to mature (Loewenberg and Dolgoff, 1992; Reamer, 1995). In fact, it was not until the mid 1970s—some three quarters of a century after social work's formal inauguration—that a critical mass of literature exploring ethical issues in social work began to emerge. Charles Levy's *Social Work Ethics,* published in 1976, foreshadowed a number of significant publications on social work ethics. Before this period there was a mere smattering of writings on the subject. One problem, then, is that a very substantial percentage of contemporary social workers were educated at a time when there were very few scholarly works available on ethical issues in the profession.

A second problem is that most social workers have not received much, if any, formal education on ethical issues. Only a handful of social work education programs requires students to take a full, discrete course on social work ethics. Some undergraduate and graduate programs offer an elective on the subject. Most social work education programs, however, do not offer a course—required or otherwise—on social work ethics (Black, Hartley, Whelley, & Kirk-Sharp, 1989).

That is not to say, of course, that social work students are not introduced to the subject at all throughout their formal education. Actually, I suspect that most students are, in fact, introduced to the subject in the context of required and elective courses. It is not unusual, for example, for social work practice, policy, and research courses to include a session or two or three on ethical issues. Moreover, there are compelling arguments that sprinkling this content around the curriculum, instead of force-feeding it through a required—and, perhaps, resented—course is more effective pedagogically (Reamer & Abramson, 1982). Actually, I find this argument persuasive.

The rub, however, is that what sounds appealing in principle is not being implemented very effectively throughout all, or even many, social work education programs. Although many talented and committed social work educators have taken the time to learn something about ethical dilemmas, professional ethics, and ethical theory, most know only what they were exposed to as graduate students, and, typically, that does not include the significant amount of social work ethics literature penned within the past two decades (and most of that within the past decade). As a result, most students are still receiving fairly superficial and, perhaps, outdated introductions to social work ethics, often consisting of little more than a cursory review of core social work values and some of the more common ethical issues germane to practice.

The problem is exacerbated by the fact that many, probably most, practicing social workers do not receive periodic continuing education on social work ethics, either in the form of conference presentations or in-service training. If we were to count heads, I am sure we would find that only a small portion of the profession has received any kind of in-depth introduction to the subject.

To be sure, not all of the news is bad. All social workers have received a systematic introduction to social work's core values and the NASW Code of Ethics. That is a staple of every social work education program and of much of the profession's introductory literature. Furthermore, most social workers have received at least a superficial introduction to common ethical dilemmas in the profession, perhaps in the context of a course on social work practice or in field placement. The subject of ethics is also showing up more and more in presentations at professional conferences, such as those sponsored by the National Association of Social Workers (both national and statewide conferences), the Council on Social Work Education, and various specialty organizations (for example, the National Association of Pediatric Oncology Social Workers or the National Network of Social Work Managers). In addition, the Council on Social Work Education took a major step when it included in its 1992 Curriculum Policy Statement—the document that guides curriculum content in social work education programs nationwide—the following mandate concerning the teaching of social work values and ethics:

> Programs of social work education must provide specific knowledge about social work values and their ethical implications, and must provide opportunities for students to demonstrate their application in professional practice. Students must be assisted to develop an awareness of their personal values and to clarify conflicting values and ethical dilemmas.

Beyond this, however, our efforts as a profession to educate social workers about ethics have been rather anemic. What, exactly, needs to be done to remedy the situation? With regard to content, social workers need more, much more, education than they currently get with respect to four topics. The first topic concerns social work values. I am quite willing to concede that most social workers receive an adequate introduction to traditional and core social work values, including those related to, for example, social justice, client dignity and self-determination, equality, respect for diversity, and privacy.

But values-related issues do not stop here, and social workers need to be able to deal with a variety of other challenges that pop up from time to time. One issue concerns conflicts between social workers' and their clients' values. How should a social worker deal with a client who routinely expresses racist or homophobic views? Should one challenge these views assertively; simply express one's opposing opinion in a mild-mannered fashion and move on; say to the client, "What I hear you saying is that you don't really like (fill in the blank) people."; or ignore the matter all together and pretend that the client did not make the scurrilous comment? This is a complicated phenomenon, and social workers need to confront it head on.

Another difficult values-related issue concerns the goodness of fit between the social worker's values and the values of one's employer and the social work profession itself. How should a social worker handle a situation in which his or her personal values clash with his or her agency's clearly enunciated position on an issue, such as abortion-related services? What if a social worker's values contradict a position adopted or endorsed by NASW? What if a social work student admits, with remarkable candor, that he only wants the MSW degree to be eligible for third-party payment for clinical services and has no interest whatsoever in social work's deep-seated and historic commitment to social justice issues?

The second topic concerns ethical dilemmas in practice. Within the past fifteen years or so, professionals in general, such as nurses, physicians, journalists, engineers, accountants, dentists, and police officers, have developed a much more mature grasp of the ways in which practitioners can encounter confusing and troubling conflicts among professional duties and obligations, that is, ethical dilemmas. Journalists, for example, occasionally have to choose between the public's "right to know" and someone's privacy rights, for example, when a reporter gains access to highly sensitive but confidential material concerning a prominent public official's private life. Nurses may have to choose between their obligation to "follow doctors' orders" and to promote patient well-being, in instances in which it seems that to obey a physician's order would be harmful to a patient. Accountants sometimes discover that their clients are involved in illegal activity and have to reconcile their loyalty to their clients with their duty to disclose serious wrong doing.

Not surprisingly, social workers face their own forms of ethical dilemmas. Some of these dilemmas involve direct practice, that is, the delivery of services to individuals, couples, families, and groups. They may involve choices between respecting clients' right to confidentiality and protection of a third party, or between respecting clients' right to self-determination and interfering with clients to protect them from themselves.

Other ethical dilemmas involve social policy or work with communities and organizations. For instance, a social worker employed as a community organizer may have to decide whether to side with a community group—the "client"—that wants to displace low-income residents of a particular neighborhood to allow commercial development that is likely to strengthen the community's overall economy. A social worker employed as an agency administrator may have to figure out how best to allocate scarce resources (funds) to divisions within the agency, knowing full well that even the "best" option is going to mean a significant cut in important services to vulnerable people.

Still other ethical dilemmas involve social workers' relationships with colleagues. These situations often involve painful choices between loyalty to a colleague and disclosure to a superior, a licensing board, or professional organization concerning the colleague's misconduct. Such whistle-blowing cases can present social workers with exceedingly difficult choices.

This brings us to the third topic, which involves specific concepts that can enhance social workers' ethical decision-making skills. Professional literature now abounds with various frameworks for ethical decision making. Most serious discussions begin with an introduction to key ethical concepts that are rooted in centuries-old moral philosophy theories. Among these core concepts are the distinctions between metaethics (fairly abstract discussions about the origins, nature, purposes, and validity of ethical principles and guidelines) and normative ethics (the application of ethical principles and guidelines to the analysis of actual ethical dilemmas); the concept of ethical dilemmas (conflicts among duties and obligations); and differences between deontological and teleological, or consequentialist, ethical theories. (Deontological theories are those that claim that certain actions, such as keeping promises, obeying the law, and punishing innocent people are inherently right or wrong, or right or wrong as a matter of principle, and teleological theories are those that claim that the rightness or wrongness of any particular action is determined by the goodness of its consequences. These are fundamentally different approaches to the analysis and resolution of ethical dilemmas and are usually contrasted with each other.)

These ethical decision-making frameworks also typically include a series of steps that professionals can take as they navigate through an ethical dilemma. These may involve identifying relevant ethical and values issues; identifying the individuals, groups, and organizations who are likely to be affected by the ethical decision; exploring possible courses of action and likely risks and benefits; considering relevant ethical theories, principles, and guidelines, codes of ethics, and personal values; consulting with colleagues and appropriate experts; making the decision; and monitoring and evaluating the decision.

The final topic concerns a troubling and painful aspect of social work practice: malpractice and ethical misconduct. Like many other professions, in recent years social work has experienced an increasing number of ethics complaints, malpractice claims, and lawsuits filed against practitioners. It is not clear whether the increase in complaints, claims, and lawsuits reflects an increase in actual incidence of malpractice and misconduct, or whether clients and others simply are more inclined to pursue these matters aggressively through the courts and by initiating disciplinary proceedings.

Whatever the explanation, there is no doubt that social workers are being named as respondents and defendants more often than in any other period of the profession's history. Hence, social workers need to be informed about these matters that, historically, have not been included in social work education. Social workers need to know what constitutes malpractice and negligence, and about such concepts as misfeasance, malfeasance, nonfeasance, acts of omission and commission, assumption of risk, comparative and contributory negligence, joint liability, and standards of care (Reamer, 1994). This kind of legal language can be intimidating, of course, but social workers need to understand what these terms signify. Social workers also need education about the kinds of complaints and claims being filed against practitioners alleging such activities as sexual misconduct, confidentiality breaches, undue influence, failure to protect third parties, contract violations, improper termination of services, negligent consultation and referral, defamation of character, negligent intervention, fraud, and so on.

The bottom line is that, as a profession, social work is much wiser than it used to be about the nature and magnitude of ethical issues in practice. However, although a segment of the profession has developed a firm grasp of these issues, a significant portion of the profession has not received in-depth, systematic training on the subject. Although many social workers have been introduced to the topic—in the context of their social work education, agency in-service training, or continuing education—most have received only rudimentary instruction.

To keep pace with developments in the field, social workers need to mount much more ambitious efforts to educate practitioners about professional ethics. Social work education programs, both undergraduate and graduate, need to strengthen their course offerings. Social service agencies need to include the topic on their in-service education agendas routinely. Individual practitioners need to pursue continuing education on professional ethics, and continuing education programs offered by educational institutions, social service agencies, NASW, and other professional associations need to sponsor such sessions.

When all is said and done, social work ethics is at the heart of the profession. The profession's mission is couched in ethical terms and social workers' efforts are guided ultimately by ethical considerations, commitments, and concerns. If social work is to fulfill its honorable and noble mission, its practitioners must be thoroughly acquainted with what are now widely recognized as the essential components of social work ethics.

REFERENCES

Black, P. N., Hartley, E. K., Whelley, J., & Kirk-Sharp, C. (1989). Ethics curricula: A national survey of graduate schools of social work. *Social Thought, 15*(3/4), 141–148.

Loewenberg, F. M., & Dolgoff, R. (1992). *Ethical decisions for social work practice* (4th ed.). Itasca, IL: F. E. Peacock.

Reamer, F. G. (1994). *Social work malpractice and liability.* New York: Columbia University Press.

Reamer, F. G. (1995). *Social work values and ethics.* New York: Columbia University Press.

Reamer, F. G., & Abramson, M. (1982). *The teaching of social work ethics.* Hastings-on-Hudson, NY: The Hastings Center.

Rejoinder to Professor Reamer WENDY KUGELMAN

Part of Dr. Reamer's response is logical. All professional groups must become better at teaching ethics (or any other topic). He lists four areas that need more attention: values, ethical dilemmas, ethical-decision making skills, and malpractice and ethical misconduct. It is a good list. I agree—these areas need more consideration in the literature and classroom.

However, the main point of Dr. Reamer's argument is: social workers are not trained to deal with ethical problems. We need specialized curriculum changes to be competent/ethical practitioners. If we take Dr. Reamer's argument literally, the conclusion is: social work has a history of unethical or uninformed practice. If we assume this is true, we must also assume that—as a group—we have been unable to deal with ethical problems. The field spans a century. Ethical problems have gone hand in hand with social work practice—today and during the settlement workers days. If we agree with Dr. Reamer's analysis, we must assume (and he states this) that our teachers, role models, scholars, and mentors have not adequately dealt with or helped us deal with the ethical aspects of our profession. Have we been so lost?

I must recast some of Dr. Reamer's argument. It is axiomatic that social workers and social work scholars/educators need to bolster the ethics/value component of their thinking. This does not mean that we have been practicing in a ethical vacuum. We have not been unethical or uninformed during the past one hundred years. Historically, the field was linked to the social sciences. This tie to the social sciences connected us to the study of ethics and morality. It might mean that because of the nature of contemporary problems, resource scarcity, and the need for specialization, we are (unfortunately) less involved with the social science literature and more specialized in our thinking and research. It does not mean that new practitioners, their mentors, and the mentors before them have been unable to think about social work ethics.

The real trouble with Dr. Reamer's analysis is how he has divorced us from the social science literature. He takes a separatist attitude when he says: "it was not until the mid 1970's . . . that a critical mass of literature exploring ethical issues in social work began to emerge." This leaves us having to reinvent the wheel. I do not believe that Charles Levy was reinventing the wheel. He was helping to codify centuries of thought (some of which was informed by Judeo-Christian history). If we view ourselves within the social sciences then we can come to terms with what we have not accomplished—but also with what we have accomplished.

Are Professional Practitioners Ethically Bound to Keep Abreast of the Research Literature in Their Respective Fields?

EDITOR'S NOTE: Debates about different ways of knowing are prominent. These increasingly include relativistic views suggesting that one person's truth is as good as another's. What are the implications for clients and for professionals of different views about what knowledge can be gained about our world? If one view is as good as another, why bother reading the professional literature? Or, if views presented mislead rather than inform, why bother reading? Conversely, if there is knowledge to be gained (information that helps clients attain outcomes they value), are not professionals obligated to be informed about this? Whatever side we argue, should we not apply the same reasoning to what we ourselves would want? For example, do we want our own physicians to be "abreast of the research literature" related to a serious medical problem of our own?

Cheryl Richey, DSW, argues YES. She is Professor, School of Social Work, University of Washington, where she teaches graduate courses in direct practice and research. Topics of recent articles include social support characteristics among nonclinical African American and Filipino-American parents, effectiveness of respite care in reducing caregiver burden, effectiveness of social-support skill training with multiproblem families at risk for child maltreatment, and developing and implementing a group skill training intervention to reduce HIV/AIDS risk among adolescents in detention. Current interests include participating in collaborative projects with Professor Sohng and others in the School's Multicultural Research Group.

Sung Sil Lee Sohng is Assistant Professor, School of Social Work, University of Washington, where she teaches cultural diversity and social justice, participatory action research, and social work practice with families and groups. Her recent publications deal with supported housing for the mentally ill elderly, research as a tool for empowerment, and practical approaches to conducting and using research for school social workers.

YES

CHERYL RICHEY

The NASW Code of Ethics states that part of the social worker's *ethical* responsibility is fully using knowledge for professional practice. It also clearly states that the knowledge base for professional practice comes from both research knowledge and practice wisdom. Thus, the Code posits that ethical professionals do not rely solely on their own perceptions of clients, situations, or solutions, but also take steps to learn about the body of research germane to their practice and profession. In committing ourselves to the status of professionals, we pledge to honor high standards of conduct. This includes taking the time to read and reflect on what is known, what is not known, and what needs to be known in relevant fields of practice.

The Research Literature

The research literature reflects what other professional social workers view as relevant for advancing practice knowledge. It includes individual case studies, surveys by questionnaire or interview, historical studies of published and unpublished documents, analyses of social policies, intervention outcome studies, ethnographies of a particular group or community, and meta-analyses of a cluster of studies. A research-based approach requires evidence for a particular position. Scholarship goes beyond expositions of personal opinions, evocative testimonials, propaganda, and marketing claims based on clinical intuition or political expediency. It is systematized knowledge that is critically amassed. Scholarship requires a careful account of events that may involve both qualitative and quantitative description, a thorough analysis of confirming and disconfirming evidence, the integration and interpretation of available knowledge, and acknowledgment of possible limitations of what is known.

The research-based literature allows for and even promotes public or peer surveillance. The peer-review process practiced by most professional journals requires that papers be critically reviewed by other experts in the field who are blind to the identity of the author. The anonymous peer-review process provides some quality control of what is published because reviewers recommend publication based on the quality and relevance of a paper, not on the reputation of the author.

Benefits for Practitioners

The issues addressed by researchers can provide valuable information to practitioners at all levels of practice. For example, by reviewing scholarly work that documents barriers to service access, the needs of high-risk groups, typical stress reactions and coping patterns, client feedback on specific program components, and recommended program and policy changes, social workers can make more informed case-specific decisions, as well as better program decisions and resource allocations.

Also valuable for practice are reports of the steps of the research process. For example, articles that describe what is known about a problem and what more needs to be known can provide a useful summary of current knowledge to social workers practicing in a particular field. Also informative for practice are articles reporting: (1) the characteristics of specific client groups or subpopulations that serve as study participants; (2) the relative success of various outreach or recruitment strategies with high-risk individuals who agreed or declined to participate in the research; (3) how innovative programs were developed and implemented in partnership with community agencies; (4) the differential reactions of clients to an intervention based on such characteristics as client age, ethnicity, social class, gender, or family support levels; and (5) the relative merits of measurement instruments or assessment procedures that were developed or modified for a particular project.

Studies that report client reactions to services communicate viewpoints of consumers that might not otherwise be directly accessible to the practitioner. Clients are often reluctant to provide direct negative feedback to individual service providers for fear of offending them. Without explicit safeguards, subtle or overt pressure to give a certain kind of feedback likely promotes polite if not positive appraisals by clients of services rendered even when this is not the case.

Another important aspect of scholarship is that it is cumulative. Few studies could stand alone as the foundation for knowledge in a particular area of practice. Most academic researchers come to realize early in their careers that few studies ever produce the definitive answer or the paradigm-shifting discovery that forever changes the course of practice. More likely, each discrete research endeavor is like a pebble tossed on the road that alone is hardly noticeable, except as a little bump. But, when more and more pebbles are strewn in a general area or deliberately piled up in a single mound, the effects become noticeable, worthy of comment or concern, and possibly a detour or new arterial.

Therefore, when professional social workers are encouraged to keep abreast of the research literature, in truth, there is a body of emerging knowledge that the practitioner must access. Because it identifies what has been done, what is being done, and what should be done, it is growing and dynamic. The knowledge base presents, sometimes in deliberate and connected ways, sometimes in haphazard and unconnected ways, the thinking, discoveries, successes, and mistakes of our foremothers and forefathers, our colleagues, and yes, our adversaries. Therefore, to ignore the research literature is like ignoring the sage advice, musings, and debates of our elders and our contemporaries—those who have passed by or are passing by tossing pebbles as they go. As professional social workers, we are ethically bound to join with and learn from this legacy and developing dialogue. It documents what we have tried, what has been important to us, what has been successful, what has failed, what we disagree about, and what still needs to be discovered.

Keeping up with the professional literature reduces insularity. Insularity from the main conduits of scholarly work in the field can promote stereotypic or automatic responding and decision making; a mindless, rigid, or overconfident approach to practice; intolerance for alternative viewpoints and solutions; and burnout in the form of hopelessness and exasperation when one's personal well of knowledge runs dry. Without a continual feed on research literature, professional decision making is done in a closed system that simply recycles and reconfirms personal biases, preferences, and traditional ways of doing business.

Getting Beyond Personal Experience

If social workers draw exclusively on their own personal experiences, or on the experience of clients, colleagues, or "experts," service decisions are no longer individualized. Important social class differences and ethnic and cultural factors including family role expectations and religious prescriptions may make generalizing from one's own experience or subjective knowledge to those of clients very hazardous.

Although a practitioner's own experience with a problem can enhance empathy with a client facing a similar situation, the social worker will be better able to serve each client individually if he or she has taken the time to review and reflect on what is known about the problem and the solutions that have been tried. In most cases, professional decision making is like a "recipe" that combines parts of many information sources in various combinations, depending on the particular circumstances. For instance, a typical formula might be, combine and mix: 1 part published research findings; 1 part consultation with supervisor or other expert/informant; 1 part client input, including client perceptions of problems, goals, and solutions; 1 part practitioner deliberation based on practice experience/ wisdom and agency/case realities.

In addition to reducing insularity, accessing data from samples larger than one's own practice, host agency, or community enables professionals to catch a glimpse of the bigger picture of social phenomena. For instance, studies that present data on incident rates (e.g., hate crimes against sexual, religious, and racial minorities), or numbers of people who are or are not able to access services (e.g., number of homeless individuals turned away from shelters, number of abused women securing or not securing shelter), provide powerful information that can be used by social workers in their roles as advocates, program managers and planners, and policy makers. Few funders would likely grant support for innovative or expanded (or even continued) services if data were not presented that supported their critical need.

Information about the bigger picture also allows the direct service practitioner to put into perspective the experiences of individual clients and their families (e.g., the nature and magnitude of people's reactions to traumatic events; incidence of caregiver burden among family members of the elderly; unemployment statistics and rates of substance abuse or domestic violence).

Keeping up with the published literature in other disciplines related to one's field of practice also offers glimpses of the bigger picture by providing alternative explanations for and solutions to social problems. Access to perspectives outside of social work can stimulate one's thinking about ways of looking at people in their environments, and support creative approaches that break out of familiar mindsets. Computer-assisted searches of on-line databases can produce expansive surveys of published and unpublished literature in many disciplines.

A strong case can also be made for keeping up with the research literature on diverse populations and problems that are outside of the experience of the practitioner. For example, with the changing demographics of most U.S. cities, few can claim to have personal knowledge of individuals who differ from ourselves on such factors as ethnicity, culture, linguistics, religion, sexual orientation, physical ability, age, social class, and gender. Keeping abreast of the literature in social work and related fields provides another avenue for becoming acquainted with the experiences of diverse groups.

The recent emergence of many new social work journals that address specific populations, problem areas, or specialized areas of practice gives testimony to the growing demand by professionals for new practice knowledge. Many of these journals (e.g., *Affilia: Journal of Women and Social Work; Journal of Multicultural Social Work; Journal of Gay & Lesbian Social Services;* and the *Journal of HIV/AIDS Prevention & Education for Adolescents & Children*) publish research-based articles that present innovative approaches to the design, evaluation, and delivery of social services; papers that provide reviews of the research literature; and discussions connecting research with theory and policy.

Meta-analyses of a number of studies about a particular issue provide important information about how consumers view their service needs or have responded to particular intervention elements or programs. For example, meta-analyses of dozens of studies, which often represent hundreds of clients, have reported what appear to be consistently effective interventions for children and adolescents in outpatient psychotherapy, and for chronically mentally ill adults in inpatient and outpatient mental health settings. Although direct generalization from a synthesis of various studies to one's own practice is challenging, to turn away from findings that reflect the feedback of hundreds of clients seems not only unprofessional, but particularly irresponsible, reckless, even arrogant.

Finally, keeping abreast of the research literature helps professionals to avoid ineffective or harmful practices. For example, current research now debunks the widespread notion of several decades ago that families, particularly mothers, were to blame for schizophrenia. Past authorities characterized the mothers of schizophrenic individuals as cold and overcontrolling, or communicating mixed messages that resulted in double-bind situations. These beliefs resulted in families being viewed as dysfunctional and dangerous, which promoted an adversarial worker–family relationship. Vilifying parents also resulted in additional guilt, remorse, and pain for family members who were already coping with a child's illness. Recent research now suggests that biological factors, not bad parents, contribute to the onset of schizophrenia. Blaming parents for causing schizophrenia only exacerbates family stress and emotional conflict. Thus, by not keeping abreast of knowledge developments, social workers could continue to make decisions that result in useless or harmful services.

Conclusion

This essay began by referring to the NASW Code of Ethics, so I conclude by returning to it. The Code of Ethics, Section II-F, states: *The social worker's primary responsibility is to clients.* With this ethical standard in mind, social workers who choose to disregard new information based on research that may challenge established beliefs seem particularly unethical because their disregard may have direct negative consequences for their clients, whom they are suppose to be serving with *devotion, loyalty, determination, and the maximum application of professional skill and competence.*

Rejoinder to Professor Richey
SUNG SIL LEE SOHNG

I appreciate the thoughtful and convincing arguments made by Dr. Richey. I find myself agreeing with her on many points, especially in areas where she emphasized the role of research as a vital source for practitioners to critically reflect on "personal biases, preferences, and traditional ways of doing business"; to consider alternative ways of knowing the world and the human condition; and to expand their practice perspectives. However, there are some areas where I hold contrasting views, and I will briefly comment on them.

Knowledge as Process

Although we need to understand what others have said and done before us, scholarship envisioned in the notion of interactive and critical knowledge involves more than "the process of piling pebbles on the road." This perspective reifies the social and historical conditions in which scholarship is produced and reproduced. Constructing interactive and critical knowledge emerges more as breaks and ruptures than as a cumulative development. Scholarship in this reconstructed sense denies the objective status of knowledge and concerns itself with a process that informs knowledge.

Knowledge development is a dynamic process, involving a continual process of reconceptualization. The work is never done. It is not another pebble on the road, but itself part of the continual process of "re-visioning." That is, an act of looking back, of seeing with fresh eyes, of entering an old text from a new critical direction, and finally of sighting possibilities and thus helping to bring about what is not yet visible, a new ordering of human relations.

Poverty of the Dichotomies between Objective and Subjective

Conventional ways of talking about published research scholarship as "blind, peer-reviewed," and thus objective and accurate, provide little understanding of the underlying matrix of assumptions, dispositions, questions, and procedures that constitute the production of knowledge. Challenges to the notion of "objective" scholarship have come from many quarters, largely on the grounds that it is conducted by people, and people cannot divorce themselves from their social environments. To those who believe that individuals may be biased but multiple "reviewers" may not be in the aggregate, it must be pointed out that Kuhn's (1970) work became so salient because his thesis was that all the scientists in a particular field at a particular time may share the same set of fallacious and unacknowledged assumptions that enter into their evaluations of the scholarship. Feminist scholarship has made us aware of sexism, classism, and racism in social science knowledge. All researchers construct their object of inquiry out of the materials their culture provides, and social values, struggles, and interests play a central role in this ideologically and historically embedded project that we call scholarship. The separation of objective and subjective into opposing poles is misleading, obscuring, and often mystifying to such research practice.

Instead of "objective/subjective dualism," feminist standpoint theory may help us grapple with the complexity of the interrelation of objectivity and subjectivity. Standpoints involve a critical consciousness on two levels: a person's location in the social structure and that location's relationship to the person's lived experience (Collins, 1990; Hartsock, 1987). Standpoint theory maintains that all research must include explicit reflexivity, that is, researchers need to examine the role of their own social position as they conduct research. Researcher reflexivity is particularly consonant with social workers' commitment to professional self-awareness. Researchers need to examine critically the sources of social power in their lives and how these sources appear in their research. Their class, culture, ethnicity, gender assumptions, beliefs, and behaviors must be placed in the frame of analysis and in the research report. Ultimately such an emphasis involves a cross-checking mechanism on power relations that underlie the formation of knowledge itself. Conventional approaches to objectivity are inadequate and incapable of identifying social and cultural values and interests—biases shared by researchers as part of their culture. Such an explicit, open, honest research processes is necessary and ethical to produce a more complete and less distorted social analysis.

By deconstructing assumptions of "rigorous," "objective" knowledge, research literature becomes a much contested cultural space, a forum for surfacing what it has historically repressed. Analytically, deconstruction moves from the either/or logic of ranked binaries to the both/and logic that probes "unsaid" and "hidden." It fights our own tendencies toward imposing order and structure and encourages the ambivalence, ambiguity, and multiplicity that reflect our practice world.

Although Dr. Richey and I started from an opposing position, we converge through our shared commitment to promoting "mindful practice"—in Dr. Richey's words, "continual awareness of new information," grounded in social work values of self-determination, empowerment, and liberation.

REFERENCES

Collins, P. H. (1990). *Black feminist thought: Knowledge, consciousness, and the politics of empowerment*. London: Harper Collins.

Hartsock, N. (1987). The feminist standpoint: Developing the ground for a specifically feminist historical materialism. In S. Harding (Ed.), *Feminism and methodology* (pp. 157–180). Bloomington: Indiana University Press.

Kuhn, T. (1970). *The structure of scientific revolutions* (2nd ed.). Chicago: University of Chicago Press.

NO

Sung Sil Lee Sohng

The Consumption of Research

To consume the knowledge produced by others is the role that the marketplace assigns to the masses of a contemporary knowledge society. Most writers on this topic uncritically espouse research utilization as central to the profession and professional activities. They maintain that the vibrancy of social work as a profession is linked to the ability to generate, disseminate, and apply information based on research (Bloom, 1978; Fischer, 1976; Grasso & Epstein, 1992).

Such a stance largely ignores the sociopolitical and moral contexts where social work practice and research occur, and thus reifies a technological and instrumental view of the practice/research activity. Research that claims innovative and significant advances in social work knowledge production should be cast in a perspective of such central questions as: What models of research underlie the prevailing research literature? What procedures and rules of investigation does it justify and authorize? What kinds of knowledge are produced, by whom, and for what purpose? Are these models of research relevant and valid for social work practice? Treating research utilization as simply a technology, without consideration of its philosophical and sociopolitical dynamics, mutes the imperative for political challenge.

In this debate, I present a critical evaluation of the relationship between professional competence and research-based knowledge. I consider two issues: (1) a widening gap between research and the realities of practice and (2) an often futile quest for technical solutions to social problems that diverts attention from their structural origin. I then provide the basis for new models of knowledge and a political strategy for what we must do.

What Kind of Knowledge Does Research Literature Produce?

Over the last three decades, social work researchers have embraced the empirical/rational model of science, motivated by reformist zeal, concern for improving practice, and for legitimizing its claim to professional status in academic settings where positivism is the primary approach in the social sciences. Positivism assumes that "objective" knowledge is possible—that value-neutral observations can be made that are not affected by the wishes, hopes, expectations, category systems, and the like, of observers. This perspective recognizes only two forms of knowledge—empirical and logical—as having any claims to the status of knowledge. Emotions, intuition, practice wisdom, and one's own experience are viewed as mere "subjective" speculation, because they are verifiable neither by empirical observation nor by logical deduction. Positivism rests on the objectivist's view, the existence of the world outside the mind. This world is assumed to be lawfully ordered and deterministic in its manifestations. The major task of science is therefore to describe this order so that, once the laws of nature are known, prediction is possible. The objectivist's world view maintains that it is both possible and essential for the research to adopt a distant, noninteractive posture. Following from this are several consequences: (1) a stress on developing better techniques of measurement; (2) a move toward experimentation and laboratory sciences; (3) analytical reductionism (breaking an observed relationship down into variables); and (4) a distinction between fact and value with science dealing only with the former. Forms of practice that adhere to these rules are "scientific."

This has contributed to social work making tremendous strides in both incorporating and contributing to advances in social science empiricism. These strides can be seen in the growth of Ph.D. programs that focus on training researchers and educators, as well as in the proliferation of new journals dedicated in research. Consequently, by the 1970s, practice expertise was no longer sufficient to qualify for a social work teaching post. Instead, one needed a Ph.D. (or DSW) and a demonstrated commitment to research and publication.

The Effectiveness Debate

Another manifestation of positivism in social work research is the effectiveness debate, a twenty-year exchange, still going strong, fueled by the observation that clients seemed equally likely to deteriorate or improve after casework intervention. Today, the question, "Is casework effective?" remains unanswered and probably unanswerable. The "optimists" can point to some improvement in outcomes over time, albeit from a dismal baseline (Fischer, 1976; Reid & Hanrahan, 1982). Reid and Hanrahan (1982) take note of the evolution in social work research methodology from "researcher as evaluator" to "researcher as developer" of models. The new look in methodology—research and development, or R & D—is characterized by experiments in which developers of practice methods devise and implement experiments to test them (Rothman, 1980; Rothman & Thomas, 1994; Thomas, 1989). Thomas (1989) states that the outcomes of developmental research are "products" that are the technical means of achieving social work and social welfare objectives.

Although the logic of a positivist approach is straightforward and compelling, its uncritical application can lead to the enthronement of research and development (R & D) as substitutes for social reform. Interventions are tested and evaluated, but on a small scale, in controlled settings, on the assumption that those found promising may then be more broadly adopted. But research-based practice models is constrained by three factors. First, what works on a small scale, where investigators have greater control of the variables, may not be easily transferable to other settings. Second, the interventions often fail to address underlying structural problems or resource availability. Third, legislators and other policymakers like symbolic programs that cost little and offend few while demonstrating their concern about the issue. In this way, R & D projects may serve to "cool out" a problem, showing that something is being done. Thus, social welfare research and development became a key component in the ongoing dynamic of cyclical reform. Innovations are developed, tried on a small scale, and found to show promise in support, but fail when attempts are made to implement them more broadly. The cycle is repeated when a new innovation is introduced. Meanwhile, the problem remains, and conservatives find confirmation of their view that "nothing works."

The Schism between Expert Knowledge and Client Empowerment

Scientific theory and methods produce specialized, clearly bounded knowledge in which social workers become expert. As a privileged knowledge holder, the "expert" practitioner plays the role of adjudicator of what is "real" or "true." Clients who experience problems of living may gain valuable knowledge and insights, but their knowledge is given little weight because it is not scientific. Therefore, decisions affecting clients are shown to be based on "expert" knowledge, and any attempts by clients to counter these decisions are labeled as "uninformed," or not capable of making a "good" choice. By believing that professional knowledge is the most reliable form of knowledge, social workers inevitably consign clients to a position in which they cannot possibly determine what is best for themselves.

If this is the case, can the prevailing research literature that gives privileged status to scientific knowledge support the guiding principles of social work practice—self-determination, empowerment, and liberation? The idea of mobilizing a person's inner resources and wisdom underlies much of empowerment practice. Bertha Reynolds spoke of the value of inner wisdom and the need to stimulate clients' capacity to solve their own problems. Others underscore the power of self-determination that places the client's own knowledge of self at the center of social work practice. Attempting to assess people's capacity for action on their own behalf within the context of expert knowledge can only lead to a weak and dubious agreement about the meaning and application of self-determination and client empowerment.

Rethinking Knowledge and Methods

A growing body of literature calls not only for critical evaluation of the scientific paradigm but for use of new models of knowledge. Schon (1983) made a case for professions to reunite the concepts of knowing and doing and to consider that much of the knowledge practitioners seek resides in the action rather than preceding it. He called his approach "knowing-in-action." His central critique is that the human mind does not consist merely of an intellect driven by analysis, rationality, and logic. In many cases, practitioners know intuitively what to do or how to do it as events unfold. Knowing-in-action holds that intelligence resides within the act of using one's body and mind together to meet some challenging or changing aspect of the environment. This inner capacity for knowing is the ground from which social work knowledge must be generated. This perspective is gaining attention in the growing fields of feminist research and participatory research that emphasize the construction of interactive and critical knowledge as important sources of knowledge for the profession.

Interactive Knowledge

In living with other human beings, we come to know them in an interactive sense. This knowledge does not derive from analysis of data about other human beings but from sharing a life-world together. Although scientific knowledge requires separateness and externalization, interactive knowledge is predicated on connectedness and inclusion, the social and emotional bonds among people. This is what Gowdy (1994) describes as path with a heart or Berman (1981) as participating consciousness.

Interactive knowledge embraces physical, emotional, intellectual, social, and spiritual dimensions of knowing. It recognizes the uniqueness of individuals, the importance of relationship in human growth, and the interpersonal and subjective nature of knowledge building that is an essential aspect of social work practice. Practice wisdom, folklore, popular knowledge, or means of survival are all examples of interactive knowledge that have allowed people to survive, interpret, create, produce, and work throughout human history. Such knowledge is not valued in research literature, and its validity has been suppressed by the rational scientific method. This form of knowledge cannot be dealt with objectively, that is, scientifically; it can only be experienced.

Critical Knowledge

There is a kind of knowledge that comes from reflection and action, which makes it possible to deliberate questions of what is right and just. Although this kind of knowledge is an essential aspect of social work practice, today its pursuit is relegated as secondary to scientific analysis. This leaves issues having to do with what social goals should be pursued in an intellectual and moral vacuum. The development of critical knowledge is premised on three principles: (1) the meaningful involvement of people in addressing the concerns that affect their lives; (2) purpose of knowledge as power to ordinary people; and (3) commitment to a process of critical action and reflection. Social work history provides models of such knowledge development. The work of Jane Addams at Hull House demonstrated an understanding of research as reflection and action for social change. At the heart of social work is the fundamental interconnection of people, power, and social action. Likewise, the development of social work knowledge should promote sustained collective action in the struggles over power and resources, and generate change-oriented social work theory. Such a stance reasserts ethical choice, value, and history into the production of social work knowledge.

Conclusion: Turning the Issue Upside-Down

I have argued that the widening gap between the realities of practice and research can be traced to a flawed conception of professional competence and its relationship to rigorous professional knowledge derived from scientific and scholarly research. The question of the relationship between practice competence and research-based knowledge needs to be turned upside down. It is not that practitioners ignore the research literature; it is that they question its legitimacy. We should start, therefore, not by asking how to make better use of research-based knowledge but by asking what we can learn from a careful examination of a world of intuitive knowledge, emotional connectedness, and critical reflection—in action already embedded in competent social work practice. These are the natural resources on which to generate social work knowledge. Social work practitioners *do research every day of their work lives,* as they spontaneously engage in skillful judgment, decisions, and actions without being able to state the rules or procedures they follow. The legitimation of the role that subjective, interpersonal, ideographic, value-laden, and interpretive experience plays in knowledge building has important reparative implications for the rift between practitioners and researchers and brings the conduct of social work research into harmony with social work practice. Researchers and research publishers are ethically bound to embrace a more expansive notion of knowledge, find new ways to communicate with diverse social work communities, and join together in a new vision of the scholarly community in which researchers work *with* people rather than *on* or *for* people.

REFERENCES

Berman, M. (1981). *The reenchantment of the world.* Ithaca, NY: Cornell University Press.

Bloom, M. (1978). Challenges to the helping professions and the response of scientific practice. *Social Service Review, 52,* 593–594.

Fischer, J. (1976). *The effectiveness of social casework.* Springfield, IL: Thomas.

Gowdy, E. (1994). From technical rationality to participating consciousness. *Social Work, 39,* 362–370.

Grasso, A. J., & Epstein, I. (Eds). (1992). *Research utilization in the social services.* New York: The Haworth Press, Inc.

Reid, W., & Hanrahan, P. (1982) Recent evaluations of social work: grounds for optimism. *Social Work,* pp. 328–340.

Rothman, J. (1980). *Social R & D: Research and development in the human services.* Englewood Cliffs, NJ: Prentice-Hall.

Rothman, J., & Thomas, E. (Eds.) (1994). *Intervention research: Design and development for the human services.* New York: Haworth Press.

Schon, D. (1983). *The reflective practitioner: How professionals think in action.* New York: Basic Books.

Thomas, E. J. (1989). Advances in developmental research. *Social Service Review, 63*, 578–597.

Rejoinder to Professor Sohng CHERYL RICHEY

I wholeheartedly concur with a number of Professor Sohng's basic premises, including social work practice and research must be viewed in a sociopolitical context, research is valuable if it provides change-oriented knowledge for practice and social reform, and responsibility for building and disseminating knowledge-for-practice should be shared by all members of the profession. With these shared overarching premises in mind, I offer for the reader's consideration, the following counterpoints and challenges to Sohng's position that professional practitioners are not ethically bound to keep abreast of the research literature in their respective fields.

In addition to questioning the *research* enterprise, as advocated by Sohng, in terms of the models of knowledge production that underlie the procedures and rules of investigation, I believe we must also critically examine the models of thinking and worldviews of *all* producers and disseminators of knowledge that might influence the practice of social work with real people. This means that ongoing, critical examination of the sociopolitical and moral contexts of social work knowledge development should not be limited to researchers and their work. Social work practitioners, educators, and administrators are equally vulnerable to political challenges that their work has questionable relevancy for addressing many of society's ills that are rooted in structural inequities and require social welfare solutions applied on a grand scale.

If we are to achieve what Sohng states is the heart of social work—the fundamental interconnection of people, power, and social action—then *all* members of the profession need to work together to promote change-oriented knowledge for practice and sustained collective action. Therefore, although I agree with Sohng that researchers and the publishers (and funders) of research need to take responsibility for producing and communicating knowledge that advances effective practice with people, I do not believe that this expectation releases professional practitioners from their ethical responsibility to keep abreast of the literature. In fact, the absence of ongoing monitoring and input by practitioners as to the relevance and applicability of published research findings would only continue to enable those who are able to get their work published to shape the knowledge landscape into the twenty-first century.

If social workers are not keeping abreast of the professional literature, how will they know if and when it gets better; how will they access the new and more relevant sources of practice knowledge promoted by Sohng? It seems more likely that social workers who have shunned the research literature because they view it as irrelevant to their work will be suspect of any research-grounded knowledge, even approaches labeled "feminist" or "participatory."

To mobilize practitioners to participate in knowledge construction for their respective fields, a more useful recommendation would be that they regularly read, respond to, and challenge the professional literature. This recommendation empowers practitioners to take an active role as critical consumers of published literature vis-a-vis its relevance for practice in the real world.

As critical consumers or consumer advocates, social work practitioners could engage in a dialogue or interaction of sorts with researchers in several ways. First, practitioners could get more detailed information on specific procedures or interventions by writing directly to the author for copies of program manuals, assessment or intake protocols, and so on. Second, after receiving requested materials, practitioners could follow up with additional questions, as well as report back their positive and negative experiences with program replication. Third, practitioners could write to journal editors about articles found helpful or not helpful. This correspondence might be published as *Letters to the Editor* for the review and consideration by other readers, or it might be shared with members of the editorial board.

In conclusion, by keeping up, speaking out, and talking back, practitioners can develop and nurture better interconnections with current knowledge-development activities in their fields of interest. These interconnections can be forged by field testing innovative program materials, communicating with authors and editors about the relevance of research for practice, participating in regional and national conferences where research is shared and knowledge constructed, and networking with colleagues for professional development and collective social reform.

Is It Ethical to Presume the Competence of Runaway/ Homeless Children Who Are Seeking Care at a Runaway and Homeless Shelter?

EDITOR'S NOTE: Self-determination is a key value in social work. Essential to self-determination is making our own decisions. Under what circumstances is it ethical for social workers to remove agency from people—assume they are not competent to make their own decisions and to make decisions for them? This question is more difficult to answer when children and youth are involved. When is a child or youth competent to make his or her own decisions?

Joanne M. Remy, CSW, who together with Linda Glassman argues the YES position, received her MSW from Fordham University. She served as the Clinical and Program Director for Covenant House—Under 21/New York for several years. She has directed a National Business Education Initiative for the National Child Labor Committee. She is currently an independent consultant for youth programs in the New England area.

Linda Glassman was trained as a Marriage, Child and Family Therapist and received her Master's Degree in Clinical Community Psychology from California State University, Dominguez Hills. She has administered programs for runaway and homeless youth in New York and California. Ms. Glassman was the former chair of a statewide consortium of youth and family service providers, and of the Los Angeles County Delinquency Prevention Association. She is currently Executive Director of the Corporation for AIDS Research, Education, and Services.

Karen M. Staller, J.D., M.Phil., argues the NO position. Currently a doctoral candidate at Columbia University School of Social Work, she headed the Legal Department of Covenant House—Under 21/New York and has been a consultant for a number of youth programs in New York City.

Stuart A. Kirk, DSW, who joins in the NO case, is the Ralph and Marjorie Crump Professor of Social Welfare at the University of California, Los Angeles. He has published on deinstitutionalization, research utilization, and mental health. He is co-author, with Herb Kutchins, of *The Selling of DSM: The Rhetoric of Science in Psychiatry.*

YES

JOANNE M. REMY
LINDA GLASSMAN

We believe that youth who have requested services at a youth shelter should be presumed competent to make decisions about their own lives. We begin our arguments by exploring the circumstances that lead youth to decide to seek services at a shelter. Such youth, by the very fact that they have voluntarily sought services, have demonstrated that they have the cognitive skills necessary to understand that they are in need of assistance. Having made this initial decision without adult assistance, most young persons in shelters are certainly competent to make subsequent ones, especially with the help of social work staff.

Young people should not be denied the right to make decisions that will impact the rest of their lives merely because they have not reached a specific age. We argue that no social or child care worker, however skilled, knows enough about any client culturally, socially, emotionally, and economically to develop an appropriate plan without that client's full participation. Even if such an omniscient professional existed, there would be little likelihood of the client following a plan that the client did not help to create.

Social workers and child care staff have an opportunity and ethical obligation to assist the client in exploring the options, resources, feelings, and possible consequences of the life choices they are faced with making. This helps the young person become even better and more responsible decision makers.

Reasons Young People Decide to Seek Shelter

It is important to understand what has brought youths to the shelters in the first place. Such shelters are no longer referred to as "runaway" shelters, but rather as "runaway and homeless youth" shelters. This change in terminology reflects the fact that many of those being served, like their adult counterparts, are impoverished young persons who need assistance with basic needs. A study conducted by the National Network of Runaway and Youth Services indicated that 39 percent of the youth shelter client population came from families living below the poverty level (NNRYS, 1991).

Other young people can no longer live at home because of physical or sexual abuse, or parental alcoholism or substance abuse. They do not have the option of staying at home in a supportive family environment; by leaving home and seeking shelter, many youth are attempting to acquire more stability and support than they currently have. Seeking assistance is certainly not a sign of incompetence, but rather of cognitive and emotional maturity.

Competency and Age

Few guidelines exist to help professionals grapple with the issue of competence and age. Legally, youth as young as twelve years are permitted to decide whether they wish to be adopted or remain in foster care. Minors older than twelve years of age are assumed to have the capacity to understand the oath that witnesses take, and thus, have the ability to testify in court proceedings. Eighteen is the age that persons are considered competent to vote. Young people's rights regarding medical care change according not to their age, but to their pregnancy status. Even young adolescents are assumed to have decision-making capability in many important matters.

The NASW Code of Ethics presumes that clients are competent. This is evident in the mandate to social workers regarding client self-determination. The mandate strongly supports the notion of client responsibility for decision making, viewing clients as being in the best position to know their needs and decide on a plan that makes sense for them.

Learning to Be Competent Decision Makers

Youth who have sought care and services at runaway and homeless youth shelters have already made at least one positive decision. Unlike most who have left home, they have sought help in an appropriate environment. A study by the Research Triangle Institute of 600 youth living on the street indicated that 56 percent had not sought services from a youth shelter program. (Greene, 1995). Those who have, have demonstrated the ability to know when help was needed, the willingness to ask for it, and the resourcefulness to know where to ask for it. These represent strengths that should not be ignored, but rather, cultivated.

Anthony Maluccio (1983) proposes a model of working with clients that builds on such strengths. He discusses the need for practitioners to understand each client's competence and the multiple factors affecting it by clarifying the competence of the client system; clarifying the characteristics of the environment that influence the client's coping and adaptive patterns; and clarifying the goodness-of-fit between the client system and the environmental influences (Maluccio, 1983, p. 144). The presumption of client competence thus allows the social worker and the client to identify the strengths within the "client system," determine the obstacles that exist in the outside environment, and find a way of grappling with these obstacles in a manner that uses the client's strengths, thereby further increasing competence and problem-solving skills.

Maluccio defines the client system as abilities, skills, attitudes, and potentialities. (Maluccio, 1983, p. 145). He suggests that these can only be identified if the human service professional is looking for them; that is, if competence is presumed. Once these are identified, they must be reinforced and mobilized to support the process of change (Maluccio, 1983, p. 143). Runaway and homeless youth have skills and abilities and a wealth of life experience. What they need is guidance to further develop these competencies to create positive change.

Maluccio considers the impinging environment to be the external demands and challenges as well as resources and supports that are a part of a client's reality. (Maluccio, 1983, p. 145). These may be issues such as neighborhood violence and housing problems that represent obstacles. Examples of supports or resources might be caring family members or good health care services. The social worker cannot presume to know what these might be; the client must educate the social worker about the realities of his or her external environment. It is only through the client that one can adequately determine which environmental factors will create obstacles or represent true supports in the quest for change.

Lastly, Maluccio talks about the "goodness of fit" between the client system and the impinging environment. This is an assessment of what needs to be done. Maluccio discusses the need to assess how nutritive the environment is in relation to the client's needs. What needs to be changed to make the transaction mutually rewarding and to achieve a more adaptive fit? What new activities should be planned? (Maluccio, 1983, p. 145). These kinds of questions appropriately highlight the importance of the client's participation in formulating the goals and the case plan. The client must work with the social worker to answer these questions. If one imposes goals and objectives on youth, there can be no goodness-of-fit, and there is likely to be only resistance.

Our experience in working in youth shelters has taught us that Maluccio's model is a very practical one. We have often found ourselves working with young persons whose life experience has been so tragic that we have been awed by the very fact of their survival. We also know that the realities in which they must continue to live are ones that only they themselves can fully understand. Even with (or because of) our professional training, we recognize that we are ill equipped to make life decisions for another human being. And telling young people what to do does not work: they do not do what we tell them. We see our role as assisting young people in making their own decisions, reminding them of their inherent strengths and previous successes. We also make it clear to them that they have the ultimate responsibility for the decisions they make, and it is they who must live with the consequences.

We know that all of the decisions they make are not good ones. We do our best to be clear with young people about what we think the probable consequences of poor decisions might be, and if we determine that what they are doing is about to cause serious harm to themselves or others, we attempt to prevent them from doing it. However, just as with the adults with whom we work, we know that ultimately, our adolescent clients must take responsibility for their behavior. They can only do so if we have treated them as competent people, capable of making their own decisions.

Conclusion

Young people who seek services at youth shelters should be presumed to be competent unless, as with adults, there is some disability such as severe and chronic mental illness, developmental disability, or incapacitating substance abuse. This presumption of competence results not only in the young person's rights being recognized, but in the creation of case plans in which young persons have participated and thus are much more likely to follow. By engaging youth in making decisions about their future, social workers can teach skills that will be useful not only in the current situation, but when they encounter subsequent challenges.

Perhaps the most important reasons for presuming client competence is that most young people do their best to live up to expectations. If we expect that they are too immature or "damaged" to make competent decisions, they, most likely, will behave that way. If, however, we work as Anthony Maluccio does at identifying strengths, it is much more likely that the youth with whom we work will exhibit them. It is thus our professional responsibility to presume that our clients are competent and treat them accordingly.

REFERENCES

Greene, J. M. (1995). *Youth with runaway, throwaway, and homeless experiences: Prevalence, drug use, and other at risk behaviors.* Vol. I Final Report, February. Washington; DHHS.

Malucchio, A. N. (1983). Planned use of life experiences. In A. Rosenblatt & D. Waldfogel (Eds.) *Handbook of clinical social work* (pp. 134–159). San Francisco: Jossey-Bass Publishers.

National Network of Runaway and Youth Services. (1991). *To whom do they belong? Runaway and homeless and other youth in high-risk situations in the 1990s.* February. Washington, DC.

Rejoinder to Ms. Remy and Ms. Glassman KAREN M. STALLER
STUART A. KIRK

Remy & Glassman put forth three arguments. We examine each in turn.

Reasons Young People Decide to Seek Shelter

First, our opponents argue that an exploration of the reasons young people seek youth shelter services will lead us to conclude that these youth are making competent decisions. They identify two reasons for shelter use: escaping poverty and escaping extremely troubled home environments. The authors conclude that the act of seeking shelter, under these conditions, is a sign of "cognitive and emotional maturity."

Although we agree that children from poverty and troubled homes fill the youth shelter systems, we strongly disagree with our opponents' conclusive leap to cognitive capability. It makes little sense that children—driven to shelter systems out of poverty or abuse—are equipped as competent decision makers. It is particularly troubling that implicit in our opponents' position is a willingness to shift the burden of adulthood on poor children at young ages when more affluent families tend to prolong dependence while their children complete higher education programs.

The fact that poor children use crisis shelters is a sign that their most basic needs are not being met. Certainly, these children do not start their trek in search of professional help. If they were really seeking greater "stability and support" and exhibiting "cognitive and emotional maturity," as our opponents argue, children would turn to relatives, teachers, and friends, not to either life on the streets or the stranger–professionals they encounter at youth shelters.

Competence and Age

In their second argument, Remy & Glassman search the legal system and the NASW Code of Ethics for age guidelines to use in determining competence. They note that the presumption of minor incompetence is lifted at different ages under different circumstances. The authors conclude that youth shelter clients are competent to make decisions because "even young adolescents" are permitted to make important decisions in "other areas."

We agree that young adolescents have latitude in making some important decisions but disagree this extends to the youth shelter setting. Minors are deemed competent to make important decisions under three conditions: First, when the breadth of the decision is narrowly circumscribed; second, when the minor demonstrates an understanding of the nature of the decision and its consequences; and finally, when the ultimate assessment of competence is retained by an adult—usually a parent, doctor, or judge. We argue that for social workers to presume the competence of minor clients in youth shelters violates each of these premises.

The Runaway and Homeless Youth Act (RHYA) effectively lowers the age of adult decision making. Participation in the youth shelter program—no matter what the age of the youth is voluntary and protected from outside intrusion. This means that the child can override parental authority during their shelter stay. Social workers who presume the competence of their clients avoid the adult check that is usually in place when minors assert their independent rights in other narrowly circumscribed areas. Youth shelter social workers taking this position run the risk of becoming advocates against existing social structures, including family, school, and other supports, under the guise of client self-determination.

In addition, our opponents find support for their position in the NASW Code of Ethics. We do not. The Code is a document written for adult clients, and to the extent it applies to children, their competence is not assumed. Although the Code explicitly mandates that social workers foster maximum client self-determination, it explicitly excepts clients when "another individual has been legally authorized to act on behalf of a client." Parents are not only legally authorized but primarily charged with the care of their minor children. There is no support in the Code for social workers claiming that authority.

Learning to Be Competent Decision Makers

In their final argument, our opponents turn to the Maluccio model and assert that, to develop client decision-making skills, social workers must build on the positive decision of youth to seek shelter. We disagree with their characterization that Maluccio starts from a position of presuming client competence because the mere act of "clarifying the competence of the client system" sounds like a dubious presumption (at best) and with the applicability of the model to the shelter youth population.

Central to the Maluccio model is the notion that clinical social workers must build on a client's life experiences, which requires a "commitment to the view of human beings as striving, active organisms who are *capable of organizing their lives and developing their potentialities* as long as they have *appropriate environmental supports*" (Emphasis added) (Maluccio, 1983, p. 136). Building on life experiences necessitates both appropriate environmental supports and sufficient core material from which to develop. Youth shelter populations are so deprived in these areas as to violate the basic tenets of social justice. They cannot reach Maluccio's starting gate.

We return to Wakefield's words of warning that justice does not mean giving the client whatever is wanted; it "requires that the client be given whatever is fair in relation to the minimum level of goods that a sense of justice demands" (Wakefield, 1988, p. 208). Child clients should be treated with respect. They have the right to be taken seriously, but we continue to maintain that prematurely presuming their competence has lifelong and debilitating consequences.

REFERENCES

Maluccio, A. N. (1983). Planned use of life experiences. In A. Rosenblatt & D. Waldfogel (Ed.), *Handbook of clinical social work* (pp. 134–159). San Francisco: Jossey-Bass Publishers.

Wakefield, J. (1988), Psychotherapy, distributive justice, and social work, Part 1: Distributive justice as a conceptual framework for social work. *Social Service Review, 62,* pp. 187–210.

NO

KAREN M. STALLER
STUART A. KIRK

. . . with liberty and justice for all.

Each year, thousands of young people appear at runaway and homeless youth shelters. They share two characteristics: they are looking for a place to spend the night and doing so without the expressed permission of the adults in their lives. Their immediate care needs are easily met but the next step, to develop and execute a workable case plan, is more difficult and routinely falls onto the shoulders of the agency social worker. Should the minor be treated as competent to engage in self-directed case planning?

We argue, first, that the NASW Code of Ethics, current legal standards, and agency culture do not provide useful guidance for workers in this environment. Next we trace the relationship between the ethical principles of self-determination and competency to their professional and social value underpinnings. We argue that the crux of the debate rests in a conflict between the liberty-based principle of self-determination and the justice-based principle of competency. As a way to resolve the conflict, we apply Wakefield's conceptualization of the organizing value of the social work profession: minimal distributive justice. We conclude that presuming client competence in runaway shelters violates the basic value tenets of the profession. Therefore, we answer "no" to the question of whether social workers in runaway shelters should start from a presumption of client competence.

The Code of Ethics, Legal Standards, and Agency Culture

The NASW Code of Ethics explicitly mandates that social workers foster maximum client self-determination. The only explicit exceptions are for clients who have been "adjudged legally incompetent" or when "another individual has been legally authorized to act in behalf of a client" (NASW Code of Ethics). The application of these provisions to minors is not easy. Generally, the law presumes that children, under the age of majority, have limited capacity to make decisions about their lives. Parents are legally authorized, and primarily charged, with the care of their minor children. What happens when a minor asserts his or her independence?

The majority of states presume minors are incompetent unless there is an affirmative showing of competence in a specific limited area. For example, in New York, a minor's ability to get married requires a combination of parental and judicial consent at different threshold ages. This approach to legal competence attempts to account for individual differences in the maturation process, but provides little additional guidance for social workers in runaway shelters, where youth seek to exercise comprehensive authority. Because sheltered youth are substituting their judgment for their caretakers' judgment, the social worker is called on to evaluate the minor's competence with a degree of breadth that the legal approach generally seeks to avoid. Because neither the NASW Code nor the law provides much guidance, we turn to the nature of the agency environment.

As an organizational entity, runaway shelters possess a unique history. They have their roots in the 1960s and fill a service vacuum resulting from changes in the juvenile justice system. During the 1960s, youth of the counterculture congregated in cities such as New York and San Francisco. Their immediate shelter needs were met by "crash pads," which were unlicensed facilities run by sympathetic adults. In general, the shelters favored the autonomy of youth and fostered a rebellious attitude toward family and society.

Youth's primary contact with authority was the juvenile justice system. Judges enjoyed substantial judicial discretion in tailoring remedies, including incarceration, found to be in the "best interests" of a particular minor without distinguishing between rebellious youth and those who had committed serious offenses. So state legislatures began distinguished troublesome but noncriminal behavior, such as running away, by extracting it from juvenile delinquency statutes and creating a new category of "status offenses." In 1974, status offenses were decriminalized, thus eliminating incarceration as a judicial sanction. Juvenile courts were left with jurisdiction in three distinct categories of cases: abuse and neglect, juvenile delinquency and status offenses. The role of the state is clearly formulated in the first two categories. In status offender cases, however, judges were left with little disciplinary authority and no designated child welfare system for the referral of troubled children.

The resulting service void was filled by the crash pad shelters, which Congress legitimized in 1974 with legislation now known as the Federal Runaway and Homeless Youth Act. The Act was justified on two grounds: concern for the safety of children and an express desire to remove the problem from the hands of law enforcement officers. Legislative sanction shielded shelters from criminal charges of "custodial interference" and afforded youth a period of immunity from parental control, thereby vesting minors with autonomous authority. The legislation favors child autonomy and yet seems to delegate paternalistic responsibilities.

Social workers operating in a runaway shelter environment do so where the public interest is not clear, where there is a substantial heritage of treating youth as independent decision makers, and where the environment is heavily steeped in anti-parent and anti-establishment sentiments. Social workers must shape their role based on an understanding of the goals and values of their profession.

Professional Ethics, Social Values, and Minimal Distributive Justice

Social values, professional values, and professional ethics are distinct concepts related by common threads. Professional values represent preferences from among a list of competing social values and professional ethics serve as value guidelines for practice. Justice and liberty are core American values. Liberty is concerned primarily with individual rights; justice is concerned with the relationships of individual and social interests. The ethical principle favoring client self-determination is derived from a liberty-based social value. Clients should both be free to choose their own life plan and free from undue interference or restrictions on that choice. As a social value, justice is associated with notions of equality and fairness and concerns itself with individual or group interests in relation to others. As an ethical concern, competency is justice based because it requires evaluating individual or group ability (i.e., children, the mentally ill) against social norms. Liberty-based values justify limiting the social workers' interference, whereas justice-based values permit the social worker to take an active role negotiating between the client and the client's position in society. Therefore, the relationship between self-determination and competency is explainable, in part, as a tension between liberty and justice values.

Ethical dilemmas arise when values conflict. The question posed to social workers in runaway shelters is how to preemptively choose between justice-based competency restrictions or liberty-based rights of self-determination in their practice with minors clients. One approach to resolving value-based ethical dilemmas is to isolate a single organizing value unique to the profession and from which resolution of value conflicts should logically flow. Wakefield (1988a, 1988b) argues persuasively that "minimal distributive justice" (hereafter MDJ) is the organizing value for the social work profession. We endorse his position and further argue that it serves a crucial role in resolving value-based ethical dilemmas within the profession.

Wakefield's conceptualization of MDJ is derived from John Rawls (1971), who asserted that in a just liberal state each participant must have a meaningful opportunity to pursue his or her own life plan, which requires participants to possess a fair share of socially produced resources. Distributive justice refers to the fair allocation of those requisite resources—called primary goods (Wakefield, 1988b, p. 356; Rawls, 1971).

Central to this conceptualization of distributive justice is the notion of a "social minimum" (Wakefield, 1988b, p. 356). Distributive justice requires a safety net for the most marginal members of society. When the requisite minimal distribution of primary goods is not met, "deprivations" exist (Wakefield, 1988a, p. 205).

Social work concerns itself with providing for the basic needs of the most marginal members of society. The goal of the profession is to provide resources that "promote the abilities of autonomous persons to pursue their own distinctive visions of their lives" (Wakefield, 1988a, p. 208). Therefore, the profession's unique responsibility rests with preventing deprivation and correcting inequities that threaten the ability of persons to pursue their own life plans (Wakefield, 1988a, p. 205). Social workers function as transfer agents in areas where deprivations occur, thereby ensuring MDJ (Wakefield, 1988a, p. 205). MDJ links liberty and justice because distribution of primary goods resulting in deprivations are unjust, by definition, and consequently inhibit freedom by impeding an individual's ability to pursue his or her own life plan.

MDJ, Social Workers, and Youth Shelters

Using MDJ to analyze the conflict presented in this debate entails three steps. First, we identify primary goods in children. Next, we examine the general state of primary goods as they exist in the population of sheltered youth, and finally, we conclude that the appropriate professional role of social workers calls for them to resolve the present conflict in favor of presuming incompetence.

Rawls did not address the issue of primary goods in children, but children must have those things during childhood that will allow them to participate in the "central institutions of society" as adults (Brown, in Gaylin & Macklin, 1982, p. 214; Wakefield, 1988). Maintenance, protection, and education of children underlie the obligations of families. Maintenance includes providing essential elements of life: food, clothing, and shelter. Protection includes physical safety, emotional safety, and supervision. Education includes formal schooling and informal education. Informal education, or socialization, includes factors associated with healthy psychosocial development. Maintenance, protection, and education not only are issues of vital social interest but are important to the developmental needs of children and are crucial prerequisites for adult freedom. They constitute core primary goods specific to children.

Deprivations refer to an unequal distribution of primary goods that causes "substantial impairment in the effectiveness of the basic goal-oriented behavior of a person" (Wakefield, 1988b, p. 373). Evaluating deprivations in children not only involves asking whether deprivations exist but whether they will impinge on future autonomy. In the shelter population, deprivations in maintenance exist by definition. Minors leave home with next to nothing and have little capacity to provide for their immediate needs (Brennan, 1978). Family estrangement serves as a rough proxy for measuring maintenance deprivation, and the ever-increasing list of descriptive labels—runaways, homeless, throwaways, shoveouts, system kids, and street kids—is testimony to family estrangement.

Shelter youth have been repeatedly victimized. They have suffered from neglect and abuse—both physical and sexual (Bass, 1992; GAO, 1989; NNRYS, 1991). Runaway behavior is correlated with unsafe activities, including survival sex, drug dealing, drug and alcohol dependency, as well as medical problems, including HIV infection, and mental health problems, including extreme depression (Bass, 1992; Rotheram-Borus & Koopman, 1991; Stricof, Kennedy, Nattell, Weisfuse, & Novick, 1991).

Shelter youth have serious problems with both formal and informal education. Almost half have had "trouble with school" or have dropped out, been expelled, or suspended (Bass, 1992; GAO, 1989). Abandoning formal education results in the youth's premature disaffiliation from one of the primary institutions of socialization and lowers self-esteem. They exhibit compromised problem-solving and social skills, are socially isolated, and many are attached to "street life" (Janus, 1987).

In sum, shelter youth exhibit deficits in all three primary social goods—maintenance, protection, and education—that fall below social minimums and constitute deprivations. Deprivations violate the rules of social justice and seriously impinge on the future ability of this population to function as autonomous adults.

The primary mission of the social work profession is to correct the unjust distribution of primary goods. Shelter youth do not possess the minimally acceptable primary goods requisite for autonomous functioning as adults, so it is incumbent on the social workers to attempt to alter the course of deficiencies in maintenance, protection, and education. This role stands in direct conflict with the autonomous behavior that the youth are exerting. The temptation to treat them as autonomous decision makers is embedded in the legislation and the agency culture. Congress delegated responsibility for a group of unsafe and under-socialized youth to the workers in runaway shelters. Wakefield warns that justice does not always entail giving the client whatever is wanted; justice "requires that the client be given whatever is fair in relation to the minimum level of goods that a sense of justice demands" (Wakefield, 1988a, p. 208).

MDJ resolves the conflict between liberty-based self-determination and justice-based incompetence. Self-determination must be curtailed when the competence necessary to pursue one's life plan is in question. Social workers in youth shelters should presumptively favor the justice-based notion of incompetence over the liberty-based value of self-determination. To do otherwise, in the long run, allows the youth to disaffiliate from the traditional institutions of socialization; allows the child to bond with the street culture; and gives tacit approval to running away as an acceptable problem-solving strategy.

Conclusion

Social workers are charged with the difficult task of changing the self-destructive life course of these deprived youth and making liberty and justice real for them. It is easier to participate in the conspiracy that permits premature autonomy, but to do so allows self-determination to masquerade as freedom. Self-determination must be limited by recognizing client incompetence. To do otherwise not only violates the central mission of the profession, but it forsakes justice by permitting these particularly marginal minors to run away from their very freedom.

REFERENCES

Bass, D. (1992). *Helping vulnerable youth: Runaway & homeless adolescents in the United States.* Washington, DC: NASW Press.
Brennan, T. (1978). *Social psychology of runaways.* Lexington: Lexington Books.
Gaylin, W. & Macklin, R. (1982). *Who speaks for the child: The problems of proxy consent.* New York: Plenum Press.
Government Accounting Office. (December, 1989). *Homelessness: Homeless and runaway youth receiving services at federally funded shelters.* GAOL/HRD-90-45.
Janus, M. D. (1987). *Adolescent runaways: Causes and consequences.* Lexington: Lexington Books.
National Network of Runaway and Youth Services. (February, 1991). *To whom do they belong? Runaway, homeless and other youth in high-risk situations in the 1990s.* Washington, DC: Author.
Rawls, J. (1971). *A theory of justice.* Cambridge, MA: Harvard University Press.
Rotheram-Borus, M. J., & Koopman, C. (1991). Sexual risk behaviors, AIDS knowledge, and beliefs about AIDS among runaways. *American Journal of Public Health, 81,* 208–210.
Stricof, R. L., Kennedy, J. T., Nattell, T. C., Weisfuse, J. B., & Novick, L. F. (1991). HIV Seroprevalence in a facility for runaway and homeless adolescents. *American Journal of Public Health, 81* (Supp.), 50–53.
Wakefield, J. C. (1988a). Psychotherapy, distributive justice, and social work. Part 1: Distributive justice as a conceptual framework for social work. *Social Services Review, 62,* pp. 187–210.
Wakefield, J. C. (1988b). Psychotherapy, distributive justice, and social work. Part 2: Psychotherapy and the pursuit of justice. *Social Services Review, 62,* pp. 353–382.

Rejoinder to Drs. Staller and Kirk

Joanne M. Remy
Linda Glassman

Staller and Kirk rightly argue that youth coming to shelters are often seriously lacking in basic needs. However, they justify taking control away from these youth and presuming them incompetent by arguing that they are perhaps too deprived to make their own decisions. We would argue that many youth exhibit enormous strengths. Hardship, even for youth, does not necessarily result in incompetence. We have seen many youths coming from very difficult poverty and home situations who have had realistic dreams and goals for themselves and a desire to help their families.

Staller and Kirk would use control over the youths' plans to provide them with services and resources that would presumably give them a better advantage in society. Certainly, social workers have an ethical obligation to assist youth in obtaining the services they need to do so. However, making decisions and setting priorities for clients raises many practical as well as ethical questions. Will clients follow plans that are not meaningful to them? Will young people seek services from agencies that insist that they relinquish control over decision making? Should social workers have the power to impose their values and agendas on others? Are social workers able to sufficiently account for the cultural differences between themselves and their clients when developing plans for them? Will social worker control necessarily result in better plans? To all of these we would answer no.

We seriously question the notion that taking control away from youth is in some way better for them and for the society at large. Being in shelter is short term. In a relatively short period, youth will be facing the world as decision-making adults. For these adults, as well as the society at large, it is beneficial for them to have acquired skills in identifying their needs, setting priorities, identifying resources, making choices, and dealing with consequences. Not having provided them with an opportunity to develop and enhance such skills seems, at best, short-sighted.

Finally, we would argue strongly that there are inherent dangers in assuming incompetence because of deprivation. This argument justifies the notion that the right to liberty depends on personal qualities or circumstances. It justifies one person having the right to control another person until they meet certain criteria.

We understand that the intent of our opponents' argument is to provide deprived youth with basic needs and to ultimately advance their quality of life within society. However, in addition to the practical problems we have discussed, we believe that there are inherent dangers for abuse when one group of people have the ability to declare another group of people incompetent and to make decisions for them because of differences in life circumstances.

Is the Number of Social Workers in Private Practice a Measure of How Far the Profession Has Strayed From Its Historic Obligation to Serve the Poor?

Editor's Note: To many, the origins, central mission, and moral legitimacy of social work are tied to its involvement with the poor. In their minds, nothing so pollutes this vision as the growing number of social workers who turn their careers to private practice. To counteract this trend, some graduate schools, such as the one at the University of California, Berkeley, offer generous financial incentives to students who agree to work in the public sector after graduation. As one of the debaters here makes clear, however, those who endorse private practice do not concede that it represents a turn away from the poor. The other debater makes the even rarer argument that social work's commitment to the poor is not nearly as historic as almost everyone believes.

Gary Lowe, Ph.D., answers YES. He is Dean of the School of Social Work at East Carolina University. His publications are concerned with social work education and the history of the profession, as well as matters related to South Africa, where he once served as a Senior Lecturer at the University of Cape Town–South Africa.

P. Nelson Reid, Ph.D., who argues the NO position, is professor of social work in the Division of Multidisciplinary Studies at North Carolina State University. He is the co-author of *The Moral Purposes Of Social Work,* the "American Social Welfare History" entry in the Encyclopedia Of Social Work, and numerous articles in social work journals. His teaching specialities include social welfare history, social policy, and ethics.

YES

GARY LOWE

Social work's historic obsession has been with professionalization, not serving the poor, resulting in a confused, at best, sense of obligation to serve the poor. A central outcome of this historic obsession has been the emergence of the social worker as therapist/clinician in private practice rather than as individuals, or a collective, addressing questions of poverty. Even as the notion of the social worker as private practitioner gains legitimacy, however, social work continues to claim that it well serves the poor. The essence of the issue is not that the profession has experienced a 180-degree turn in its focus; instead, historical investigation shows that social work has been going down this path for a very long time.

I suspect that the average person-on-the-street, if asked to describe the job of a social worker, would respond, "Oh, they work for (the) 'welfare'." Conversely, those in therapy rarely identify their therapist as a social worker even when he or she is. So the person-on-the-street thinks social workers engage the poor in some fashion or another, and others who are social workers, or served by social workers in a therapeutic relationship, do not identify themselves as social workers or know their helpers are really social workers, rather than clinicians/therapists/psychotherapists. This is a strange and troubling paradox.

The Myth of Working "with" the Poor

Social work has constructed a powerful myth that its roots are deeply embedded in a "historic obligation to serve the poor." Admittedly, early social work and its members worked among the poor. The activity of the early reformers made them unique because they alone would actively work with these outcasts. It is important to understand the motives underlying the services rendered to the poor by early social workers and their influence on how the occupation has evolved. Our historical giants were not, in a current political sense, conservative, but they were certainly "conventional" in their attitudes toward those in need.[1] As Lubove (1973) succinctly observed, "...charity was essentially a process of character regeneration, not social reform, and involved the direct influence of successful, educated, and cultured representatives of the middle class upon the dependent individual or family" (p. 12). Therefore, "It was unlikely that Miss Richmond's colleagues, the agents and visitors of the charity organization societies, would be stampeded into drastic social action. Their focus upon the individual case and upon the moral roots of dependency precluded any such possibility" (Lubove, p. 11).

Certainly, early founders of social work were reflections of their own times. But what is often missed by present-day social workers is that the fundamental attitude and orientation reflected in the sentiments of a Josephine Shaw Lowell or a

Mary Richmond and others set the direction of social work's development in the direction that has led to the current motif of private professional practice.

Casework and Psychology— Coincidental and Complementary

The articulation of casework as social work's nuclear skill paralleled the emergence of psychology, particularly Freudian. These two elements laid the foundation for what is now an increasingly dominant theme in social work practice: the clinician in private practice defining themselves as "psychotherapist." Furthermore, social work's virtual obsession with obtaining professional status combined with the casework/psychology development, initiating a historical process that even the Great Depression could not thwart.

On the eve of the Great Depression, social work was abandoning its still young reform tradition and clearly replacing it with a reach for professional status in all of its attribute glory: scientific base, central skill/technique, and the like. This aspect of our past is not news, or should not be news, because a number of histories have been written detailing this process of occupational self-interest (Ehrenreich, 1985; Katz, 1986; Leighninger, 1987; Lubove, 1973).

Casework as a core technique was clearly oriented to an atomistic approach to intervention, and at the time of its articulation it was also informed by an ideology of adjusting the individual to the larger environment. The culture's fascination with psychology and its hoped-for promise to aid in explaining how we behave fit nicely with the casework notion. The two elements provided an apparent hook on which to hang social work's professional quest. With the two elements well established in our history, I think a thoughtful analysis of the subsequent decisions reached by social work leaders shows an inexorable march toward the ultimate social worker role as "shrinkette."

The Social Worker as Clinician, or Is It Therapist?

The latest edition of the *Encyclopedia Of Social Work* has an extensive entry on "clinical social work" (Swenson, 1995). This entry articulates a definition of "clinical" that is so broad it manages to encompass virtually any social work activity and ultimately implies that "clinical" contains a direct individual/family therapeutic emphasis. The *Encyclopedia's* entry on "Private Practice" (Barker, 1995) notes that in a 1991 NASW survey, of 134,000 members, an estimated total of 55,000 members were involved in private practice (15,000 in primary roles/ 40,000 in some part-time role). The entry on "Poverty" (Coulton and Chow, 1995) restates the usual mantra that "Social workers were historically the predominant profession working with and on behalf of poor people . . . Today the role

of social workers with respect to poverty is not as pervasive or well defined "
(p. 1876). These entries provide some indication of the level of confusion about
the nature of just what it is we social workers actually do when we pull on our
professional galoshes.

We have an unexamined history that, if studied carefully, would reveal a
clear movement, not so much away from the poor, but toward a more desirable
goal of professional status. Our alleged "obligation" to serve the poor in the past
was tenuous at best and is even more so in the present.

Conclusion

The current political scene is filled with raucous debate and an inevitable outcome
will be some form of so-called "welfare reform." Even though NASW has lobby-
ists operating at the national level, and each state chapter has some effort directed
toward lobbying, it is still rare to have social work sitting at the public debate table,
much less in the policy room. The current debate is being framed by lawyers, public administration and management types, professional politicians, and obviously
well-organized public interest groups with strong antiwelfare ideologies.

Social work has reaped what it has sown: we have established a status-seeking
professional goal that has promoted a private practice service norm. No amount of
framing the discussion in terms of privatization, fee for service, or competition
leading to improved quality of service can change the clear movement within social work toward individualized or family therapy as a preferred mode of practice.

The issue debated here implies that there may be something amiss if indeed
private practice is taking social work away from its commitment to the poor. The
issue is not one of right or wrong, but one of understanding our roots, if you will.
By casting the issue(s) in win/lose terms we gain little insight and risk asking the
same questions over and over again.

So, my answer to the question is in the affirmative: yes, we have strayed
from serving the poor, but this is not a recent development. The significance of
my affirmative position is not to say that something is amiss in social work but to
try to understand how it has come to pass. As we all should know, it is often more
important how a question is asked or issue framed than how it is answered. My
answer has been historical, arguing that an increase in a private practice orientation is a significant factor leading social work ever further away from addressing
issues of poverty and the poor. But it is important to realize that this movement
away from the poor was not perpetrated by someone else: it is the culmination of
our own choices over a sixty-year period.

Social work has important and vital insights to offer to the enterprise of addressing human needs and dependence for the poor and the nonpoor. Being realistic, the therapist is with us and their private practice activity as well and I want
to be the one training/educating the therapist rather than some other discipline.

I still rankle at the social worker who chooses the label of "therapist" rather than identifying themselves as a social worker who does therapy (the now deceased Virginia Satir comes to mind). The important point is that, because one is social work trained and prepared, my bias leads me to believe that they are probably more complete practitioners than if they had been trained in another disciplinary setting.

NOTES

[1]Linda Gordon's (1994) recent important history, *Pitied But Not Entitled,* struggles with this "conventional" dynamic widely shared by many of our acknowledged significant professional forebearers.

REFERENCES

Barker, R. L. (1995). Private practice. In R. L. Edwards (Ed.-in-Chief), *Encyclopedia of social work* (19th ed., Vol.3, pp. 1905–1910). New York: National Association of Social Workers.

Coulton J. C. and Chow, J. (1995). Poverty. In R. L. Edwards (Ed.-in-Chief), *Encyclopedia of social work* (19th ed., Vol. 3, pp. 1867–1878). New York: National Association of Social Workers.

Ehrenreich, J. H. (1985). *The altruistic imagination: A history of social work and social policy in the United States.* Ithaca, NY: Cornell University Press.

Gordon, L. (1994). *Pitied but not entitled: Single mothers and the history of welfare.* New York: Free Press.

Katz, M. B. (1986). *In the shadow of the poorhouse: A social history of welfare in America.* New York: Basic Books.

Leighninger, L. (1987). *Social work: Search for identity.* New York: Greenwood Press.

Lubove, R. (1973). *The professional altruist: The emergence of social work as a career, 1880–1930.* New York: Atheneum.

Swenson, C. R. (1995). Clinical social work. In R. L. Edwards (Ed.-in-Chief), *Encyclopedia of social work* (19th ed., Vol. 1, pp. 502–513). New York: National Association of Social Workers.

Rejoinder to Professor Lowe
P. NELSON REID

Lowe makes a compelling case that the "historic obligation" of social work to the poor has been overstated and that the "historic obsession" has been with professionalization. Social work has fostered the "myth that it has a legitimate claim to having served the poor." This posturing, according to Lowe, is made transparent by the "true nature" of the professions original service to the poor, which is represented by J. S. Lowell and Mary Richmond, both believers in "character regeneration" as opposed to social action and consequent social reform. Lowe goes on to say that the principal model of social work practice derived from social work's early days, casework, is not only not a suitable method to attack poverty but a method that lends itself to status seeking, and "social work, then, has reaped what it has sown." Having sown casework, it reaps clinicians and "shrinkettes."

I take issue with Lowe's implication that the social work's early involvement with the poor was less than an expression of genuine commitment. He quotes Lowell and Richmond to point out that early social workers were cultural conservatives who believed that the poor could benefit from moral and character development as well as material aid. No doubt they believed it, as did most of their nineteenth-century colleagues. But they did not invent it, nor is there evidence to suggest that the motivation for their belief was professional gain. They were reflecting strong currents of social and moral thought and no doubt were strongly committed both to the rightness of their thinking and to the objects of their work, the poor.

This sort of *ad hominem* argument avoids the necessity to actually deal with the ideas of Lowell and Richmond, ideas that cannot be so casually dismissed as Lowe suggests. Indeed, I would go further and say that social work as represented by Lowell and Richmond, and later by Addams, Lathrop, the Abbotts, and others (all of whom Lowe would find more politically correct) accepted the responsibility to be the profession that would specialize in dealing with the social problems represented by the poor and dependent.

Social workers, of both the COS and Settlement variety, accepted professionalization as a desirable social strategy, and as such thought it proper to delegate the problem to a group of people trained and committed to dealing with the problem in the society's larger interest. I would say this is quite evident from social work's role in the creation of ADC in the Social Security Act and the strong insistence that discretion and casework be established as the service model as opposed to a simple economic security payment. It would be a later generation of social workers that would refuse this social responsibility and would say in essence that we do not want to work with the poor in the way the larger society expects.

The public no longer looks to social work as a solution to the problem of poverty because as a profession we said we did not have the solution and increasingly appeared to be unconcerned with the dependence and social deterioration of the poor. As the lastest round of welfare reform demonstrates, the profession is hardly on speaking terms with the ideas and ideals that are guiding social policy. This will only alienate us further from an active policy role and the realities of the poor.

Both consequences Lowe would deplore. He is surely right to point out that this commitment to the poor was never the unalloyed militant advocacy of the poor that a Piven or a Cloward or an Alinsky might find satisfying, but he is wrong to argue that social work was obsessed with professionalization to the point that it did not reflect serious thought and genuine purpose. To the contrary, I find more serious thought and purpose reflected in the writings of a Lowell or Richmond than is apparent today. The intellectual life of the profession has in recent decades been rather confined and rather left. Oddly, in so being, social work has abandoned the strategic and larger policy issues to others. What is left to us is the social service delivery role, one aspect of which is direct practice. How is this role to be carried out best? Through a consumer-focused, market-based model.

NO

P. Nelson Reid

Private practice does not represent a decline of professional commitment on the part of social work to service for the poor. To the contrary, it is a superior model of service delivery. Superior, not only in the sense of effectiveness and accountability, but in the moral sense as well and, as such, will benefit the poor as it benefits other social service consumers. It represents not a straying from historic obligation so much as a deviation from the historic form of service delivery based on paternalism and state monopoly. The increase in private practice is part of a larger transformation of the social and human services that is producing a more competitive, effective, and diverse mix of service providers. For the traditional users of social services, including those with low income, this will mean more individualized service, more concrete task-specific service, and more service choice. In addition, this transformation of social services will alter the relationship of worker and client in ways that will be to the client's benefit.

I will argue this position by making the following points: (1) the traditional public service delivery model is based on paternalism and social control; (2) the professional commitment to individual clients, as opposed to the poor as a political class, is greatest in the private practice model; (3) the "commercialization" of the social services represents an extension of consumer sovereignty, typical of services to the middle classes, to the poor; (4) the market-based private practice model breaks down ideological and political definitions that have constrained support for the social services, and brings social work as a profession into greater conformity with the dominant professional service delivery models in the United States; (5) the private practice model solves the eternal dilemma of the client–worker relationship in monopolized, state-imposed social services.

The Public Service Monopoly

Every student of social welfare has wondered why it is that certain professional services are delivered in an individual, consumer choice system and others are delivered as public services. Those delivered as individualized services, such as legal and medical services, are historically characterized by high levels of consumer choice, consumer responsibility for payment, some measure of competition (often suppressed by professional groups), some profit orientation, and largely collegial control of the service organization. The public service model involves effective monopoly provision with minimal consumer choice, public budgeting of costs, top-down determination of service needs and provision, a supervisory structure that emphasizes accountability inward and upward rather than to the client, and a reward system based on organizational conformity to rules, procedures, and supervisory satisfaction.

Social services for the poor in the United States developed as social work established itself as a profession specializing in the solution of problems of dependence and deviancy. The poor were regarded as reformable, and the profession had the knowledge and skill to engage in effective reform of both the poor and their environment (Reamer, 1992). As Ehrenreich (1985) notes, the social work profession was the social policy response to the poor for the first third of this century and the development of social services related to child welfare and Mothers' Aid established a pattern of service organization that would remain largely intact for the remainder of the century.

That model emphasized the necessity for professional and lay control of the definition of problems and the delivery of the services (Gordon, 1994). The idea that individual poor persons could select among competing available services was never seriously considered. Professional and class arrogance and paternalism, combined with a belief that the poor were best understood as a group, a captive social caste, and a commitment to public responsibility all combined to produce the inevitability of public monopoly provision.

Commitment to Client

In a private practice–based system of social service, the client comes first. This is so because whether the client pays out of pocket or has some third-party payer (insurance, government, or otherwise), the social service provider will not be paid without attracting clients to the service. In the best of circumstances, the consumer has a choice among competing providers, and those providers are treating consumers as knowledgeable and responsible and providing the information that allows an intelligent choice.

To be sure, private providers would like to establish effective monopolies and gain control over a captive share of the market. As we know from corporate history, the government is not the only source of monopoly. But whether it is railroads and tobacco early in the century, or medical care or job placement now, monopoly provision is inherently costly, inefficient, and less effective. Monopoly provision is, by definition, nonmarket; that is, consumer interests and individual choices are limited or nonexistent.

In the social services, this produces standardization of services and procedures, the categorization of consumer needs and problems, loss of sensitivity to individual consumers, and organizational patterns that serve organizational and professional interests rather than consumer interests. This may be as simple as not opening for evening hours and closing for lunch or as complicated as incorporating faddish practice models that are of great interest to sometimes bored professionals but neither have clinical research support nor fit well with the agency client base.

Studies of client satisfaction with social services show that one of the more common observations of social services users is that they feel dehumanized and boxed in by the process (Reid, 1983). In these and other ways the monopoly-like organization shows that its priority is accountability inward and upward, and not to consumers. No matter the individual commitment to clients that a social worker may have in such an organization, the character and culture of the organization will overwhelm both worker and client.

Commitment to an individual client is not to be confused with ideological commitment to the interests of groups of people, for example, the poor. When critics of privatization complain that private practice undermines concern for the poor, they seem to be mostly concerned with commitment to the poor as a social class, that is, as a political matter (Keith-Lucas, 1992). They fear that the fragmentation and individualization of social services will integrate services for the poor and nonpoor, as in the case of health services. They fear that focus on individuals will lessen the understanding of the poor as a single social caste. And they fear the dismantling of large-scale public organizations that have often been the source of effective political advocacy of the presumed interests of this unified class of poor persons.

All of these fears are well founded, but the truth is that all of this is part of a twentieth-century welfare state past and the intellectual, ideological, and organizational elements of that past are dead and dying in the United States and elsewhere. We are moving to a new paradigm, and in any case, optimum professional service to the poor and everyone else cannot be provided through state monopolies.

Commercialization of Social Services

Decentralization and commercialization of the social services has been progressing steadily in the United States for at least 25 years. It is a product of a combination of political, cultural, and economic forces, including the decline of collectivist ideology and its emphasis on state centralization, a rediscovery of the market as a social ideal, the cultural commitment to individualism, the emergence of ever-smaller interest groups in politics, including the resurgence of neighborhood politics in American cities, and the emergence of technology that allows information storage and decision making to occur at disparate sites (Gilbert & Gilbert, 1989).

Privatization is not a temporary political slogan; it is widely shared belief in the value of market allocation and "business" principles. The market is valued as a means to control production, distribution, and pricing because it is based on the individual as the primary unit and because it requires no overall planning or administration (Smith's unseen hand). The alternative is to place production, distribution, and pricing decisions in the political venue, and that sort of thing on a wide scale is discredited as leading to the economic and political collapse of eastern Europe and the no-start economies and strongman governments of the third world.

If competition is good for automobiles and soft drinks, if the market reflects accurately what individuals want and are willing to pay for, if the market keeps efficiency high and innovation in gear, then why is it not good for the social services? The logic is compelling, and in the absence of any alternative rationale that holds that social services are different and need to be centralized and produced in public organizations, then the marketization of the social services will continue.

One can make a case that education, especially at the lower age levels, is properly a social, collective responsibility because the public good depends on a certain commonality of both knowledge and experience among our citizens. We are as a nation debating this issue, but at higher levels of education and training, in regard to health services, or legal services, or housing, or child care, no one argues that these services should not be provided to individual consumers in ways that reflect individual consumer interests. If you want that, you must choose the market.

The problem in social welfare services for the poor is that the poor do not have much money, and therefore one might think it is necessary to provide them with the desired service or good in a nonmarket way. Just set up public housing or public mental health services or free child care for those below a certain income. But this has proved neither necessary nor desirable. If the problem with the poor is one of income insufficient to purchase the available service, then that can be fixed through third-party payment, like Medicaid, or through vouchers, like food stamps. In these and virtually every other case, there is no need for the state to produce the services in question. They are already being produced, probably in a reasonably efficient and effective way.

The problem is getting the poor access to the system of services and goods that have already developed in response to the needs of the nonpoor; if the poor have special needs, and if the poor as a consumer set have effective demand, then the service pattern will shift in response as providers compete to get a share of the market. The marketization of social services, perhaps ironically to some, tends then to promote social equalization by promoting the participation of the poor on an equal consumer unit basis with the nonpoor, and it renders the poor less the dependent supplicant waiting in line for the state's charity and more the rational consumer choosing among willing providers.

The Decline of Ideology

The privatization of social services tends to cut across the usual political boundaries, both in the sense of incorporating "business" principles and people into the social services (Stoesz, 1986) and in rendering the social services both less governmental and more politically neutral. The old welfare state construct, both intellectually and politically, has collapsed. The sort of hostility to capitalism that was common and popular among those involved in social welfare earlier in the century may hang on among the professorate in graduate schools of social work, but it has long since dissipated among the ordinary human service worker.

The decline of traditional labor unions and the manufacturing industries in which they rooted has fundamentally altered both our economic and political life (Himmelfarb,1991). The new paradigm is what Gilbert and Gilbert aptly refer to as "the enabling state." Such a state is not motivated by class antagonism and is less concerned with transferring wealth or income, but is more concerned with opportunity and social mobility.

The welfare state assumes a certain fixed relationship between social classes, the permanence of injustice, and the necessity to redress inequality through social policy designed to transfer resources among groups (initially classes, but more recently racial or gender groups). The enabling state focuses on individuals and finds the language and concepts of welfare statism outmoded and cumbersome. In the new paradigm, the social services concerned with individualized service becomes a primary mechanism for enabling and, because social services are no longer burdened with the ideology of welfare statism, the expansion and subsidy of consumption of such services will come from those who might earlier have been reluctant.

This distinction between the "old" welfare and the new welfare of opportunity and enabling is at the heart of the opposition to private practice in social work. It is not opposition merely to a practice form, but rather to a market-based, individualistic social order and the social policy that supports it. This is not to argue that criticism of individualism in American society is without merit in every case, only to note that the American social welfare system never embraced the European welfare state construct and now leads the way in exploring alternatives. Those of us in social work who imagine otherwise have simply not grasped an evident reality.

A social work educational system that does not recognize the importance of the current trends and does not incorporate into curricula material regarding private practice and the role of the private sector, for-profit and nonprofit, does a grave disservice to our students and future practitioners. It renders the profession less able to keep up and more inclined to cultural and political alienation.

Final Point about Social Work Relationships

Much ink has been devoted to consideration of the client worker relationship in social work. Indeed the social work process is one that can only work through an effective relationship, or so it has been believed by generations of social workers. Under what circumstances is such a worker–client relationship likely to develop? Do we want a social service system that strengthens the ability of persons to assess themselves and leads to a greater sense of self and personal responsibility? Or do we want a social service system that reflects the powerlessness and dependence of its users? I think the answer to that question is evident, and that the conclusion is that a private-practice, consumer choice, competitive construct for social services represents a positive advance toward the sort of social service system for the poor that we, and they, would like.

REFERENCES

Ehrenreich, J. H. (1985). *The altruistic imagination.* Ithaca, NY: Cornell University Press.

Gilbert, N., & Gilbert, B. (1989). *The enabling state: Modern welfare capitalism in America.* New York: Oxford University Press.

Gordon, L. (1994). *Pitied but not entitled: Single mothers and the history of welfare.* New York: Free Press.

Himmelfarb, G. (1991). *Compassion and poverty.* New York: Knopf.

Keith-Lucas, A. (1992). A Socially Sanctioned Profession? In P. N. Reid and P. R. Popple. *The moral purposes of social work.* Chicago: Nelson-Hall.

Reamer, F. G. (1992). Social work and the public good. In P. N. Reid and P. R. Popple, LOC. Cit.

Reid, P. N. & Gundlach, J. H. (1983). A scale for the measurement of consumer satisfaction in the social services. *Journal of Social Service Research, 7*(1) pp. 37–54.

Stoesz, D. (1986). Corporate welfare: The third stage of welfare in the United States. *Social Work, 31,*(4), pp. 245–249.

Rejoinder to Professor Reid

GARY LOWE

Reid argues that a privatized social welfare delivery system is superior to a traditional state-operated model. By implication, social workers in a system are enhanced professionally. Most importantly, the recipient will receive superior services. All of this is asserted with the only proof being that other professions such as medicine and law successfully deliver their services to their consumers in this way.

Buried in the literature of professions is the notion of "perceived risk." That is, physicians, and even lawyers, tend traditionally to hold positions of high status because we all get ill and we certainly live in a litigious society. So, the higher the perceived risk requiring the services of a given profession, the higher the level of status and reward bestowed on that professional activity. Simply put, physicians and lawyers traditionally hold positions of high status and usually higher-than-average financial reward because people believe they will naturally or necessarily face the risks of illness and legal questions.

Services to the poor have never been seen as germane to the survival of a society by the general "haves" of that society. In short, the perceived risk of poverty as a significant social problem or threat is not viewed as very important. Many are aware that poverty and fundamental dependence exist, but few have a sense that it will ever happen to them: the active awareness of anyone thinking they might slide from middle class comfort into poverty is stifled at a minimum, and feared at worst, but rarely entertained as something that will happen to the proverbial "me." Furthermore, given our cultural norms and myths about self-reliance, even those who flirt with edges of poverty often deny their needs for assistance both social and material. Therefore, the valuing of those perceived as serving the poor is a weak currency.

If serving the poor, and social work as the profession charged with this role, were valued as a service vital to our daily life, then Reid's position has relevance and validity. But the current "welfare reform" debate shows a low level of concern held by many toward recipients of such services. Reid's alleged improvement in welfare services through a privatized model are not as obvious and predictable as he asserts.

Reid constructs a charming position resting on notions of rationality, market-driven economics, and individual choice. It is not clear how these dimensions will actually accrue to the poor, but contained in his position is the subtext supporting my position that social work has consistently moved away from the poor, because they bring lack of status as well as low financial reward in the marketplace. When applied to persons in dependent circumstances of whatever description, the determining factor that will make Reid's view an effective approach will be the possession of resources providing the access he asserts will be enhanced through privatization.

Reid does not provide convincing proof of how private practitioners or privatized agencies will improve services to the poor and dependent. Finally, Reid actually answers the question in the affirmative if one were to take his position to its logical conclusion: private practitioners place themselves into a market environment, thus laying the groundwork for serving only those who pay, whether out-of-pocket or through some other form of third-party arrangement: the poor, whether a class or an individual, need not apply.

Is There a Strong *Ethical* Case for Disallowing or Discouraging Interracial Adoptions?

EDITOR'S NOTE: Nations that permit foreigners to adopt their children are always among the poorest facing chaotic circumstances. Even when they can do little better than warehouse these children in grim state institutions with meager budgets, these countries permit adoptions by foreigners only with great reluctance and even shame. Within the United States the poverty may not be so abject and the social scene may be much more stable, but the subject of interracial adoptions evokes feelings just as strong. This is particularly true in African American and American Indian communities, where the bulk of interracial adoptions appears to have taken place.

Raymond L. Bending, Ph.D., and Teresa C. Jones make the YES case. He is Assistant Professor at the University of Washington School of Social Work, where he teaches diversity, policy, and courses related to working in minority communities. He is currently engaged in the evaluation of the Native Initiative of the Washington State Families for Kids Initiative.

Teresa Jones is a doctoral candidate in the School of Social Work at the University of Washington and a research assistant at the school's Northwest Center for Children, Youth and Families.

Christine T. Lowery, Ph.D., is a member of the Hopi-Laguna tribes of the Southwest. She is an assistant professor at the School of Social Welfare at the University of Wisconsin–Milwaukee.

YES

RAYMOND L. BENDING
TERESA JONES

Interracial adoption is antithetical to our nation's current child welfare policies that promote family preservation. The child welfare system would not be so over-crowded with minority children if more effort were put into implementing this country's current family preservation policies. Groups that oppose interracial adoption such as the National Association of Black Social Workers, the National Indian Child Welfare Association, the Congress of American Indians, and Indian tribes argue that interracial adoption is a blatant form of race and cultural geno-cide. Opponents of interracial adoption argue further that the cultural identity of minority children is severely damaged when minority children are raised in non-minority homes (Simon, 1994). Recognizing that the need for a loving and caring home is critical for children who are lost in the foster care system, opponents of interracial adoption have taken the position that interracial adoption may be used but only as a last resort.

The strongest and most convincing arguments promoted by advocates of in-terracial adoption claim that it is the only answer for many minority children who are in foster care limbo and in need of permanent homes with loving and caring families. They maintain that these adoptable children are older mixed or minority children, often emotionally troubled or physically handicapped, and therefore need special families (Simon, 1994). Biased practitioners and policy makers ar-gue that minority families cannot meet these special needs and therefore they have to turn to white homes. Yet, we now know that when there is a commitment to culture, homes become available even for difficult-to-place children. Like early assimilation polices, this is another form of discrimination hidden under the theme of the Best Interest of the Child.

The primary purpose of our argument against interracial adoptions is to stimulate a dialogue that will persuade child welfare workers, policy makers, and others that it is important to make every effort to match children with parents of the same ethnic or racial background and to make sure that the practice of interra-cial adoption is used only as a last resort.

Ethics of Interracial Adoption

Historically, the methods used in the practice of interracial adoption in the United States have been antithetical to the social work code of ethics that supports anti-discrimination, self-determination, and the civil rights of the clients. This does not mean that interracial adoption or the adoption of minority children by white families is discriminatory in itself. What is discriminating is the practice of deny-ing minorities the right to adopt children of their own race or ethnicity because of prejudices based on racial and cultural biases. An example is the implementation of federal policies intended to assimilate Indian children into the dominant culture. Private and public child welfare agencies and the Bureau of Indian Affairs believed that Indian people were not capable of providing safe and loving environments for their children. Therefore, agencies were allowed to place many Indian children in foster or adoptive homes often located great distances from the childrens' homes, extended family members, and culture of origin.

This practice was often done without tribal or family members being party to permanency planning and judicial proceedings. In states with large populations of American Indians, 25 to 30 percent of Indian children were separated from families and placed in non-Indian settings (Byler, 1977). Other minority groups in the United States have also suffered at the hands of the dominant culture. African Americans have a history of being powerless and vulnerable to the demands of a white society that has been making decisions for placing black children (Swanson & Brown, 1980). With a history of poor treatment by public systems, people of color rarely approached formal agencies. When families of color did not come to child welfare agencies asking to be adoptive and foster families, the agency practitioners and administrators concluded that minority homes were not available. Until recently, there were few outreach efforts. Such efforts still are not common. Recruitment efforts more often are directed toward white families and communities.

Effects of Interracial Adoption

Arguments on the effects of interracial adoption of minority children can be placed on a continuum. At one end, supporters of interracial adoption maintain there are no negatives. On the other end, opponents maintain that interracial adoption does have negative effects on minority children. To confuse this complex debate even more, literature on the effects of interracial adoption also have produced varying results (Zuniga, 1991). For example, Simon and Alstein's (1981) research on interracial adoption found no significant difference on measures of self-esteem between interracial adopted children and children who had been adopted within their own race. Conversely, McRoy and Zurcher (1983) maintain that the development of an unambiguous positive racial identity is a problem for interracial adopted children. In another study done by Feigelman & Silverman (1983), a larger proportion of black children adopted by white parents (31 percent) had higher maladjustment scores than white children adopted by white parents (2 percent).

Findings that interracial adoption has no negative affects must be questioned, because most of these studies were done by interviewing the adoptive parents during the child's grade school years (Shireman & Johnson, 1986). But if we look at these same children when they enter adolescence, we see a very different picture. Simon & Altstein (1981) found that interracial adoptees showed signs of stress and tension during adolescence. Although supporters of interracial adoption agree that cultural identity is an important need in a minority child's development, these same longitudinal studies indicate that this becomes less important to white adoptive parents as the child becomes older and thus is too often ignored.

As social workers, we are aware that adolescence can be one of the most vulnerable times in any child's development. Love and understanding are needed, along with discipline, to guide children through these challenging years. To illustrate the hurt that some interracial adopted minority children go through during these developmental years, we want to present the effects of interracial adoption on Indian children that we observed in child welfare practice. We see these victims of interracial adoption in the mental health system, in the streets, and on suicide lists.

The long-term effects of interracial adoption on Indian children and families are hard to erase. They go far beyond the concerns of some social workers who are only concerned about finding a child a loving and caring home. These effects have had a social and psychological impact on American Indian people that I as a former child welfare worker and now a professor of social work involved in Indian communities continually witness. I have met and heard Indian people speak of the deep wounds interracial adoption has left in their hearts. They speak of losing or not knowing their tribal culture, of having problems identifying as an Indian, facing racism as adolescents, and being caught between two worlds. Many of these former victims of interracial adoption who were seen as cute little Indian babies by their adoptive parents were later turned away because these same loving parents were unable to see or meet their needs as American Indian adolescents.

Family Preservation Policy

Two child welfare policies that advocate family preservation that social workers should be aware of are PL 96-272, the Adoptions and Assistance Act, and The Indian Child Welfare Act of 1978. The Adoptions and Assistance Act mandates that child welfare workers make reasonable efforts to keep families together. Through implementation of this act, child welfare workers have been able to avoid the removal of children from their homes and implement interventions that prevent child abuse and child neglect.

Similarly, the Indian Child Welfare Act was passed to prevent the breakup of American Indian families. It mandates that child welfare workers take active efforts to prevent the breakup of Indian families and establishes standards for the placement of Indian children in foster or adoptive homes. Interracial adoption is considered only as a last resource under these standards. When adoption or foster placement is necessary, the Indian Child Welfare Act outlines specific placement standards: First, adoption or foster care within the child's extended family must be considered. If permanent placement cannot be found in the extended family, then the worker must make active efforts to place the child within the child's tribe.

If that cannot be done, then an adoptive family should be found with a family or parent from another tribe. If all of these efforts fail, interracial adoption or placement can be considered. But even when a child is adopted by a non-Indian family, cultural ties must be maintained with the child's tribal heritage. Numerous non-Indian people of color applaud the Indian Child Welfare Act and have asked that similar placement criteria guide all placement decisions.

Family preservation policies were passed to strengthen families, not to tear them apart. Minority communities and cultural groups are like families; there is a sense of relationship that extends through minority communities and even through minority cultures. When we continually remove children from these cultures, we are weakening minority communities, their cultures, and their children. We recognize that there are times when family reunification is not the best permanent plan, such as when an entire family is so dysfunctional the child's welfare cannot be assured; when a family refuses to make the behavior change that will ensure the child's well being and safety.

However, how often are effective interventions introduced? How often are families given opportunities to heal? Child welfare workers must carefully weigh their decision to reunite children or terminate parental rights. Separating a child from his or her biological family is a painful experience with long-term negative consequences no matter how secure the new placement. Furthermore, current child welfare data show abuse in adoptive and foster homes. Why make this experience more painful by removing a child from his or her culture or heritage?

As a profession whose mission is to empower groups that suffer the effects of poverty, we should do all we can to nurture their ethnic and cultural strengths. Removing children from their group does not accomplish this mission.

Implications for Social Work Practice

Placing children of color in culturally appropriate adoptive homes is critical to their long-term emotional and social health and stability. To become secure, healthy adults, individuals must develop a sound identity throughout their lifespans. Remaining connected to one's racial and cultural heritage is an integral part of that sense of identity. To that end, child welfare professionals and advocates have the responsibility to empower and support families of color to adopt children from their communities who are in need of permanent homes.

Recruitment of adoptive families of color is critical. One of the best ways to learn how to create an effective recruitment program is to observe and get information from successful programs. There are several agencies in the country, including Homes for Black Children and The Institute for Black Parenting, whose recruitment and retention histories have proved that families of color can successfully adopt when the policies and practices of the agency are positive, sensitive, and flexible.

Agencies must make a commitment to having their staff reflect the communities and the children they serve. Currently, approximately 83 percent of the child welfare workers nationwide are white, although at least 30 to 40 percent of child welfare cases involve children of color (McRoy, 1989; McMurtry & Lie, 1992; Rosenthal, Groze, & Curiel, 1990). Prospective adoptive families need to feel welcome in and trust the agencies through which they apply for adoption. Having staff reflect the racial and cultural characteristics of their clients is an important part of the trust-building process.

People of color tend to have definitions of "family" that extend beyond the traditional nuclear family concept to which, unfortunately, many adoption agencies subscribe. Grandparents, cousins, aunts, uncles, and an array of fictive kin, who may be located miles away, often play a prominent role in the support of family members and in the raising of children. However, these family members are often overlooked as viable caretakers for children in need, despite the fact that these connections would allow the children to stay within their families and their cultural environment. Child welfare workers and agencies need to respect and acknowledge all of the family members that children have and offer these individuals the opportunity to provide homes for their children.

Agency services need to be accessible, responsive, and ongoing. Families need to know the purpose of what adoption workers are doing throughout the application process. Part of our responsibility as child welfare professionals is to demystify the adoption process. Honesty, clarity, and attention to families' personal concerns about the application process will help ensure that families of color are retained in the process.

Social workers who believe in the importance of culturally appropriate adoptive placements have a responsibility to advocate for the establishment of policies and practices that remove the barriers so that families of color can successfully adopt and provide loving homes for the children of their communities.

REFERENCES

Byler, W. (1977). Removing Indian children: The destruction of American Indian families. *Civil Rights Digest, 9*(4), 18–27.

Feigelman. W. & Silverman, A. R. (1983). *Chosen children: New patterns adoptive relationships.* New York, NY: Praeger.

McMurtry, S. L., & Lie, G. (1992). Differential exit rates of minority children in foster care. *Social Work Research and Abstracts, 28*(1), 42–48.

McRoy, R. (1989). An organizational dilemma: The case of transracial adoption. *The Journal of Applied Behavioral Science, 25*(2), 145–160.

McRoy, R. G., & Zurcher, L. A., (1983). *Transracial and inracial adoptees: The adolescent years.* Springfield, IL: Charles C. Thomas.

Rosenthal, J. A., Groze, V., & Curiel, H. (1990). Race, social class and special needs adoption. *Social Work, 35*(6), 532–539.

Shireman, J. F., & Johnson, P. R. (1986). A longitudinal study of black adoptions: Single parent, transracial and traditional. *Social Work, 31*(3), 172–176.

Simon, R. (1994). Transracial adoption: The American experience. In I. Gaber & J. Aldridge (Eds.), *In the best interest of the child: Culture, identity and transracial adoption* (pp. 136–150). London: Free Association Books.

Simon, R., & Altstein, H. (1981). *Transracial adoption: A follow up.* Lexington, MA: Lexington Books.

Swanson, A., & Brown, J. (1980). The ethnic factor in child welfare service: Some practice implications. *Journal of Humanics, 8*(1), 98–122.

Zuniga, M. E. (1991). Transracial adoption: Educating the parents. *Journal of Multicultural Social Work, 1*(2), 17–29.

Rejoinder to Professor Bending and Ms. Jones
CHRISTINE T. LOWERY

In this rejoinder, I focus on the implications of the Indian Child Welfare Act of 1978 (ICWA) not addressed by Dr. Bending and Ms. Jones. The ICWA was passed to end a long-time practice of pulling the spirits of children from their Indian families, their communities, and geographical place. There is no argument that we live in a racist society. There is no argument that one way to kill a people is to take their children. There is no argument that child welfare policies in this country come from a place of family punishment, rather than family preservation. From a social work perspective, the ICWA should be welcomed, enlighted legislation, for it turns our eyes from a deficit model to a strengths model for social work practice and acknowledges cultural, tribal ways of life.

Still, there are complex issues raised by the ICWA that social workers must face in practice. Under the ICWA, tribes may be notified of mixed-race children who may be 1/32 or 1/64 Indian, whose parents or relatives may or may not be known to an Indian community. Tribes may be asked to respond on behalf of children who are part of several tribes, whose relatives may or may not be known to these tribes. If these children have identified relatives in the tribe, but these relatives are unable to care for them, the tribe must decide whether to employ its resources to care for these children.

The resources of each tribe vary widely. Some tribes have one or two foster homes and share a traveling children's court judge with several small tribes or bands. Larger tribes have social services, foster care programs, and adoption services available, complete with experienced tribal court systems. No tribe has all the monetary resources it needs to support the needs of its tribal children in care.

The issues in some of these cases are not clearly cut or easily determined. There isn't a "right" way or an "only" way to deal within a matrix of policy, resources, rights, needs, immediacy, and future. We must do better than drawing academic lines in the sand. We must generate creative combinations to feed the spirits of our children while meeting their needs for food and security.

We have come full circle. Before the ICWA, the decision to remove children from Indian families was probably made by a non-Indian state social worker, missionary, or nurse, working by themselves and thinking they were doing the right thing, whether this was racially motivated or not. There is no reason to make the same ethical blunders.

The social worker can contribute his or her creative energy, experience, and knowledge of potential resources and community values, child development and attachment theory, social services and child welfare policies, and even help facilitate group process. Although social workers must wrestle with the ethnical and practice implications of each foster care/adoption case, it is a wise social worker who does not take it on himself or herself to make such decisions on his or her own.

Matters regarding the lives of children are serious and must be deliberated with others: the children themselves; their parents or relatives if available; various community members; children's court representatives; child welfare people. The community, whether this is a tribal community or not, must decide who its members are, who its allies are, how it will use its resources, and what options it will consider in behalf of its children. Therein lies its responsibility and its strength.

NO

CHRISTINE T. LOWERY

Hillary Clinton and Mother Theresa joined forces to open a home for abandoned children in Washington, DC in June 1995. The First Lady requested that the nation focus its attention on the 400,000 children in the foster care system and to consider adoption to help address the child welfare crisis. In light of the overwhelming number of unwanted children and the restructuring of the American family in the last four decades, the need for more options for these children becomes paramount. As we move toward a more multicultural and multiracial society, the argument for disallowing or discouraging interracial adoptions needs to be amended. The issue is not dichotomous. Real life is not dichotomous. The needs of children are not dichotomous.

When we consider the lifelong personal and societal consequences of growing up unwanted, abandoned, rejected, angry, enraged, we need to look critically at an array of options for addressing the child welfare emergency in our country. Interracial adoptions are part of an array of options, including strengthening recruitment strategies for minority foster and adoptive homes, that we should consider. If the major arguments against interracial adoption focus on issues of identity and isolation from the culture and race of the child, there are options that increase cultural and racial identity formation and decrease isolation.

Looking toward the twenty-first century, with increased exposure to cultural experiences through personal relationships, interracial experiences, common ecological concerns, global travel, and media, there is an opportunity for increasing awareness of cultural and racial life on this planet. What if we recruited adoptive parents who have living experience within the race or culture of their prospective children? And note, I said, children. Why not adopt families of two, three, or more children who share the same genes, the same relatives, and perhaps, the same cultural memories? Why not maintain ties with the family of origin? Why not "share" children?

One could argue that multicultural/multiracial familial, intergenerational understanding is enhanced when the adoptive parents have continuous, personal, nonjudgmental relationships with the relatives, biological parents, and yes, communities of their adoptive children. Such relationships can be collaborative; strengths of the adults and children can pass through a permeable, living membrane. Such relationships limit geographical displacement of children and provide an opportunity for children to know and understand their communities of origin, if these resources are known.

Cultural preparation for developing family of origin relationships would enhance the knowledge and the experiences of the adoptive parents and the "shared" children. This transcends reading a book or two, attending the annual cultural event, and eating ethnic foods at a local fair. Cultural experience and knowledge can be deepened through volunteer work with specific racial groups, political advocacy around issues that affect these groups, joining a church attended by the people of the adopted sibling group, doing library research about the history and culture of cultural, ethnic, or racial groups, talking with others of the culture or race, learning songs with the children, asking questions, and listening to the answers.

Cultural preparation and relationship building around "shared" children also provides the family of origin with the opportunity to contribute their own knowledge of their family history, their culture, their way of life, and the history and issues that have influenced their own communities. But most importantly, maintaining ties contributes a potential bridge, a measure of cultural fluidity for the children. Maintaining ties increases the opportunity to understand meaning in both groups, and provides a foundation for knowing that one can draw from both groups, that is, become bicultural, if one chooses.

Children need to know who they are spiritually, culturally, and biologically. They need to know where and whom they have come from. Children need to acknowledge the strengths and weaknesses of their own families just as they must understand the strengths and weaknesses of their adoptive parents. This understanding must extend to the cultural values in their communities of origin and to the cultural values of their adoptive communities as well. Values must be compared and contrasted, experienced, modified, revisited, and appreciated over the lifetimes of the children. They can have multiple options on which to build healthy identities. "Who am I?" can become the conscious integration of many people, including their biological and adoptive parents and many contexts, whether racially mixed or not.

Do we, in fact, want to discourage monocultural, monoracial environments for interracial adoptions? Could this be the crux of the argument as opposed to the idea of the interracial adoption itself? Children need to see parts of themselves reflected in others of their own race, in others of all ages. Can we plan adoptions for sibling groups with adoptive parents who commit to live in a racially integrated, culturally integrated life?

Some of our children are racially mixed children. Can we recruit mixed-race couples or interracial couples as adoptive parents to increase the adoptive options for these children? Although such relationships do not guarantee cultural knowledge, awareness, or openness, some of these matches may provide awareness, of racism, discrimination, and oppression felt by children of color in a white environment. In fact, this is one argument against interracial adoptions: white adoptive families cannot help children of color in a racist society. Yet, in an age of support groups, we belittle the strength of "like families" coming together to develop their own solutions for handling such issues. We also overlook the strength of the people of color in the community that can help bridge these gaps. Furthermore, we belittle the cultural work and the work of race that some adoptive couples are willing and qualified to do. Can we as social workers afford to ignore these resources?

Children of the Twenty-First Century

Not only do children need to know who they are, but particularly in the twenty-first century, they need to understand how to communicate with many people and to move comfortably among different cultures and situations. Agar (1994) introduced the concept of the MAR—mistake, awareness, repair—in a language context:

> The MAR puts you out to sea in the best sense of the word, at home between lands, able to change course and reach any of them . . . I think that sailors on the MAR are about an evolutionary human development, a shift in the human ecology that selects for the ability to take growing up in a particular languaculture as a resource rather than a conclusion. . . . The sailors, the ones who live on land or at sea, the ones who grow comfortable with the languaculture, are the guides into the next century. They're from somewhere, but they can deal with differences anywhere else. (p. 234)

The greatest problem with interracial adoptions in the past is that the process has been a training ground in a monocultural, monoracial environment, "making" children of color "white." A new interracial adoption framework requires cultural integrity and integration. Such a framework must offer cultural resources for our "shared" children to know, to use, to adapt, to learn more about so that they can deal with differences. . . . For "two people who know the MAR can talk about differences without guarding their own frames like threatened lands that others want to conquer" (Agar 1994, p. 234). This is dialogue for the twenty-first century and requisite grounding for the survival of our children.

The ethical question centers not on disallowing or discouraging interracial adoptions. What boundaries do we violate when we make well-planned, well-integrated, interracial adoption plans like those described above? We can no longer argue that there is terminal loss to the community or people of origin when education and economic factors demand that adults of all races go where they can find opportunities to support their families. However, in an interracial, culturally focused, child-focused adoptive setting, the importance of contribution to one's people can be taught. Knowing who you are is the basis for this commitment. Knowing who you are also permits you to return home again.

What is unethical, above all else, is leaving children without care, without adults on whom they can rely. This care includes the birthright to their culture, their language, their people, along with security, food, clothing, shelter, education, love, a sense of belonging and place, and the confidence and ability to contribute to others.

Collectively, we have never had our priorities in order when it comes to our children. Indeed, in a country where life as a commodity is marketed through TV commercials, where profit determines what the country values, where freedom from racism and discrimination is a never-ending battle, where ethics have to be taught in the classroom as advanced study instead of being modeled in society, the life breath of a child sometimes does not stand a chance.

Until we understand that the responsibility for ALL children is OURS, until we act on this responsibility, our life breath is limited too, whether we recognize it or not.

REFERENCES

Agar, M. (1994). *Language shock: Understanding the culture of conversation.* New York: William Morrow and Company, Inc.

Rejoinder to Professor Lowery

RAYMOND L. BENDING
TERESA C. JONES

We agree with Dr. Lowery on two major points. First we agree with her statement that it is unethical to leave children without care on which that they can rely. We also agree that interracial adoption should be an option in permanency planning. We disagree on when and how this option should be used.

We maintain that interracial adoption should be used only as a last resort. However, there is a belief that there is a shortage of foster and adoptive homes in minority communities. Therefore, interracial adoption is often used as the only option of permanency for many minority children. Is this because minority families do not want to adopt these children or is it because active efforts have not been made to recruit foster and adoptive homes in minority communities?

Dr. Lowery makes recommendations that advocate educating and preparing white families to adopt children of different races. She also recommends recruiting adoptive parents who have living experience within the race or culture of their prospective children. We ask, why cannot these same resources and efforts be put into recruiting and preparing potential adoptive parents in minority communities? We believe that families in these communities can be prepared to parent these children. Why do we have to go outside of minority communities to recruit families? Families in these communities already have the life experiences and cultural expertise. Do we choose to prepare white families to adopt minority children because we still believe that minority children will be better off in white homes that fit the dominant standards of the ideal family?

Dr. Lowery suggests that parents who are committed to live in integrated neighborhoods should be recruited to adopt these children. This implies that these families will continue to live in integrated neighborhoods. However, research indicates that though families may start out in integrated neighborhoods, they eventually move to white areas.

Dr. Lowery recommends forming adoptive parent support groups along with enlisting people in minority communities to help white parents handle identity and racial problems of adopted minority children. Again these plans sound good on the surface, but who is going to monitor the families to ensure that they do what is in the best interests of the child? Can we risk indiscriminately placing children of color in white homes with just the hope that those families will honor their responsibilities to the child's cultural identity development?

As child welfare professionals, we are advocates for the children in foster care. We are responsible for finding the best permanent home for each child. Consideration of cultural well-being of children of color must be a high priority when we make permanent decisions.

Are Private Practitioners Obligated to Serve at Least Some Clients Who Cannot Afford Their Customary Fees?

EDITOR'S NOTE: Who has a right to what services under what circumstances is a key question in professions. Urging practitioners to provide pro bono services is suggested by some people as a way to correct inequities in policies and opportunities for some of our citizens. Are private practitioners obligated to do so?

Kimberly Strom-Gottfried, Assistant Professor in the School of Social Work at the University of Minnesota, argues YES. She teaches practice and human resource management. She has conducted research and written extensively on the private practice of social work, specifically on the ethical, clinical, and educational implications of managed care.

Gary Labella and Betsy Owens say NO. Mr. Labella is a Clinical Social Worker who has worked extensively as a supervisor in the field of community mental health and school social work. He has been in private practice since 1985 and is a founding board member of a behavioral managed care company.

Betsy Owens, CSW, CAC has been in private practice since 1981. She has initiated the formation of the national private practice section of NASW, is the cofounder of Capital District Social Workers in Private Practice, and has lobbied on a variety of insurance and professional issues. She is an adjunct professor at Hudson Valley Community College, and is a founding board member of a behavioral managed care company.

YES

KIMBERLY STROM-GOTTFRIED

The word "obligation" is defined in various dictionaries as a "moral or legal duty," "a binding promise, contract, or responsibility." Although social workers in private practice may lack the legal compulsion to see clients who cannot afford their services, in every other sense of the word, they are obligated to do so. This means, in actual practice, the provision of free care—not putting clients on a sliding scale, extending their payment plan, seeing them for free after their insurance expires (until they can be referred out), or serving on a charitable board and calling it community service.

Although there are multiple benefits that accrue from the provision of free services, the obligation to do so is derived from the fact that private practitioners are, first and foremost, professional social workers, and that status as a professional carries with it certain privileges and expectations. For the past eighty years, social workers have endeavored to overcome Abraham Flexner's pronouncement that social work was not a profession (1961) and to achieve the recognition that our society bestows on its professionals. Indeed, part of the pact with society is predicated on the notion that the profession's orientation toward service and the collective good warrants the autonomy, protection, and status that society bestows. Other professions such as law and medicine do not debate their responsibility to give something back for the greater good, be it pro bono legal services or an allotment of "charity" health services. Social workers in all settings, in as much as they are part of a profession, are similarly obligated to make some of their services available to those who cannot afford them.

In private practice, there exists a much more direct link between services rendered and financial remuneration than there does in agency settings. As such, practitioners may experience "free care" as a loss of income and view nonreimbursed services as detrimental to the health of their "business." Although their setting does not exempt them from the obligation to provide some services to those who cannot afford them, there are also advantages in doing so that benefit clients, the social work profession, and private practitioners themselves. Why should private practitioners make some services available to those who cannot afford them?

It's Good for Clients

In the 1970s and 1980s, social workers fought for vendorship and other laws that have enhanced the visibility of the profession and viability of private practice. Often, this was referred to as "Freedom of Choice" legislation, as social workers made the case that their numbers, fees, geographic dispersion, and training made them the only mental health resource for many consumers. Having made this case so convincingly, it now seems disingenuous to withhold services from at least some people who need them, but who cannot afford them.

In an ideal system, people in need of health and mental health services would have the ability to access the best services available, regardless of their ability to pay. However, in the United States of the 1990s, ours is not an ideal system, and thus, the poor or uninsured have the least access to services that are both available and well qualified to meet their particular needs. Although the NASW Code of Ethics admonishes social workers to promote the general welfare and make social services more available to people, this longer-term approach to systemic change can also be coupled with change at the individual level. If one of every three or four social workers is now in private practice (Berliner, 1989; Mackey, Burek, & Charkoudian, 1987), tangible progress on access to services could certainly be made, even if each social worker only provided free care to one case at a time. In fact, the Code of Ethics of the National Association of Black Social Workers speaks specifically to personal sacrifice for the collective good in the provision: "I stand ready to supplement my paid or professional advocacy with voluntary service in the Black public interest." (Lowenberg & Dolgoff, 1992, p. 211).

Although the NASW Code of Ethics does not address free care directly, it does state that social workers should ensure that their fees are "fair, reasonable, considerate, and commensurate with the service performed and with due regard for the clients' ability to pay" (NASW, 1993, p. 1). The Code also mandates that clients should not be terminated precipitously, except under unusual circumstances. A number of private practice–related texts specifically associate this passage with the provision of free care, noting it as an option when clients' funding runs out and "client dumping" is prohibited (Barker,1992; Lenson, 1994; Lowenberg & Dolgoff, 1992). It is clear that, although the Code may not mandate the provision of free services, a number of its provisions concerning the well-being of clients support this practice.

It's Good for the Profession

Not only is the provision of free services important for meeting the needs and affirming the value of individuals in need of service, but the practice has advantages for the profession of social work as well. As noted earlier, the provision of free care is part and parcel of professional status. The consistent and intrinsic expectation that at least a modicum of free care will be provided thus reinforces our status as professionals.

Beyond parity with other professions, social work, unlike any other, has at its roots an origin of charity and social justice. The commitment to serve the poor and disenfranchised is an essential feature of the profession and is not negated because the service setting is private. Eschewing that tradition not only weakens the identity of social work among other disciplines but also becomes a divisive force within the profession as some "psychotherapists" seek to distance themselves from their social work lineage. In fact, the adoption of a clear philosophy in support of free care might diminish ongoing criticism of private practice, as reflected in the statement, "It seems a basic contradiction in terms to speak of the 'private' practice of 'social' work" (Merle,1962). In fact, even among other mental health providers without the history that accompanies social work, there exists an obligation for free care. For example,the American Psychological Association strongly recommends that all psychologists do some unpaid work. Should social workers be expected to do less?

It's Good for Private Practitioners

Finally, if private practitioners are not compelled to provide free care for the good of the profession or of their clients, perhaps they will consider the benefits they can personally accrue from the practice. Although private practice is a business and like all businesses must contend with the fiscal bottomline, the provision of free care offers both tax and public relations advantages. All businesses "give away" their services in some way, as a form of marketing and community service— whether it is an item for a fundraising auction or a donation for disaster relief. Doing so is seen as being a "good member" of the commercial community and provides name recognition as well as goodwill.

Providing some free care may also afford the practitioner peace of mind. As with any for-profit enterprise, difficult decisions must regularly be made for the health of the business. The cognitive dissonance and emotional conflicts that may accompany these choices can be diminished if the social worker has a fair and distinct policy for addressing the dilemma of clients who cannot afford his or her fee.

As opposed to merely reducing fees, free care allows a clear and defensible policy for handling clients who cannot pay. With third-party reimbursement, reducing fees or using a sliding scale becomes more precarious, as decisions to reduce fees in individual cases can affect others' rates. It is far better to apportion a percentage (5 to 10 percent) of the caseload to free care, inform appropriate clients of this option at the outset of treatment, and keep a waiting list when these slots are already full. This is also preferable to the practice of reserving "free care" only for clients whose insurance has run out, because the latter is much more difficult to predict and fairly administer.

Conclusion

The obligation of private practitioners, indeed of all social workers, to serve some clients who cannot afford their services is intrinsic to our position as professionals. Yet the benefits that can accrue from doing so stem from many sources. This argument does not imply that a standardized level of free care be implemented, nor that such arrangements be externally enforced. The choice, amount, and process of implementation of free care will always lie with the individual practitioner, hopefully commensurate with the health of his/her business, but originating in the belief that it is the right thing to do.

REFERENCES

Barker, R. L. (1992). *Social work in private practice* (2nd ed.). Washington, DC: NASW.

Berliner, A. K. (1989). Misconduct in social work practice. *Social Work, 34*(1), 69–72.

Flexner, A. (1961). Is social work a profession? In R. E. Pumphrey & M. W. Pumphrey (Eds.), *The heritage of American social work: Readings in its philosophical and institutional development (pp. 301–307)*. New York: Columbia University Press.

Lenson, E. S. (1994). *Succeeding in private practice: Business guide for psychotherapists*. Thousand Oaks, CA: Sage Publications.

Lowenberg, F. M., & Dolgoff, R. (1992). *Ethical decisions for social work practice*. Itasca, IL: F. E. Peacock Publishers.

Mackey, R. A., Burek, M., & Charkoudian, S. (1987). The influence of setting on clinical practice. *Journal of Independent Social Work, 2*(1), 33–44.

Merle,S. (1962). Some arguments against private practice. *Social Work, 23,* 12–17.

NASW (1993), Code of ethics, Washington, DC: National Association of Social Workers.

Rejoinder to Professor Strom-Gottfried

Garry Labella
Betsy Owens

Although Professor Strom-Gottfried makes many valid points, our position originates from the practice implications of reduced fees, rather than from the moral and academic perspective. Furthermore, our position is the same whether the issue is reduced fees or free service. For us, the crux is that the fees are not determined by market forces under this "obligation." Indeed, the term "obligated" in itself indicates a mandate with implications for enforcement. "Good will" will eventually not prove to be sufficient to meet this mandate.

Professor Strom is correct that practitioners will view free care as a loss of income. This fails to acknowledge that this is a different obligation than any imposed on agency practitioners. A 5 to 10 percent contribution of services appears minimal. However, it is clearly prejudicial to the independent practitioner. Agency practitioners are not obligated to return 5 to 10 percent of their salaries to charitable causes. This disparity is sure to alienate the 25 percent of the profession that is currently in independent practice. Obligatory free care will force competent practitioners to choose between their profession and their families' livelihood.

The concept of earning a living is antithetical to a primarily female profession, where we "should" promote self-sacrifice for the common good. Nonunionized, agency employment seldom offers salaries that allow practitioners to adequately support their families. It is often the private practitioners' ability to take the salary issue into their own hands that appears to run contrary to the perceived origins of the profession.

As Professor Strom notes, Abraham Flexner stated 80 years ago that we were not a profession. As an unpaid avocation, this was correct. Historical documents reveal that the founding mothers were in fact rich wives, who could well afford to work for little or no pay. Although the goal was noble, there was little personal sacrifice. Paradoxically, today, many of those who disparage private practitioners earn greater incomes than independent practitioners through unionized collective bargaining agreements (in contrast to nonprofit salaries). This strategy would be illegal price fixing if attempted by the independent practitioner.

The key to reform lies not in the obligation of any individual practitioner, but for social reform to continue through the strengthening of the public system. Serving the poor and disenfranchised should be a volunteer service only when the practitioner feels they have the wherewithal to do so.

Finally, there are no "tax" advantages as Professor Strom points out. Businesses are not allowed tax deductions for nonremunerated services. In fact, given that practitioners must absorb the cost of room rental, phones, personal child care, insurance, billing and office supplies, obligatory free care is in fact a dollar expense and not a tax advantage.

As an early practitioner, I learned about the tyranny of the "should." Dictating morality to the private practitioner will only cause controversy and dissension, a reduced level of care to the client, an abandonment of the public welfare system, and a reduction in quality social practitioners among our ranks.

NO

GARRY LABELLA
BETSY OWENS

Since its inception, social work has been seen synonymously—in both respect and in derogation—with "charitable giving." It is the root of this association that leads one to assume that obligatory sliding fees scales are appropriate professional dictates. However, as the profession has evolved from a charitable avocation to a professional vocation, there are many reasons to argue against obligatory sliding fee scales or mandatory pro bono work. This shall be demonstrated in the following arguments that pertain to legal issues; public versus private responsibility; the new influence of third-party payers; and the pernicious effect such action would have on treatment.

Legal Implications

The key term appears to be "obligated"; this raises questions as to who defines the obligation and how it is to be enforced. Pro-competitive regulations exist to ensure that the best services evolve at the lowest fees. Anti-trust laws preserve market forces and disavow attempts to set fees from within trade groups. The promotion of competition among otherwise collegial social workers ensures that the limited pool of clients drifts toward the most efficient practitioners. Anti-trust violations are not mere slaps on the wrist: individual fines can reach into the tens of thousands of dollars. Yet obligatory sliding fee scales cannot be instituted without bordering on illegality. Who would determine the details of appropriate fees? What percentage should be reduced for what unit of service? If the fees are too low, there is no recourse through collective bargaining to rectify financial inequities. Actions regarding fees, and particularly enforcement, if done from within the profession, imply illegal price fixing.

Public versus Private Responsibility

As the states increase the privatization of indigent care, we must learn from our history. The days of the charitable "poor houses," while the best we could provide at the time, were in fact blights on our provision of care. Appropriate levels of care have evolved with economic incentives. Those with greater purchasing power will inevitably receive a superior level of care. To mandate fee reductions will subsequently result in a two-tier system. The current public delivery system has effectively closed the gap; we should not look to displace this with fee setting.

Privatization and the subsequent cost-shifting of public responsibility will have the additional effect of reducing the public sector workforce. Managed care companies are already closing community mental health centers as they compete for the same contracts. To enable them to reduce their own per capita spending and produce lower bids for contracts falls into the trap of enriching managed care coffers at the expense of our profession. Ultimately, mandatory sliding scales will sabotage the public sector delivery system, with an influx of public sector employees flooding the social work marketplace. Salaried positions insulate clinical social workers from the administrative burdens of managing the delivery of services. Clinicians are free to provide treatment as they see fit, and are not constrained by reduced income due to managed care irregularities, no-show appointments, uncollected fees. Agencies are free to hire MBAs to manage rate setting. Fees are not individually negotiated but ascertained in the business office through spreadsheets and actuarial tables. Conversely, most independent practitioners are skilled therapists, not accountants. Mandatory reduced fees place a budgetary burden on the therapist that does not occur in the public sector. This alone could lead to the fiscal demise of the independent practitioner.

Third-Party Payers: A New Factor in Service Delivery

Third-party rates are based on the "reasonable and customary fees" of competing area practitioners. To engage in fee reduction within legal parameters, many states require that clients not be charged a higher fee if they have insurance coverage. However, many therapists do compromise their state certification and provider contracts to lower fees for a client when their benefits expire. Certainly, the NASW Code of Ethics does not condone acts of "dishonesty, fraud, deceit, or misrepresentation." The profession does not condone social work behaviors that triangulate the patient and the service provider. However, unless the same reduction in fees is offered to clients represented by insurance carriers, there is a complicity in fraudulent behavior.

Increasingly, a clinician's values about how to "help" are influenced by third-party payers rather than the profession itself. Insurance companies and managed care firms define care by their pressure on therapists to contain costs. Many clinicians have already found their services devalued by lower reimbursement rates. Caseloads are shrinking because of reduced and closed insurance panels.

The crux of the dilemma rests with maintaining a stable income while having two client entities with differing and opposing agendas—the patient and the payer. To maintain his or her livelihood, the private practitioner is constantly balancing therapeutic judgments against ethical, business, and contractual decisions. Economic factors may supersede the therapist's preferred model of therapy and the ability to keep treatment decision making exclusively within the therapeutic relationship.

Treatment Considerations

There should be neither prohibitions against nor mandates requiring each practitioner to negotiate reasonable fees with their clients. To mandate this practice promotes professional regression. Our professional identity has evolved from volunteer, affluent wives to professionals who could sustain and not merely supplement family incomes. Mandatory reduced fees do not take into account that, as paid professionals, we have livelihoods to support. It is doubtful that employee unions would permit the reduction of social work fees for its social work employees for moralistic purposes. Private practitioners should not be held to a different standard of practice than salaried employees.

Subsequently, for therapists who primarily support themselves through the revenues of a private practice, there is the danger of personal dissonance and professional betrayal as the value associated with "helping" becomes eroded and redefined by the pressures to earn a stable income. When counter-transference issues develop, therapeutic issues are bound to emerge. For example, the social worker may become less tolerant of the client's struggle for change and less responsive to clinical demands, and may develop strategies for avoiding or prematurely ending care. It generally requires superb skill, professional integrity, fiscal stability, and administrative supervision to ensure that the client does not become therapeutically abandoned under these circumstances.

In the eyes of the therapist who puts the needs of the client above sustaining their livelihood, there are subtle and mitigating rationalizations for dissonant behavior of this nature. The act of participating in a helping profession connotes an altruistic attribute that is sanctioned by this culture. "Giving" at the expense of the provider becomes more than a noble gesture of goodwill. It becomes a larger statement and mechanism by which society rids itself of the guilt for abandoning its impoverished.

Clearly, social workers in private practice are subject to business, clinical, and ethical factors as they attempt to establish a livelihood. We believe that we have presented a clear case to trust our colleagues to meet their ethical obligations without external mandates to do so.

Rejoinder to Mr. Labella
and Ms. Owens
KIMBERLY STROM-GOTTFRIED

In the opposing viewpoint, the authors seem to have transformed the "obligation to serve at least some clients who cannot afford customary fees" into a mandatory, across-the-board imposition of sliding fee scales. Such a shift substantially changes the issue at hand, and we are in agreement that mandated fees are both inappropriate and unworkable. Nevertheless, lost in their discussion is the importance of social workers, regardless of setting, providing at least some pro bono social work services. Some of the arguments supportive of this proposition can be found in their very arguments against it.

The authors cite anti-trust laws as a prohibitory factor in price setting. Although this is certainly a reason not to require universal fee scales, these laws in no way prohibit individual practitioners from allotting a portion of their services to free or reduced care . Similarly, the authors acknowledge the emergence in our country of a "two-tiered" service delivery system. Although some (Morreim, 1988) would disagree with their assertion that the gap between the public and private sector services is narrowing, the very existence of such disparity speaks to the worth of pro bono care. If it can be assumed that private or "top-tier" services are of better quality than those of the second or public tier, is not there merit in making some of the higher-quality services available to those who would otherwise not have access to them? This does not negate the need to work in other arenas to close the service gap, but it is an additional, visible manifestation of the profession's commitment to making quality services available to all.

As noted in my original statement, one impetus for providing a segment of totally free care is the confusion and liability that can result with third-party payers when reducing fees. Pro bono service alleviates this ambiguity and has an additional benefit for the provider negotiating with managed care companies and other third parties. When screening clinicians for inclusion in their provider networks, many payers consider a therapist's "profile" or dossier enhanced when it is apparent that they routinely offer a pro bono service or have a clear policy for doing so.

Finally, the countertherapeutic impact of reduced fees is mitigated when social workers have a clear and consistent policy that they can live with, and when they understand the personal and professional benefits that accrue from such a service. Rather than looking at pro bono work as "giving something away for free," they should view it as a "giving back" to society that accompanies professional status, and as a gesture that has long-range business benefits. If one's practice cannot withstand one or two free care cases a week, reduced rates are not the source of its undoing.

I am not arguing for a mandate of any kind, but I do think we, as professionals, need to be periodically reminded of our obligations and supported in adhering to them. In a national study of social workers in private practice (Strom, 1994), 80 percent of the respondents reported providing no pro bono services whatsoever. Although 70 percent provided services at a reduced fee to at least one of their cases, the data still indicate that perhaps trusting each to simply do as he or she sees fit is not enough.

REFERENCES

Morreim, E. H. (1988). Cost containment: Challenging fidelity and justice. *Hastings Center Report, 18*(6), 20–25.
Strom, K. J. (1994). Social workers in private practice: An update. *Clinical Social Work Journal, 22*(1), 73–89.